Bella Caledonia

BELLA CALEDONIA

Copyright 2022 Respective Authors
Published by Bella Caledonia
an imprint of Leamington Books
32 Leamington Terrace
Edinburgh

ISBN: 9781914090493

Book design and layout by Joshua Andrew
Editorial by Ambrose Kelly
Production management by Peter Burnett
Cover design by Stewart Bremner
Printed by Imprint Academic, Exeter

"Work as if you live in the early days of a better nation"
Alasdair Gray

Contents

BELLA CALEDONIA

AN ANTHOLOGY OF WRITING
FROM 2007 - 2021

2007-2021

An Introduction by Mike Small

Bella started as a hobby, quickly became an obsession and got swept up and along by the events of 2014 and beyond. Between its launch in 2007 and 2021 it can be seen going through phases of idealism, utopianism (even), frequent rage, and dipping in and out of more serious interaction with policy rather than politics and with culture rather than 'the national question'. These phases were influenced by who was interacting with Bella, who pitched ideas and who came onboard at different times, plus the editor's mood, energy levels and living conditions. This collection reflects some of those phases and brings together some of the best writing we've published since 2007.

Bella formed out of a novel - or rather out of a glimpse of an idea within a novel - Alasdair Gray's *Poor Things*, his Glaswegian gothic masterpiece, and the idea of Bella as a sort of national figurehead. So it's fitting that the cover of this book is a homage to Alasdair's *Poor Things* by the artist and designer Stewart Bremner. Alasdair was a huge influencer and supporter of Bella from the start and his characteristic generosity carried Kevin Williamson and I as we tried to understand what we were trying to do. He's one of several people we've lost on the journey and we miss his wild and wonderful self but mostly just appreciate his unquestioning positivity and humble support for people trying to do something, but not quite sure what they were embarking on.

We've always been eclectic, a loose collection of multiple perspectives and tones. Sometimes this looseness has felt suitably generous and wild, sometimes it's felt that it's in danger of coming apart at the seams and becoming incoherent. I knew from the beginning that the thing that was holding it together was the idea of 'becoming', the idea of 'self-determination' being explored from all angles - but I worried that wasn't spelt out clearly enough or widely understood. But then sometimes things are better when they are implicit. This collection reflects some of those dynamics and contains poetry, articles, essays, rants and polemic and contributions from writers who are famous or infamous and those that are neither. The articles are laid out chronologically though it seems they are not a linear route. Instead they gnaw away at the same questions over and over asking: how do we do this? Trying to build on waves of anger and discontent measuring spoonfuls of rage and hope, idealism and ideas charting the disintegration of the British state and the very idea of Britain alongside fleeting glimpses of an emerging other.

Bella's identity has evolved over time and this is reflected here. Our actual political outlook hasn't changed at all but we have evolved from a journalism that was entirely free, entirely 'amateur' in the best sense to one that has (tried) to become more professional. It's ironic that as part of the 'mainstream' media imploded for a variety of political and technical reasons many freelance journalists came to the 'new media' and the distinction became a bit blurry.

Although we were frequently bundled in with other 'blogs' we've never really been a blog. We have always tried to avoid what Mark Fisher called: "the solitary urinal of male subjectivity." Too many blogs (so many) are the outlet for single men of a certain vintage and hue and we have never wanted to be that thing, though the battle for greater diversity and plurality in publishing is ongoing and not confined to the print media. Part of the evolution was my own personal and political journey. Some of this is reflected in the various slogans and taglines we've adopted since 2007. At first we had 'fresh thinking for the new republic' which was suitably idealistic and beautifully naive for the moment. Then, at some point we went with "it's time to get above ourselves" which came from a conference in Glasgow organised by Bronagh Gallagher when the question being asked was "What Time Is it?" I really liked it because it spoke to a key theme of Bella's over the years, the yearning for Scotland to really throw off some of the self-inflicted shackles and restraints we've created for ourselves over history. It allowed us to step away from the victim and grievance narrative that was popular in some quarters which I always found strangely disempowering.

Another slogan that appeared and faded was "independence - autonomy - self determination" which attempted to place us in some European political tradition of autonomism and Negri & Hardt, but also to begin to look at the idea of "self-determination in a deeper sense beyond just constitutional change. The aim was always (and remains) - to transform Scotland not just gain independence. We were asking: what would and could 'self-determination' look like from an individual perspective, or a neighbourhood, or a comm-unity or a for a city??

All of this annoyed lots of people. The vitriol that has rained down on Bella for years is quite a phenomenon. People told me that if you're "getting abuse from all sides you must be doing something right" but that's easier to say than experience.

A prevailing, and I think profoundly wrong, orthodoxy in the nationalist movement went something like this: "We'll talk about radical politics and change AFTER independence", just now "don't rock the boat or scare the horses", or whatever craft or equine species needed undisturbed. For some independent thinking itself was frowned on and the emphasis should always be on unity and movement-harmony. I think this outlook was at times cripplingly stupid and strategically wrong. Allied to these thoughts was a pernicious idea that "unity" should prevail above all else. It's something I never adhered to. False unity is disempowering and confusing. This doesn't mean you shouldn't work with and collaborate with people you disagree with, but you need to have enough aligned values, common purpose and agreement on ends and means to make this meaningful.

Unity isn't everything.

I suppose this break with the wider independence movement was amplified by our need (and demand) for critical thinking. Our argument, or certainly my argument, was that "we" need to be self-critical about ourselves, about our movement, about our country and its cultures. This was not popular, and often misunderstood. It's difficult in a country that is trying to assert itself, in a country that still has issues about recognising its own culture and language as being valid to be self-critical. But if that is difficult it is also essential and it's something we've tried to do.

Looking back at our contributors few have been professional journalists. Looking at the list I can see only two or three. Others are land activists, poets, peace campaigners, nature writers, playwrights, feminists, writers, academics, wanderers, climate researchers, and some (many) who are none of the above. Some sadly are no longer with us.

In the beginning **Andy Wightman** wrote about the possibility that the Windsor's didn't actually own Balmoral and we should organise a community-buyout. It's one of several Bella projects that didn't quite get off the ground. **Alan Bissett** is the sole poet in this collection, and he's not really, or rarely, an actual poet but his Vote Britain was one of several additions that went viral or had a significant political 'moment' that's worth marking. It's spitting with righteous rage and contempt. **Brian Quail,** the veteran peace campaigner has been writing for Bella since the beginning, always about the same issue, the issue that won't go away until we are independent, the issue of weapons of mass destruction located on our land and in our lochs.

George Rosie explores the old canard of separating-off Shetland or Orkney (or more recently) the Borders, the 'Balkanisation' tactic used by unionists for decades to undermine the very idea of a unified coherent Scotland.

Observing a sperm whale in Oban Bay **Kathleen Jamie** muses on our relationship to the deep sea and the sense of wonder they elicit. She does this in review of Philip Hoare's *The Sea Inside* ('An astounding account of wilderness and beauty, of whales and birds and humans and the sea inside us all'). It's a double-trend we have tried to develop on Bella: featuring the new trend of nature writing and also creating a space for review of books, something that is sorely lacking in Scotland.

Playwright and author **Peter Arnott** has contributed to Bella since 2014. His brilliant essay in July of that year 'Dinner with No Voters' or "What I wanted to say before the Pudding hit the fan" was a spark of the summer - I remember people printing it and sharing it at meetings and it is reproduced here. It challenges the narrative of the No voters about how "divisive" the referendum was and their wish that all of this would all just "go away".

It's an echo to some of that debate today: "I take issue with my friends, who are still my friends I hasten to add, is in their imagining that a No vote somehow cancels the uncertainty and division. That life can ever again be like this never happened. I think that to imagine some kind of 'return to normality' is not only deluded, I think it is a positively dangerous complacency about the way things have already, irrevocably changed. And more, how things will change after a No vote, as well as after a Yes."

"If a Yes voter has to take on board the moral hazard of whatever happens for good or ill in an independent Scotland, a No voter must equally accept moral responsibility for having given Westminster permanent permission to do whatever it likes forever. No questions asked."

Arnott was pretty straight with his reader and with No voters: "David Cameron wasn't offering us a choice between different forms of democracy. He was offering us the choice between shutting up and fucking off. And fucking off might well have its difficulties, but we should be in no doubt that shutting up is exactly what is demanded of us if we don't have the guts to fuck off.

"A replacement for Trident? You don't want that? Shut Up. A slashing of consequential health spending as privatisation of the NHS in England and Wales speeds up? You don't like that either? Shut up. You voted for it."

Scott Hames has been a sceptical friend to the emergent democracy movement bringing light and insight to our often highly charged political debate. Here he looks at the discussion about the Scots language (mostly) and how the shame and contempt for our own language(s) has blindsided us to both its revival and importance and the need for a critical eye (or ear).

If Peter Arnott's essay was a viral spark, so too was **Laura Eaton Lewis** who wrote on leadership and gender. Written in September 2014 just a few weeks before the referendum it spoke to the strong current of feminist politics that ran through the campaign and the movement. We reproduced it in our print publication Closer and and also do so here. Laura wrote: "There's rich debate taking place right now in Scotland that has revolutionised people's participation in politics and the governance of our society. People who until now have not been admitted access to mainstream political processes have grasped the possibilities the independence referendum has brought about for future change. The public have themselves devised and led actions which are spreading like wildfire across the nation. It's a fertile time. We're all thinking about leadership, the way we want to be represented in politics, and how we might participate in the processes of governance in the future."

She the listed a series of gender leadership traits and experiences that had many men blushing in recognition and women cheering and raging in the same recognition, including: Men tend significantly to take credit for women's work; Men tend to delegate the admin work to the ladies; Men are significantly more likely to self-select for the spotlight; Men often leave the shitty jobs to 'someone else'; Men are very likely to talk over women; Men frequently bellow in meetings, they interrupt, they don't leave space in the conversation or look to women to give them the opportunity to talk; Men will usually ignore a woman saying the same thing as a man; Men will tend to offer 'opinion' as argument, yet demand 'evidence' from women.

This was the independence movement at its very best, mining down into power relations as part of a far deeper wider debate about how we operate and how we (re) create a better functioning society.

We have constantly tried to keep an international perspective for Bella, though this is difficult on meagre resources. So we were delighted to publish **Meghan Delahunt**'s essay reflecting on the similar energies of the Yes movement and the campaign of the Former Prime Minister Gough Whitlam, "the great, progressive politician of our youth." Written in October, just after the defeat of the Yes movement, Meghan is strangely upbeat:

"So. I've now lived through two great progressive upsurges – and two 'defeats'– in two different countries. The first as a child in Australia, the second as an adult in Scotland. How fortunate I am! I take heart from the fact that lessons learned young are lessons which endure. Through the Referendum in Scotland a whole new generation was politicised – just as I was during the Whitlam years. A whole new generation of artists and writers will come into their own, just as they did in Australia. We are still living through a revolutionary period in Scotland – nothing is settled, everything is up for grabs. How fortunate we are."

Bella has been perilously close to closing on several occasions and has only survived by pursuing people to let us publish or re-publish their thoughts and by the generous contributions of many people for free. I am sorry/not sorry for being the person doing the pursuing. On the moment of being awarded the Heine Prize in Dusseldorf, Germany, we hassled the writer **AL Kennedy** into letting us re-produce her acceptance speech.

In it she describes Britain as "a country where the public discourse is a hell's broth of gossip, malign invention, racism, rabble-rousing hatred and smut."

In a powerfully, though barely restrained tirade she writes: "As Germany clings to the lessons it learned about cultural toxicity long ago, I speak to you as a citizen of the UK, a country where books do not have to be burned – epidemic library closures and a massively compressed literary culture quietly prevent books ever being read or even born. Mine is a country which would rather leave traumatised and undefended children in the Calais mud, or now who knows where, than offer them the welcome we once extended to the kinder transports and to 100's of thousands of refugees before and after World War II."

"This is a country which tortures in black sites abroad and police stations at home, which incarcerates citizens without trial. This is a country with a wrecked education system for the masses based on monetisation and testing and an emotionally traumatising and entitling education for the elite."

"This is a country where – as the UN recently pointed out, our government's treatment of the disabled contravenes their human rights and where there is no need for an equivalent of Aktion T4 to organise the extinction of human beings with disabilities. We have simply withdrawn all their means of support, subjected them to official harassment and mass-media demonisation and waited for them to die in their tens of thousands – of stress, starvation, or else driven to suicide by their pain and despair. Make no mistake; we have been lost for some time – long before Brexit advertised that fact to the world. There is no morning when I could not wake up and say, like Max Liebermann – who once illustrated an edition of Der Rabbi Von Bacherach – "Ich kann gar nicht soviel fressen, wie ich kotzen mochte." [There's no way I could eat enough to vomit as much as I would like to.']

I include her piece because it marks the moment we enter a new phase of constitutional mayhem, from the independence moment to the Brexit vote - two events that are often super-imposed onto each other as if mistaking birth and death.

In the same year **Alistair Davidson** wrote a short and simple piece called 'The trouble with the council tax is the sound your buzzer makes' about the relentless stress of poverty and precarity, a theme that runs through Bella's output like a scar.

If the indyref was superseded by Brexit it was soon joined by the mesmerising phenomenon of the Trump presidency and the orgy of racism and reactionary politics it came from and re-produced. **Alastair McIntosh** examines the psychohistory of Trump's extraordinary reign arguing: "When I look at Donald

Trump – his colossal egotism, his grandiosity, his disconnect from empathy – I see a man who nurses a narcissistic wound, a wound to his primal integrity from places that he probably doesn't even know about. And that's just on his mother's side. Like those plantation managers in the African trade of whom Lord Tarbett spoke, his capacity to be and inwardly see – his capacity even to have an inner life as distinct from it all being on the outside – has been cut off by his deracination, his uprooting, from holding in his community."

"Such is the tragic dynamic by which – not inevitably, but very often – the oppressed turn oppressor. It is why Paulo Freire said that the great task of the oppressed is to liberate their oppressor as well, otherwise there can be no lasting freedom."

As contemporary Scotland continues to 'grow up' so too does the public sphere engendered by the Yes movement. **Katie Gallogly-Swan** was a key Yes campaigner and has continued to contribute hugely as an influential researcher. In *Getting out of the Kitchen* she writes: "For many women, publishing their work is a radical act."

"The past few weeks have seen more than a stramash in the womenosphere of Planet Scotland. The #GlasgowEffect saw a female artist lose days of sleep because of the abusive language on her Facebook page, while a regional newspaper published a picture of her home with no thoughts to her safety. A high profile twitter spat between J.K. Rowling and Natalie McGarry MP have seen both the object of twitter vilification. Scotland's ever-shrinking mainstream media lost respect in sacking Angela Haggerty at the behest of the Rangers' board—ironically less than a week after her article detailing the systematic misogyny and abuse she continues to receive from Rangers supporters as a result of her journalism. And in the latest instalment of why being a woman with a profile needs a health and safety protocol, anti-feminist supporters of Roosh V were encouraged to document details of women vocally opposing their network, in order to 'exact furious retribution' after an uproar about the 'gathering' of his supporters in Glasgow and Edinburgh this weekend."

I'm delighted to be able to re-produce **Maxwell Macleod**'s astonishing memory story about his father, George Macleod, the founder of the Iona Community. The past few years have been exhausting as political turmoil has churned on and on. So I have made no apology for occasionally turning away from the political to the deeply personal and am glad Bella has been peppered with such pieces of writing. It's referred to in the comments section as "sublime" as indeed it is. This is possibly one of the finest pieces of writing I've ever had the privilege to publish, and, besides, you really don't want to read the author's views on the constitution.

One issue that gnawed away at me for all of this period was the fraught issue of 'means and ends'. The movement was driven by strands of people who were desperate, for very good reason, and often persuaded by malignant forces that the best way forward was to propel bile and vitriol against their opponents. In her 2017 piece 'Means and Ends' **Caitlin Logan** quietly demolished such an approach. She writes: "…this has as much to do with the 'how' as the 'what' we want to achieve."

"If we hope for an independent Scotland to represent something genuinely different, it won't do to replicate the same structures, systems and dynamics which have failed us in the past."

"It would be far too easy, but tragically unwise, to take for granted that we can offer that hopeful vision to people without first embodying it ourselves."

Logan quotes the American writer Audre Lorde: "The master's tools will never dismantle the master's house. They may allow us to temporarily beat him at his own game, but they will never enable us to bring about genuine change."

She writes echoing the last embers of the fine idealism of 2014: "As it is, we are standing on the precipice of the future and we have a serious choice to make about the tools we want to use, and the nation we want to build."

I love the fact that in these pages and on Bella new writers rub shoulders with hugely influential writers like **Irvine Welsh**. In 2017 Welsh writes on the automation of work and what this means for our social relationships:

"As citizens, we justly mistrust the 'unprecedented times' mantra. After all, it would seem to give implicit emergency powers to elites whose behaviour has precipitated such crisis. Most people, justifiably, want to simply get on with life and make progress without being burdened by external threats and upheavals. Indeed, much of Conservatism's power as a political creed is that it taps into the compelling illusion of this possibility. But in an era where we face species-threatening imperatives on population, climate, a broken financial system, flatlining growth and real wage reductions, it's fanciful to imagine that we can sustain this delusion.

"These factors, in conjuncture with our information technology revolution, are pushing us towards a different set of social relationships and a new type of society. Now the dispassionate view is one that used to be reserved for neo-Marxists; it sees Western capitalism in technologically driven decline, with its ability to provide economic growth and employment prospects for its citizens rapidly receding."

One of Bella's most ethereal and haunting writers has been the traveller **Paul Tritschler.** In a series of essays spanning many years Paul's writing defies categorisation. Is it memoir? Family history? Social history? I don't really know. In 'Defence of Nostalgia' he writes about "nostalgia as a discrete aspect of memory" and the Clyde, and Notting Hill, and Christmas Eve and Tolstoy and his family and scented candles and the South of Scotland Electricity Board.

As we push on to 2018 we paused to reflect on the the 50th anniversary of May 1968. **Chloe Farand** looked at the destruction of the ZAD protest community, and what it tells us about Macron and Macronism.

Debates about language and identity and culture have raged across the pages of Bella for years, and we have been delighted to publish in both Gaelic and Scots to host some of that rage. But it's also delightful to publish a piece by **Abi Lightbody** that is characterised by joy in 'Learning Gaelic, Learning Scotland: Normalising Language'.

Like Kathleen Jamie's, **Dougie Strang**'s writing defies the description of 'nature writing'. With a background out of the School of Scottish Studies, Strang is part ethnologist, part performer, part gardener in the best Scottish tradition of generalism. He has tended to epic solo walks across the highlands and here considers landscape, history, bothy culture and MacDiarmid.

From the start we've tried to represent many Scotlands and the country and the culture beyond the central belt. Few have contributed more towards this aim than **Mairi McFadyen,** here writing about 'The Art of Living Together' and the potential of the commons to resist the "enclosure of the mind":

"In the 21st century, it is not just land and resources that have been enclosed by capitalism, but almost all aspects of life itself. The modern tendency towards turning relationships into services, commons into commodities, human into machine has been described by commons scholar David Bollier as 'the great invisible tragedy of our time." The 'new enclosure' can be seen in the patenting of genes, lifeforms, medicines and seed crops, the use of copyright to lock up creativity and culture, academic knowledge behind paywalls and attempts to transform the open internet into a closed, proprietary marketplace, shrinking the public domain of ideas, among many other examples.

The endgame of this process is the enclosure of the mind and the co-option of dissent."

The itinerant **Christopher Silver** has been a huge figure in the democracy movement for years and a long-standing Bella contributor and here coruscating Edinburgh's Adam McVey about the capital's disastrous commitment to over-tourism and the death of the city..

George Gunn has been writing the longest running column for Bella - From the Province of the Cat - from Caithness for many years, a sort of deep long-time literary historical vision of the world from Scotland's north east coast, like a metronome corrective to our intrinsic central belt bias.

George Kerevan has written an economic column for Bella for several years bringing a laser like pen to the neoliberal failings of the political elite.

I don't feel a shadow of embarrassment to say that **Stuart Christie** was one of my heroes and we were working on a book together when he died in August 2020. The previous year we had published his account of being arrested in Madrid by the Gestapo-trained* Brigada Político-Social (BPS) for trying to assassinate General Franco. We re-publish his account in memory and honour for one of Scotland's unsung heroes.

Iain Mackinnon has made a huge contribution to Scotland's public life focusing on traditional knowledge systems and land-based cultural practices of Scottish Gaels. Here he brings revelations disclosing connections between landownership in the west Highlands and Islands of Scotland and the profits of plantation slavery.

I said at the beginning that Bella was a broad church teetering on the edge of incoherence and I love the fact that we can attract and publish people like the writer and activist **Dougald Hine** who has been behind so many projects. From 2009 to 2019, he was a director of the Dark Mountain Project, which co-founded with Paul Kingsnorth. Originally from England, he now lives in Sweden where he is developing a school called HOME in collaboration with his partner, Anna Björkman. He spent a period as a commissioning editor for Bella outlining a series of cast long-form essays that would become a book. It's difficult to even capture what this was about other than the vast mesmerising collective experience we are going through and it's deep roots.

One of the beauties of this space is the exchange between reader and writer: "I must say that I enjoy reading your essays but there is an utter disconnect between my world and yours" (William Ross) to which Dougal responds: "William – Thanks for reaching out so honestly across the gap between our worlds. We'd all be the better for it, if people did so more often in online spaces." The details are less important than the tone of openness.

In 2021 the full horrors of the Ireland's Mother and Baby Homes Commission Report came out. From the perspective of the London-Irish dinner of boiled ham, cabbage and spuds, a 'tricolor feast of green, white, and rose-gold', somehow **Cait O'Neill McCullach** makes sense of it all as the full horrors of post-theocratic Ireland came into the light, horrors that whilst shocking also were part of a cathartic unravelling that has made Ireland a new place that Scotland can only yet dream of.

Raman Mundair is an Indian born writer, artist, playwright and filmmaker. She identifies as a Queer, disabled, British Asian intersectional feminist and is an activist based in Shetland and Glgasow. In 2020 she was a commissioning editor for Bella and here presents the idea – akin to the Bechdel Test – on how we should assess the artistic and creative representation of people of colour (PoC) in theatre and other forms of broadcasting.

In characteristic long-form rambling wonderfulness, **Neil Cooper** takes in the Eurovision Song Contest spanning Ted Heath, Jean Luc Godard, Bonnie Tyler and Ultravox in a kind of trans European Express of post-Brexit melancholia as ephemera from Scotland's finest arts critic emerges like detritus from his brilliant muddled Scouser's back catalogue. This sentence almost does justice to his fine contribution to Bella over many years.

Like most of us **Alison Phipps** watched in horror as the Trump cavalcade rolled in and out of office in America a grotesque menagerie of 'populism'. Here she quotes Syndey Carter, the English songwriter and poet coming from a: "tradition of whole-souled non-violence and whole-body listening which is fiercely contemplative, critically liberatory and hopeful in song, and lamentation.

It is a song for a people made in a strand of the religion which calls itself Christianity which sits with deep unease under such a label today, and for good, good reasons.

But it is equally a strand passionate about the enduring truth in the goodness of news of the life-giving force of forgiveness, mercy, justice, repentance, liberation. It imagines a better way of being together. A commonwealth of love."

Entering the mire of "free speech" activism - in this case around the politics of Steve Bannon, **Amna Saleem** writes: "Regardless of the topic, like most women of colour, I can't tweet, write an article or appear on TV without receiving racial abuse, whether that be someone taking umbrage with my skin tone, referring to me as a terrorist or accusing me of trying to implement Sharia law. In order to pursue my career, I have to accept racism fuelled by the likes of Bannon as a consequence of my ambitions. It's especially wild when you realise I'm just a young working class Muslim woman from a small town in Scotland who spends most of her time discussing pop culture and writing comedy."

In 2019 Creative Scotland's rejected the *Scottish Review of Books*' funding application. The follow-up controversy captured some of Scotland's worst networks of patronage and chumminess and the deeply conservative and reactionary voices of many at the top. **Claire Squire** investigated.

Neil Cooper has been an arts and cultural writer for decades and a long-term Bella contributor. Here he says goodbye to Europe through the lens of the history of the European Song Contest, Lulu's 'Boom Bang-a-Bang', and *It's a Knockout*.

This selection of writing is only a fragment of our output over the years, but I hope it represents a little of the rich diversity of Bella and that some of the huge changes Scotland is going through. We have a long way to go.

Balmoral Buyout

Andy Wightman

Any serious attempt at dismantling the concentrated pattern of private landownership in Scotland will get nowhere if it does not face up to the fact that the Queen's ownership of Balmoral is a central part of the problem. It remains a totemic obstacle to radical land reform since its continued existence legitimises large scale private landownership. It's time to buy-out Balmoral.

Andy Wightman, one of the foremost architects of the land reform movement of the 1990s, and now one of the people behind the Common Good movement, writes from Addis Ababa, Ethiopia

When Alex Salmond visited the Queen at Balmoral earlier this autumn, I doubt that he said much about his administration's plans for land reform. It would be a breach of Parliamentary etiquette if he had (Parliament should normally be the first to hear). But it is probably as much to do with the fact that there appear to be no such plans.

Which is a pity, since there is much that Alex Salmond has said in the past he wishes to do. In an article he wrote in the *Sunday Express* in November 1995 he argued that the unregulated land market in Scotland was intolerable, that absentee landownership was an inappropriate qualification for landownership and that all

29

land should be controlled by a democratically elected Land Commission.

Since the establishment of the Scottish Parliament, much has in fact been done. On 28 November 2004, the system of feudal tenure in Scotland was abolished although you'd be forgiven for not having noticed since a few individuals continue to own the vast majority of privately owned land in Scotland. Indeed, it is one of the curious things about attitudes to the question of landownership that there is general approval of the abolition of feudalism but little antagonism to this concentrated pattern of landownership.

The one issue around which much of this ambivalence revolves is the Queen's ownership of Balmoral Estate which induces everything from anger to romantic enthusiasm. Although Balmoral is the private property of the Queen (except it isn't quite this simple as we shall see), it is also an indispensable part of the constitutional furniture. This is partly because she spends so much time there (the film *The Queen* starring Helen Mirren provides an entertaining portrayal of her time there) and partly because she uses the time there to entertain such figures as Gordon Brown and Alex Salmond. Who could not fail to be impressed by the employment she generates in Upper Deeside, the spin offs in tourism and the fact that munificently, she provides all of this out of her own funds?

But many of Scotland's landowners are charming, polite, eager to please and undertake good works in the community. So what? Just as a benign dictator who is popular with the masses does not diminish one iota the case for democracy and human rights, so the presence of so many charming members of the nobility still lording it over huge swathes of Scotland (but doing a splendid job) does nothing to detract from the case for radical land reform.

Of course, many will argue that it matters little in the overall scheme of things that the Queen owns Balmoral. What matters is the symbolism and what this says about or attitudes to who owns our country because, for a start, we know so little about how land is owned and by whom. For example, Queen Victoria is popularly believed to have fallen in love with Balmoral and purchased it in the

19th century. She didn't. Likewise, the Queen is regarded as the owner of Balmoral Estate. She isn't.

If you look at Balmoral's website (balmoralcastle.com) you will see the following claim:

"Purchased by Queen Victoria in 1848, the Estate has been the Scottish Home of the British Royal Family ever since."

and

"The Estate is owned and funded by Her Majesty The Queen personally rather than as Sovereign."

Both claims are wrong.

Queen Victoria took a lease of Balmoral Estate in 1848 from the Trustees of the Duke of Fife. The estate was then purchased in 1852, not by Queen Victoria, but by Prince Albert since the 1760 Civil List Act meant that any property bought by the Monarch would become part of the Crown Estate (the revenues of which are surrendered to Parliament in return for the Civil List). It was thus necessary to pass the Balmoral Estates Act in 1852 to confirm the legality of the purchase and to enable Victoria to inherit Balmoral following Albert's death. The Crown Private Estates Act was then passed in 1862 to permit the further purchase of land in Scotland.

Balmoral Estate is, furthermore, not owned by the Queen. It is owned by Trustees Nominated and Appointed by Her Majesty Elizabeth the Second. The Queen is the beneficiary of this Trust. In 1997, the Trustees were Rt. Hon. David George Coke Patrick Ogilvy, Earl of Airlie (Cortachy Castle, Cortachy, Kirriemuir, Angus), Sir Iain Tennant KT LLD (Lochnabo, Llanbryde, Moray), and Michael Charles Gerard Peat CVV, Keeper of the Privy Purse (St James Palace, London)

The reason for this arrangement is to be found in Section 4 of the Crown Private Estates Act 1862 which stipulates that the Queen's private estates in Scotland shall be held by Trustees.

Balmoral Estate has thus been exempt from inheritance taxes and death duties ever since as Trusts don't die. The Crown Private Estates Act is a reserved matter for the UK Parliament so there's not much the Scottish Parliament can do about any of this.

The Queen's personal estates in England and Scotland are, furthermore, subjects of a range of special exemptions. For example, under the Animal Welfare Act 2006, the Queen is exempt under Section 60(6) from having Inspectors enter her land.

No power of entry conferred by or under this Act may be exercised in relation to land belonging to Her Majesty in right of Her private estates.

Similarly, in the access provisions of the Land Reform (Scotland) Bill, the Queen's private estates were initially exempt until Denis Canavan MSP proposed an amendment to remove it.

So, what do the Queen's Trustees actually own?

First of all, they own the Balmoral Estate itself which was extended in 1947 by the purchase of lands in Angus (Bachnagairn and Whitemounth in 1947 and Glen Doll in 1997). In addition, the Trustees have a long lease of Abergeldie Estate and bought the Delnadamph Estate in 1977 and 1980. In total they own around 61,500 acres and have a long lease of the 11,700 acres of Abergeldie (see map). This makes them the 25th largest private landowner in Scotland (up from 68th in 1970).

Despite this, the Scottish public by and large continues to be seduced by nobility and to approve of the Monarchy. Politicians know this but what is conveniently forgotten by today's political classes (who seem more intent on securing good headlines next day than tackling deep seated political issues), is that landowning in Scotland continues to be an institution dominated by a tiny number of people. In the Highlands and Islands for example, fully half of the private land – over 3.6 million acres, is owned by fewer than 100 landowners and three-quarters of it is owned by around 300.

Such a pattern is remarkable in itself but what is even more astonishing is the way in which the landowning establishment itself is not merely a collection of random individuals but a tightly knit network of power and influence extending into the fields of politics and finance. The small numbers involved facilitate the operation of this network and its effectiveness which extend to the highest levels of British society.

This pattern of influence and landed power has lasted right up until the very end of the 20th century bolstered by wider networks within politics, finance and the law. Such intimate relationships promote social cohesion among landowners which makes them readily distinguishable today as a discrete class with its own values, internal networks, and related social institutions.

Private landownership in Scotland remains a small, interrelated and privileged club which is proud to have the Queen as a member. But with land reform such an important part of public policy, what message does it send out when the Queen continues to play the role of Highland Laird? The Queen is supposed to set an example. In Scotland, public policy on land reform is to secure a "rapid change in the pattern of land ownership". The Queen is running counter to that by being the owner of a large and expanding estate.

The Queen, who, like other large landowners, owns estates to provide her with a place to spend her holidays can continue to enjoy her holidays as others do by renting a castle or country hotel. Under state or community ownership, the Queen could even continue to enjoy holidays at Balmoral if she wished.

To counter such suggestions and to promote its role as a modern and progressive estate, Balmoral Estate makes much of its economic impact on the local economy and in a recent study it claimed that:

> "…employment impacts total approximately 340 full-time equivalent jobs in Upper Deeside or 400 full-time equivalent jobs in Aberdeenshire. These employment impacts generate household income of over £6 million per year in Upper Deeside or £7 million in Aberdeenshire. The 340 full-time equivalent jobs in Upper Deeside (including Aboyne) represent up to 20% of the area's total employment."

The problem with these studies is that the figures, whilst appearing impressive, actually bear no evidential relationship to ownership by the Queen. Such impacts are no doubt partly a consequence of the royal connection but they could equally arise (or be different) under any alternative form of ownership since the assets of the area would remain the same and the royal history would still be there.

Any serious attempt at dismantling the concentrated pattern of private landownership in Scotland will get nowhere if it does not face up to the fact that the Queen's ownership of Balmoral is a central part of the self-same problem. It remains an obstacle to radical land reform since its continued existence legitimises large scale private landownership.

This is exacerbated by the fact that Balmoral will be inherited by Prince Charles as heir to the throne. Not only will he pay no inheritance tax (although the Queen's estate is subject to inheritance tax), bequests from Sovereign to Sovereign are exempt for the rather bizarre and illogical reason given on the Monarchy website that:

> "This is because the Sovereign is unable to generate significant new wealth through earnings or business activities, and to recognise the requirement for the Monarchy to have a degree of financial independence."

Whilst increasing numbers of ordinary members of the public face 40% inheritance tax bills on their parents' house (and quite rightly so), the Queen's heir will not. And whereas many ordinary people will have to sell inherited assets to pay the bill, the argument is that the Sovereign does not generate enough wealth to do this. But Prince Charles (who would have to foot the bill were he to be liable) earned over £15 million last year from the Duchy of Cornwall.

Moreover, when any normal family inherits property, each child will usually receive an equal share, the Sovereign is still subject to the laws of Primogeniture so Princess Anne, Prince Andrew and

Prince Edward will inherit nothing of Balmoral. If they did, it would at least do something to break down the pattern of ownership.

Any moves to change the pattern of ownership should not be regarded as an attack on the Queen personally (her attitudes about how to manage Balmoral are as progressive as those of many modern landowners) but a challenge to the idea that Scotland can ever truly create a modern democracy when its land continues to be in the hands of so few people.

By way of contrast to the regulatory regime surrounding land ownership, in Inverness there are 50 civil servants spending around £1.5 million pounds regulating 17,000 crofts whose influence extends individually to a few acres of bog and rock. Their ability to assign their croft, sub-let it, decroft it, split it, amalgamate it, even their competence to use it are governed with what some might argue is an inappropriate and outdated form of paternalism but which, nevertheless, recognises in principle that the regulation of occupancy is in the public interest.

Remarkable then, isn't it, that at the same time the 100 people who between them own over half of the entire Highlands and Islands of Scotland are subject to no regulation. There is no Landowners' Commission, no consideration of local needs, of the best interests of the community, or of taking action against absentees.

Endless paperwork can surround the assignation of the tenancy of a few acres of heath above Newtonmore whilst on the other side of Strathspey 40,000 acres of internationally important land in Glen Feshie are traded between strange people in the VIP lounge at Heathrow Airport with not so much as a cursory glance at any wider public interest.

In 1999, something remarkable took place. The ownership of 26 iconic properties such as Edinburgh Castle, Stirling Castle, Linlithgow Palace, Holyrood Park, Arbroath Abbey and Dunfermline Palace were transferred by the Crown Estate Commissioners to the Secretary of State for Scotland (within a few months Scottish Ministers then took over ownership). Quite why this was done is not entirely clear but the symbolism was evident (despite there never having been any publicity about this extraordinary dowry to devolution). The Crown Estate Commissioners appeared to believe that such properties were more appropriately held by representatives of the Scottish people.

Balmoral Estate is a block on land reform and for so long as it's ownership remains unquestioned so too will the wider pattern of large scale unregulated private ownership. Balmoral is the personal property of the Queen rather than part of the Crown Estate but the time has come to end this peculiar situation which continues to stand in the way of meaningful land reform.

Vote Britain

Alan Bissett

People of Scotland, vote with your heart.

Vote with your love for the Queen who nurtured you, cradle to grave,

Who protects you and cares, her most darling subjects, to whom you gave the glens she adores to roam freely through, the stags her children so dearly enjoy killing.

First into battle, loyal and true. The enemy's scared of you.

That's why we send you over the top with your och-aye-the-noo Mactivish there's been a murrrderrr jings! crivvens! Deepfried-fuckinmarsbar wee wee dram of whisky hoots mon there's a moose loose aboot this smackaddict

Vote, Jock. Vote, Sweaty Sock. Talk properly.

Vote with those notes we scrutinise in our shops.

(might be legal tender but looks dodgy to me)

Vote for the Highland Clearances. Baaaaaaaaaa.

Vote for nuclear submarine in your water

Vote for the Olympic Games you didn't vote for

(but you'll pay for it, you'll pay for it).

Vote Conservative. Vote Lib Dem. Vote Libservative. Vote Condabour.

Vote with the chip on your shoulder.

Vote Labour. New Labour. Old Labour. Scottish Labour.

(Get back in line, Scottish Labour, HQ in Solihull will issue their commands shortly,

Just keep the vote coming in from up there thanks goodbye).

Subsidy Junkie

Vote for any argument you construct in your defence being 'anti-English'.

Vote for Scots who make their career in Scotland being 'unambitious'.

Vote for enjoying your own culture being soooooooo parochial.

Vote God Save the Queen and that bit about us crushing you all.

Hush. There there.

Vote for Scotland being referred to as a 'region', like, say, Yorkshire? Or East Anglia?

Vote for our voices dominating your media, but in no way telling you what to think.

Take a drink. Go on, son, take a drink.

Vote for oil revenue, which we ensure flows directly from us into you.

Vote for being told you're the only country in the world that could not possibly survive and that without us you'd fall to pieces like children abandoned in the wild, caked in faeces.

Vote Daily Mail and Rupert Murdoch and

illegalimmigrantskilledPrincessDiana and

London London London most exciting city in the world darling

(Glasgow *is* a very violent place, is it not. Do you have art?)

Vote with your heart. Vote Empire. Vote tradition.

Vote for our proud shared history of

enslavingothernationsandstealingtheirnaturalresources

Bringing Wealth and Prosperity to the World!

being on the right side just *once* and that's only because it was against yer actual fucking Hitler

38

Vote for the #ScottishConspiracy at Westminster

(who really runs the show here eh – Blair, Brown – got your own in that time, we aren't allowed to vote in Holyrood but there's Archie McPhee pulling wee strings in our parliament when we wouldn't even *think* about interfering in how you run your own affairs but while we're at it, this referendum eh? A so-called referendum, is it? Have it *now*, make sure it looks like *this*)

Vote for very, very, very rich people patronising you.

Vote for Glasgow having the highest knife-crime rate and lowest life expectancy in Europe

due to our generosity. You may thank us at your leisure.

Vote for the absence of your history in our schools.

All Brits together.

Vote for our shock at your ingratitude!

Vote for us saying 'Eh? Eh?' when you open up your porridge mooth.

Vote for bafflement about why you want the England football team to lose.

We always want the Scots to win (except in referenda).

Vote for psychopathic villains with your accent in a soap opera.

Vote for tuition fees and student loans, ensuring that the brightest of your working-class

(since you still insist upon the term, although Our Leaders had it banned)

will one day rise and take their place in this great land.

Vote for us deploying strategic references to Braveheart to dismiss you all.

Vote for Robert Burns being called by Paxman 'sentimental doggerel'.

Vote for The Iron Lady. Such a *strong* leader, gave this country *backbone*

(you didn't really want the unions, industries or council homes, just made the place look tatty)

Vote for a deregulated banking class, lionising of the hardworkingwealthgeneratingjobcreatingentrepreneurs who you will in no way refer to as 'greedy, selfish bastards'. Give them your taxes.

Vote for foreign wars.

Yes, sadly, some of you will die. But you will return to a hero's welcome

Jock

the Union Jack, proud symbol of integrity and honour, draped across your coffin

while your mother, dabbing at her eyes, recalls the words she learned in school

in Kircudbright

'There is some corner of a foreign field that is forever England.'

Vote with your heart.

Coulport, Devo Max and Imperial Britain

Brian Quail

Henry 1st of England is reputed to have died of a "a surfeit of lampreys". These days, I am getting the same feeling of being stuffed to death with Unionjackery. What with Betty Windsor's Golden Jubilee and then Olympic hysteria, it's the Butcher's Apron everywhere you look. And this is having the intended effect. Recent polls show a significant fall in support for Scottish independence and a rise in support for "devo-max" – whatever that means.

All rather depressing, I fear. But depression is a luxury we can't afford; there's too much to be done. First and foremost, we must get people to realise that devo-max is a dead end. Because it is the least demanding of change, and the least radical of options, it has a certain superficial attraction for the faint-hearted, and a seductive appeal to the politically naive. But it leaves us with no control over the – literally – life or death question of war and peace. We would still have Trident, and the biggest arsenal of nuclear missiles in Europe (at Coulport), and we would still be dragged into foreign wars in distant lands, in the interests of American foreign policy, and Big Oil.

There was a fascinating photo in the Herald recently. Joann Lamont, Ruth Davidson, and Margaret Curran all beams and smiles shaking hands with Alastair Darling at the launch of the Better Together campaign. Tory and Labour united in defence of the Great British State. The new loyal imperial British Labour Party, lost in a love-in with the Tories, all sweetness and light. Class war – what class war? That's all over now – just don't ask me who won. Keir Hardy would be burling in his grave.

So we are "Better Together", are we? Funny, there's many a woman managed to struggle out of an abusive and violent relationship would dispute the optimism of this breezy slogan. Women who are glad they are not "together" with former partners, happy to escape at last their domination and bullying.

In a similar way, Scotland has suffered too much and too long from our 300-year-old partnership with our larger neighbour. We have too many empty landscapes, depopulated through ethnic cleansing, (clearances which the Lowland factors were more than happy to enforce). We have a de-racinated and alienated working class, ignorant of its own history, and of the struggles fought in the past. Numbed by the mindless cult of celebrity, dreaming of escape through instant lottery wealth, the people sleep walk in an unreal world. But the inanities of *Big Brother* and the *X-Factor* will not satisfy the desire for meaning and purpose in life. "Unless the people have dreams, they perish."

In the past, we have sent too may brave young men to die in foreign wars. Today at Coulport, we have the biggest arsenal of nuclear missiles in Europe. Why? Because we are British. We are home to the world's most powerful machine for the mass killing of human beings, Trident. Why? Because we are British. We pay a terrible price for being "together" with England in the imperial British state. Time for a divorce.

We suffer from the most powerful and effective form of control; that is, the oppression which is internal and self-imposed. This is so effective, it does not even recognise itself as oppression, but sees it as self-definition. We are proud to be British, and independence is a denial of Britishness. So, we accept our allocated subservient role proudly and dutifully.

In post-Cold War Europe, independence is in fact the norm. What we in Scotland are seeking is regarded as self-evidently just and desirable. The barriers to us achieving this gaol arise from "the mind-forged manacles of man" – to use William Blake's lovely phrase. It is not somebody or something "out there" that is holding us back, but we ourselves, our own lack of imagination, failure of insight and courage.

Economics are invoked; threats of financial disasters are raised as a spectre to browbeat us. Everybody knows we in Scotland are just not capable of conducting our own affairs, and ruination will be the consequences. Well, to coin a phrase, "Frankly, my dear, I don't give a damn". Bean-counting was never my forte, and, as Wordsworth said, "high heaven rejects the lore of nicely calculated less or more". Let me just observe that Estonia, which has a smaller population than Strathclyde, can manage its own affairs quite nicely, thank you. So, why not Scotland?

No self-respecting independent country would tolerate our shameful subservient situation. Unionist hostility to independence is in fact the hostility of unthinking nationalism – British nationalism. The present conflict is not, as often portrayed, between Scottish nationalism and the "normal" Unionist rest. It is between two conflicting nationalisms. Scottish, which is fundamentally communitarian and internationalist in its outlook, and British nationalism, which is inherently imperialistic.

It was ever thus. Since its creation by massive bribery and corruption in 1707, the British state has been congenitally and irredeemably, an imperialistic construct. I expect the conservative right to deny this – they would, wouldn't they? But I am surprised at the persistence of the Brit left in resolutely defending the imagined benefits of remaining in imperial Great Britain.

National aspirations of all other former colonial states are approved, but the desire of the very first British colony – Scotland –for normal independence is somehow considered reprehensible. Why so?

The Sea Inside

Kathleen Jamie

The sea surrounds us. It gives us life, provides us with the air we breathe and the food we eat. It is ceaseless change and constant presence. It covers two-thirds of our planet. Yet caught up in our everyday lives, we barely notice it. In 'The Sea Inside', Philip Hoare sets out to rediscover the sea, its islands, birds and beasts.

In April this year a sperm whale appeared in Oban Bay and remained there for nine days, long enough for word to spread and various experts to pronounce. That it wasn't set upon, tortured and speared to death, as would have been the case not so long ago, surely marks a sea-change in human sensibility. On the contrary, if anyone had harassed the creature, well, they'd have been the one flensed.

I happened to be passing through Oban en route to Mull so I joined the small group assembled behind the pizza parlour and public toilets on the pier. Fishing boats were tied up, and across the bay the island of Kerrera lay in the first spring sunshine. The whale had chosen a spot just outside the Kerrera marina, so it was in full view, and its behaviour was predictable. Every 45 minutes or so it surfaced for a couple of minutes, blew, then dived again. The group I joined consisted in Easter holidaymakers, workmen in overalls and

45

an elderly lady perched elegantly on a capstan, who perhaps knew this would be her only chance to see a great whale. Or maybe she'd seen hundreds and was coming back for more. They are a bit addictive. Some people preferred to gaze over the water in silence as they waited, others were inclined to show off their knowledge. I overheard phrases: 'When we were in New Zealand,' 'When we were in Cape Town.' 'Of course, sperm whales are usually well out into the Atlantic.'

It's true that sperm whales are deep-sea animals and it's highly unusual to have one arrive, as it were, on the doorstep. Local newspapers kept up reports but thankfully didn't give the whale a silly name. The creature might have been resting following an injury or illness; it didn't seem unduly stressed. It was echo-locating nicely and knew its own situation. The best policy was simply to leave it alone. The alternative would have been to try to shoo it back out to sea, but how do you shoo a whale? The attitude that arose was part protective, part *laissez-faire*. CalMac diverted their ferries around the beast's haunt, people came and went on the pier, and the whale remained in the bay until the next very high tide, when, buoyed by the extra water, it swam away.

I didn't see the whale from the pier. I had to leave for the ferry before it appeared but the ferry terminal windows overlook the same waters so I kept an eye out while queuing to board. Then there it was! Like a range of low grey hills, with sunlight gleaming on its flanks. A sperm whale! In Oban Bay! Having surfaced it sent up a satisfying bush of spray two or three times. I couldn't contain myself. 'Look!' I said to the woman next to me. 'Look! There's that whale!' But she didn't look. She just turned away, saying: 'I am not a whale watcher, thank you.'

The world is full of wonders and mysteries, cruelties and colourful characters, and occasional flashes of enlightenment, as Philip Hoare's book reminds us. Chief among the enigmas are other people. Until that moment, I'd thought the whale unfathomable. A half-fabled creature, emerging from the deep in a holiday resort. But that woman was now the greater puzzle. What was going on in her head?

Hoare's previous book, *Leviathan*, was a lengthy and engrossing disquisition on whales, whale lore, whale hunting and humanity's abrupt volte-face about these creatures. He was also co-curator of the Moby Dick Big Read, an online extravaganza which involved all 135 chapters of Melville's book being read, a chapter a day, by people as different as Stephen Fry, Tilda Swinton, even David Cameron, as well as ordinary folk. *The Sea Inside* is most at ease when, again, he is in the company of whales.

Companionable and entertaining, the book follows the recent fashion for combining memoir, travelogue, historical byways, natural history and lore. This can suggest a hoarder's fear that something might be left out. Or perhaps it's a bid to escape categories in favour of an appropriate fluidity. 'The sea defines us, connects us, separates us,' Hoare writes. 'Most of us experience only its edges, our available wilderness on this crowded island ... Perpetually renewing and destroying, the sea proposes a beginning and an ending, an alternative to our landlocked state, an existence to which we are tethered when we might rather be set free.' 'Being 50 per cent water,' he goes on, 'we all contain the sea inside us.' The sea becomes a medium, and Hoare delivers an enthusiast's compendium, a cabinet of curiosities linked by the notion of the sea.

The book opens and returns to Hoare's home port of Southampton. A suburban sea, he calls it, where he swims, apparently every day, and in doing so offers digressions on birds and container ships, and plenty of the fascinating facts that characterise his work. Southampton, originally a Roman settlement, now with a shore-side oil refinery, chemical plant and power station, is where the inhabitants of the South Atlantic island of Tristan Da Cunha were brought in 1961, after being evacuated to escape a volcanic eruption. But digression is the wrong word, because these explorations are not deviations from the main point, they are the point. Everything connects.

Southampton is connected by water to the Isle of Wight, where we encounter the pioneering photographer Julia Margaret Cameron, born in 1815, who lived there 'swathed in purple paisley'. Cameron was born in Calcutta, but on the Isle of Wight she 'presided over an unlikely irruption of bohemianism'. She died in Ceylon, so in a skip and a jump we are looking up at the Ceylonese stars, and wondering how we got there. The Isle of Wight also means Tennyson, and his Kraken — a deep sea connection. There are ravens on the sea-cliffs and following the ravens takes us to the desert saints, whom ravens befriended. The desert, we might complain, is far from the sea, but a sleight brings us back to the Vikings, who carried ravens as navigational aids, and thence to St Cuthbert, and yes, cetaceans. St Cuthbert, himself a great one for chilly dips in the sea, is associated with a minor miracle involving dolphin flesh. The flow of thought and association enriches the book, although cetaceans remain the fleshy centre of the watery world.

Certain of the paths are well trodden. Barely a 'nature book' is published today without homage to J.A. Baker, or Gilbert White, or stern collectors like the 18th-century surgeon John Hunter, who dissected everything, including any hapless whale that wandered into the Thames. Much is fresh, though. When we reach New Zealand, the discussion turns to the relationship between the Maori and whales. And the Moa, the giant, now extinct, bird. And Te Pehi Kupe, a warrior richly adorned with facial tattoos, who in 1824 blagged a lift to Liverpool on a merchant ship. It's testament to Hoare's skill as a writer and companion that his work, a crammed treasure chest, doesn't irritate. He isn't a show-off. In *The Sea Inside,* you can go with the flow.

All the lore and wonders are fascinating, but in New Zealand, as in the Azores, as in Provincetown, it's the cetaceans who steal the show. It's just typical of us as a species to invent the exploding harpoon long before we came up with scuba-diving gear. Now, though, it's possible to swim among dolphins and whales. What they think of it we can only speculate, but it's certainly not the worst thing we've done to them. The book's most original sections are Hoare's accounts of doing just that, diving with whales, an experience he calls 'truly dreamlike'. In the Azores, he swims among a pod of sperm whales. Despite their size, the animals flit from view. 'Like birds that vanish in mid-air, they seem to disappear in the sea. It's an impossible feat of prestidigitation. Over the waves

I can see the whale, quite clearly close; under the water, nothing. Then suddenly there it is – a big beautiful animal held in the surf, stilled within the surge as I am flailing.' He says later: 'Nothing else matters. I feel nothing bad can happen if I'm with a whale. As if its grey mass insures against all the other evils.'

In New Zealand, its dusky dolphins, a super-pod of at least two hundred. He is in the water.

I look round and see dozens of dolphins heading straight at me, like a herd of buffalo. For a moment I think they are going to swim right into me. A ridiculous notion. They, like the whales, register my every move, my every dimension, both inside and out, my density, my temperature, what I am and what I am not. A dolphin's sonar, which can fire off two thousand clicks a second, is able to discern something the thickness of a fingernail from thirty feet away. At the last minute the animals swerve aside, under my legs, by my side, past my head ... I feel the sensual power of their bodies as they race past.

I wonder if it was this cetacean sensuality the Oban woman registered and refused.

Is this then a pelagic travel book? In a sense, because if you want to hang out with whales you have to go where they are. Although Hoare's whale-road takes him all around the world, he's glad to get back to Southampton. Even before he sets out, he refers to himself as 'philopatric': home loving. By the end, when he's had enough of travel, the book almost becomes a meditation on home, and what home is. Unusually for a man in his fifties, Philip Hoare lives in the house he grew up in. Ghosted in the background are his parents, now both gone, and the business of clearing his mother's room which he left untouched for years after her death, even the bedclothes. His seafaring and whale-swimming over, he appreciates his garden and lets light into his mother's room at last, concluding paradoxically: 'There's no such place as home. And we live there, you and me.'

The Shetland Card

Gerorge Rosie

For the last couple of years, the Liberal MSPs Tavish Scott (Shetland) and
Liam McArthur (Orkney) plus the Tory relic Malcolm Sinclair (Earl of
Caithness) have been sounding off about the right of the inhabitants of
Orkney and Shetland to vote to stay within the UK in the event of the rest
of us voting for an independent Scotland. They claim that their message is
meeting a receptive audience in the islands where folk are quite content
being ruled by London. There's a nice irony there. Whether or not they
know it – and I suspect they don't – Scott, McArthur and Sinclair are
dancing to a tune composed by that wily old Yorkshirman Bernard Ingham
back in the 1970s when he was top press officer at the now-defunct
Department of Energy (DoE). Ingham, of course, went on to become one
of Mrs Thatcher's most loyal and zealous acolytes.

I suppose it might be argued that Ingham was playing into the
Shetlanders' lingering distaste of Scotland and of Edinburgh in particular.
That does exist. In the summer of 2012, I was wandering the old grey
castle at Scalloway, once home to the King's man in Shetland, Sir Patrick
Stuart. I came across a bunch of local primary school kids and their
teachers one of whom was relating the story of the castle. Her instructions
were every time they heard the name Patrick Stuart they were to boo and

hiss – which they did with great enthusiasm. It wasn't much but it was enough to get me thinking.

And I don't think Bernard Ingham was alone in his enthusiasm for driving a wedge between Shetlanders and the rest of Scotland. There's good paper evidence that this particular wheeze was popular in the upper reaches of Whitehall and Westminster as a way of both 'dishing' the Nationalists and keeping oil and gas revenues out of the clutches of the Scots. So far as I can see, the first sign of this ploy came from Ingham's colleague at the DoE, an Under Secretary called Graham Kear.

At the end of April 1975 Kear circulated a report entitled *Scottish Devolution and North Sea Oil*. While most of it is a run-down of the offshore oil industry the report contains an intriguing political suggestion. In Section 32 Kear points out that, 'If Scotland and the Orkney and Shetland Islands are both regarded as States, separate from the rest of the United Kingdom, median lines can be drawn to divide the United Kingdom Continental Shelf between, Orkney & Shetland/Scotland and between Scotland/England.'

And in Section 33 he goes on, 'On this basis 53% of the oil reserves in existing discoveries "belong" to the Orkney/Shetland islands, 46% "belong" to Scotland and the remaining 1% "belong" to England.' And in section 34, 'The majority of future oil discoveries are expected to be in "Scottish waters" or "Orkney/Shetland waters".'

In Section 40, of his report Kear conclude that 'The paper also demonstrates the importance of the Shetland and Orkney islands: any consideration of the effects of Scottish separation must take into account the possibility of pressure for the separation of the islands from the Scottish mainland.'

Which is the first airing, in black and white at least, that I can find of what became known as 'The Shetland Card'. But there's no doubt the mandarins of Whitehall thought that this was a jolly good idea. Because early in 1977 Anthony Crosland, then Foreign Secretary, wrote to Prime Minister Jim Callaghan to say that some of his *civil servants* had reported that this was one way to keep the North Sea oil fields out of the hands of the Scots.

The stratagem was exactly as Graham Kear and Bernard Ingham recommended: change the undersea border between Scotland and

England so that it ran northeast instead of directly east and then persuade Orcadians and Shetlanders to declare UDI from Scotland and extend *their* subsea borders to the southeast. Simple! That way the southern oilfields would be English and the rest would go to the Orcadians and the Shetlanders. The Scots would be left with hardly any oil and all the steam would go out of the SNP's idea of an oil-rich independent Scotland.

Because, Crosland warned, something had to be done to stop the SNP bandwagon which was rampaging across the land. Otherwise, Britain would pay a serious price. Crosland's diplomats and civil servants were telling him that foreigners were beginning to talk. They were beginning to wonder how much longer Britain could hang on to North Sea oil. This speculation, Crosland told Callaghan, 'could damage our international creditworthiness.' And with the British economy in a sorry state Britain needed all the creditworthiness it could get. North Sea oil was the 'collateral for UK borrowing'.

Crosland declared that the idea of diverting the Scotland/England sub-sea border could be spread by planting it among 'selected public opinion formers' (i.e. well-placed journalists) and some of the more loyal back-bench MPs. In the margin of Crosland's letter Callaghan's private secretary Nigel Wickes scribbled 'looks sensible…. If handled sensibly. Do you agree…?' It seems that Callaghan did agree because Crosland's letter was circulated among ministers and top Whitehall mandarins for their comments. They approved, with very few reservations.

Nobody agreed with the strategy more than Bernard Ingham, then the civil servant running the Department of Energy's information division. According to Ingham his division '… has sought for a long time in briefing to undermine SNP claims to North Sea oil: in the process it has played on the Shetland/Orkney uncertainty as well as the uncertainty about the angle of any dividing line between England and a hypothetically independent Scotland… Indeed, it is part of my standard "sales patter" …' In other words, Ingham had been playing the Shetland card for all it was worth.

In fact, Crosland and his men were slow off the mark. A month before Crosland recommended the Shetland Card to Jim Callaghan, the *Sunday Times Business News* had floated the notion. In a front-page splash by James Poole dated December 5th 1976 entitled '*Mapping the political power lines'* Poole examined the legality of Scotland's claim to the oilfields. The piece was accompanied by four maps showing how 'Scotland's oil' depended on where the international lines are drawn. Poole suggested that if the England/Scotland was drawn more realistically, and if Orkney and Shetland decided to opt out of any independence deal, Scotland would be left with hardly any oil. Poole played the latter point for all it was worth:–

'Scottish oil is also under attack from the North. In the clearest possible terms, Shetland has indicated that it wants nothing to do with a separately governed Scotland, be it devolved or independent. A resolution in the local council letters last week to all MPs, and a private separation bill in course of preparation, reaffirm this strong desire to stay outside "Scotland". And, like Scotland itself, the Shetlands has not always been part of the United Kingdom. It came from Norway in 1529 as a dowry to King Malcolm.' (Which is a bit of a historical howler: it was 1472 and the king was James III.)

Poole goes on 'Map Three shows how a median line could be drawn between Scotland and Shetland, based on the equidistance principle of the Geneva Convention. Two thirds of North Sea oil lie unequivocally in Shetland waters. If Shetland gets a chance to separate itself, all the indications are that the Orkneys would as well (Map Four).'

I've no doubt that Poole – who I knew as a good journalist – was aware of the Shetland card being trotted out by Bernard Ingham. But to beef it up Poole cited (and at some length) research by John Grant, then a senior lecturer in law at Glasgow University. Grant had examined Scotland's claim to the North Sea oilfields and decided that Scotland was on shaky legal ground. In the event of any independence negotiations, he argued, the existing maritime 'border' between Scotland and England would be have to be replaced by a line that continued the southwest/northeast line of the land border. Which meant that most of the southern oilfields would fall into English hands. And if the Shetlanders were allowed to extend their maritime border, then....

Poole's article based on Grant's essay did not go unnoticed by the Labour government. Michael Foot, then Lord President, wrote to assure Tony Crosland that '...we have taken a number of steps, somewhat along the lines your officials have suggested, to counteract this...' Foot cites James Poole's article and claimed that 'it was John Smith who suggested to

James Poole that he should write an article in the Sunday Times based on a first class essay on oil and gas by John Grant...' John Smith MP, then Minister of State at the Privy Council office, went on to succeed Neil Kinnock as Labour leader from July 1992 until his sudden death in 1994.

Whether the playing of the Shetland card by Westminster and its acolytes had any effect on the eventual outcome of the devolution referendum is hard to say. But it may well have done. When the votes were counted in March 1979 Shetland and the Orkneys were the only parts of the Highlands and Islands to vote against a devolved Scottish parliament. And they both voted 'no' by thumping majorities (5,466 to 2020 in the case of Shetland: 5439 to 2104 in the case of Orkney). No doubt Tavish Scott and Liam McArthur are hoping for a repeat performance in September next year.

Dinner with No Voters or: "What I wanted to say before the Pudding hit the fan"

Peter Arnott

One thing that almost all of my friends who tell me they intend to vote No in September have in common is that they wish that this referendum campaign had never happened. They don't see the need for it. They think it is needlessly sowing doubt, division and uncertainty at a time when nobody really wanted the debate to happen. They wish the whole damn thing would go away and be forgotten.

I have a certain amount of sympathy with that. I am sure Alex Salmond does too. After all, he didn't expect the Labour Party in Great Britain and in Scotland to collapse quite so comprehensively as they did in 2010 and 2011, and thus make possible the election of a majority SNP administration at Holyrood that was bound – trapped even – by history and manifesto commitments into calling a referendum that was not at the time of their choosing.

Where I take issue with my friends, who are still my friends I hasten to add, is in their imagining that a No vote somehow cancels the uncertainty and division. That life can ever again be like this never happened. I think that to imagine some kind of "return to normality" is not only deluded, I think it is a positively dangerous complacency about the way things have already, irrevocably

57

changed. And more, how things will change after a No vote, as well as after a Yes.

Part of this change is positive, of course, on line and in the meeting halls and pubs and clubs, the Yes campaign in all of its participatory variety has revealed and unleashed a new and painfully hopeful democratic culture in this country on a scale and of a quality of thought and debate that I never would have expected. I'm sure that my No voting friends don't really want all that to disappear and be forgotten.

It has also raised, less comfortably, the spectre of the crying needs genuine reform of the creaking, rotten edifice of the British State, and has revealed many less than attractive elements of its defensive, secretive, mendacious, culture of self-interested pessimism which I'm sure that all of us, whatever side we're on, would rather not have seen revealed so pervasively in institutions that once held almost universal affection if not allegiance.

In any case, despite the devout wish of many in the BBC and the Labour Party, to name but two, that this whole question had never been raised, the status quo, as I've said before, may well be on the ballot paper. But it is not on the cards. A wish for a return to normal is a wish for a stability that is already in the past.

You can't go home when it's not there anymore. Indeed, I would argue that a No vote will change the terms of that "stability" quite as radically as a Yes vote. A No vote is just as much of a vote for change. It is not only Yes voters who should be called on to look into a crystal ball and imagine a future that is radically "not the same".

Before my No voting friends dismiss that as a paradox, may I ask them to consider the following.

Every vile piece of Westminster legislation that has attacked the poor and dismantled the Welfare State, every policy that has ensured that it is only the poor who have paid the price of the recession caused by the greed of the rich, every act of economic and social vandalism – it has been the comfortable posture of the well-meaning voters of Scotland that none of these things have been your fault. That you didn't vote for them.

Well, you won't be able to say that any more.

Up until September the 18th, we have all been able to hide behind all that being someone else's fault. Either way the vote goes, Yes or No, that comfortable position has already been shattered. Either we vote to take responsibility for our own economics, our own wealth distribution, our own decisions to make war or peace…or we are voting to mandate away control over all of these matters to Westminster forever.

Either way, we will be responsible.

If a Yes voter has to take on board the moral hazard of whatever happens for good or ill in an independent Scotland, a No voter must equally accept moral responsibility for having given Westminster permanent permission to do whatever it likes forever. No questions asked.

Moral Hazard works both ways.

Whatever austerity measures are coming down the line, all those policies that weren't your fault before September 18th? After September the 18th, they will be your fault. No. Sorry. Every single one of them. Will be your fault. This is the trap that history has set you. And I understand your discomfort. I understand your wanting to wish all this away. But you can't. You're stuck along with the rest of us.

Except of course, we're going to be really, really annoying about it. We're going to make you feel bad. We will be unbearable. Every single day, we'll be reminding you. When the Tories make a formal or informal pact with UKIP and win the election in 2015, despite having no seats in Scotland? Your fault. When there is a vote to leave the EU and Scotland votes to stay but we have to leave because middle England votes Yes? Your fault.

Sorry. That's the way it's going to be. In fact, I confidently predict that at dinner parties in Scotland in 2016 it will be impossible to find anyone who will admit to having voted No, so complex and disruptive and chaotic will be the consequences, so omnipresent will the border question be in every single dispute about everything. It will feel very bad to have actually voted for all that.

But my sympathy will fail me pretty quickly. Because your No vote or your failure to vote will have signified that it in your view it is better for Scotland to suffer neo-conservative governments it didn't vote for than to take responsibility for its own affairs. You will have voted for Scotland, politically speaking, to cease to exist. So, kind of hell mend you. Sorry.

Now, hold on…is that fair? We can't be expected to have thought all that through before it happens!

Well…Think about it now. Alex Salmond, though he is deemed to be the source and fount of all evil, is not the only begetter of this referendum. David Cameron agreed to it too. Now why do you think he did that? Because he is a friend to democracy, perhaps? Surely only a very small minority of No voters believe that. No. You know and I know that Cameron agreed to the referendum in order to call Scotland's bluff. To settle and silence the "Scottish question" for a generation.

(That won't work, obviously, but that's an argument for later)

Cameron only did that because he was confident of a No vote, of course. But what have the Tories, and others in the British establishment to gain from a No vote?

I think they know that if we take independence off the table, if we remove, voluntarily, that bargaining chip from future negotiation, then there won't ever need to be any negotiations ever again. Everything will be in their gift. For a generation. And having voted for that once, we will have thrown away any electoral influence over what happens next.

Everything we have gained since devolution in terms of the painfully slow emergence into democracy we are still undergoing has been predicated on the "or else" of independence. Does anyone in the No Camp seriously expect a prize for loyalty when we remove the best card we've got from our hand? One or two of you can expect knighthoods, maybe, but what can the ordinary No voter really expect as a reward? from those people?

The Yes camp are constantly being asked about what kind of negotiations we can expect after we "reject" the United Kingdom – on currency, NATO, oil, Trident and the rest? Well, what kind of negotiations do you expect when you've said to other side; "whatever you want to do is fine with us"?

There I go again...being divisive...talking about "the other side".

Well, take a listen to the mutterings of the backbenchers from those English and Welsh constituencies who haven't had the bargaining position we've had, that bargaining position you're going to vote so happily to throw away, and see how long all those promises to protect the Barnett formula and add meaningful powers to Holyrood last.

David Cameron wasn't offering us a choice between different forms of democracy. He was offering us the choice between shutting up and fucking off. And fucking off might well have its difficulties, but we should be in no doubt that shutting up is exactly what is demanded of us if we don't have the guts to fuck off.

A replacement for Trident? You don't want that? Shut Up. A slashing of consequential health spending as privatisation of the NHS in England and Wales speeds up? You don't like that either? Shut up.

You voted for it.

Before September the 18th, nice left leaning folk in Scotland chatting about the Welfare State and the decline of local government and the miners and the poll tax and the sale of council housing and the destruction of our industries at dinner parties could say in their comfortable, pre-democratic way:

"Oh well, it's terrible. But it's not our fault. We're not responsible. We didn't vote for that." No more. After September the 18th, we in Scotland will be responsible for whatever happens to us. Our choice is whether or not we want democracy to go along with the responsibility.

Right now, thanks to the referendum, however uncomfortably or prematurely, our future is, temporarily, in our own hands. A No vote is not a place to hide from that future. It is just a vote to have no influence over that future after we deliver a mandate to whoever wins in Westminster elections that we can't influence to do whatever they like with it.

I hope you're comfortable with that, folks. Because if you win, I promise to devote every waking moment to reminding you what the hell you just did, even if there are none of you at dinner parties in a years time who will admit to it any more than you'd admit now to being a Tory.

Everything has changed. Everyone has to face the reality of that. Our only choice in September 18th is: Do we make the way we change subject to democratic control within Scotland, or do we leave the management of that change to whomever somebody else votes for.

Because, my brothers and my sisters, as George Bush once said, democracy, with all of the adult responsibilities that implies, is coming soon to a place near you. For the first time in history, for 15 hours in September, Scotland will be a democratic country, with its people responsible for themselves.

Putting your head in the sand of a No vote won't make it go away.

We need to talk about leadership...

Laura Eaton-Lewis

There's rich debate taking place right now in Scotland that has revolutionised people's participation in politics and the governance of our society. People who until now have not been admitted access to mainstream political processes have grasped the possibilities the independence referendum has brought about for future change. The public have themselves devised and led actions which are spreading like wildfire across the nation. It's a fertile time. We're all thinking about leadership, the way we want to be represented in politics, and how we might participate in the processes of governance in the future.

Regardless of the outcome of the Independence vote on the 18th of September, we can't go back to how things were.

For everyone, but particularly for women and subjugated others, the independence discussion has been a massively positive experience: we have found our voice, reached out to our neighbours, activated our networks, and discovered the power and influence that each of us could have. We must maintain the level of engagement that we are currently experiencing.

The potential for societal change is within our grasp, and yet this collective enlightenment has also thrown light on problems that still exist, and which we cannot allow to be perpetrated any further.

With boldness and a thirst for justice many of us proclaim that we want to make Scotland a nation of equals – where each of us has the power to participate in the shaping of her future. Yet we cannot forget where we are now, that we continue to experience a deeply unequal relationship to power.

Whether yes or no, we must rebuild and we cannot begin to create the blueprint of a new nation, its principles or architecture, until we accept that the very *process by which we write this future must enshrine the actions of equality at its core.*

What do I mean by that?

I mean that, right now, we have a serious problem with leadership. There's a problem with how it looks, how it sounds, what we believe it to be, HOW we think it gets done... and WHO we choose to do the job. Because ultimately, at the moment we **don't** get to choose.

'But hang on... this was meant to be about democracy... wasn't it?'

Take a look around, note who are our current leaders... by a long way you'll find they are white middle-class men who hail in disproportionate numbers from private education. You look at any platform in even the 'social justice' agenda of the referendum debate and the speakers also, overwhelmingly, represent that same demographic. Many of the people in leading campaign roles are self-appointed, others appointed sideways from similar jobs, and here we see the same demographic again. Now why is this? Are rich white boys better at leading than the rest of us? Is it inevitable that if Scotland votes to remove the Old Boys club we will end up replacing them with the New Boys Club?

That doesn't have to happen. If it did, it would undermine the purpose of the whole independence movement, so we can safely assume that, amongst those supporting the social justice agenda behind the independence campaigns, **no one** wants that to happen.

I don't think for a second that any of the intelligent and inspiring men that I work with are intentionally aiming to withhold power from women and minority groups. I really feel for our Good Men (of whom there are many), it's very difficult when you are a member of a privileged group to see the ways in which you unconsciously perpetrate structures and processes that continue to promote and maintain your privilege.

So how do we get out of this deadlock – what do we need to do?

First of all, we need to call it as we find it and realise that trying to resolve a problem is not going to put the end goal in jeopardy. It's not a spanner in the works, it IS the works. It's a design problem, and we need to recognise it when we see it and give voice to it. It doesn't mean that those who are perpetrating it are bad people, no-one should be automatically vilified; what it DOES mean that we have a responsibility to address it now.

Not at some point in the utopian future, not after September the 18th... Now.

So let's look at the ways in which this everyday power grab is happening within even the most progressive of circles and this is the science bit, numerous workplace studies which have shown the following:

– Men tend significantly to take credit for women's work

Whether that's taking credit for their ideas, using their words without credit, using their research or concepts without credit

– Men tend to delegate the admin work to the ladies.

Ah, the time-honoured practice of treating a woman as if she is your secretary. Come on dude, you're a grown-up... write your own emails and book your own taxi.

– Men are significantly more likely to self-select for the spotlight.

'Because we need someone up there that *knows* what they're doing'... Guys, it shouldn't be news that women have a head for economics, negotiating and strategic thinking.

– Men often leave the shitty jobs to 'someone else'...

This can be a subtle one, the menfolks don't tend to put themselves forward to do jobs unless they are the important ones. So often, to make sure things get done *properly* and the mission of the project succeeds, women feel they have to put themselves forward when no one else will to make sure the graft gets done. So, in an attempt to work their way *up to positions of power,* women end up effacing themselves by taking on the grunt work while the men take the spotlight and do the public-facing appearances and, again, take the credit. As councillor Martha Wardrop of the Scottish Greens said, 'women need to stop making themselves busy'.

– Men are very likely to talk over women.

Men frequently bellow in meetings, they interrupt, they don't leave space in the conversation or look to women to give them the opportunity to talk, in short...

– Men will usually ignore a woman saying the same thing as a man.

The classic scenario where a woman says something over and over again, maybe another woman picks up on the point and yet *the point isn't noted until a man says the same thing.* Then of course the man gets credit for her idea (see item 1). I've personally seen this happen hundreds of times. (see above: The Fast Show sketch 'The Amazing Invisible Woman')

– Men will tend to offer 'opinion' as argument, yet demand 'evidence' from women.

Women are held to a higher standard of performance and accountability than their male counterparts. Follow this up with the situation where a woman presents a storming case...

– Men often ignore the validity of evidence and arguments presented by women.

I don't know why this happens, this is one of the things that makes me *most* angry. Present a rational position please, but if you're not a man, the only way to make your argument visible is to get assertive about it because (item 6) 'men ignore women'. And we all know what an assertive woman is, that's right, an emotional one. Sorry lady, you didn't convince us with your 'facts' because you got all 'bossy'.

– Men frequently value women in direct relation to their perceived 'attractiveness'.

Don't pretend for a second that this isn't true. Look at the shit Hilary Clinton has put up with, even though it's pretty well accepted that she was the brains behind Bill C... she gets judged on what she's wearing, her age, and the worst... her *fuckability.* Just last week, a colleague of mine was in a discussion about the referendum, only to be interrupted (point 5) by a man who said 'I have to tell you how beautiful you are', and when she said that was irrelevant to anything she was actually saying, he repeated himself (point 7) and then to ensure she was under no illusion that her ideas weren't wanted and that only *his experience of her face* warranted discussion... repeated his line again (points 6, 7 & 8).

– Men usually insist on systems of discussing things that allow themselves to express dominance via points 1 to 9...

The following systems have the effect that only the few who are *already in positions of power (rich, white men) can have voice*: Head to

67

head debates favour the shoutiest; Panel presentations to an audience favour self-appointed 'experts' who place themselves above the audience; Questions from the floor allow the experts to 'teach' those of us in the audience, and questions generally come only from people (usually men) who already feel privileged and therefore confident enough that their voice will be valid when they face the 'experts'; round table meetings are usually conducted with a combination of all of the above – presentation, questions from floor, and head to head debate conventions, with the added problem that the agenda of what *can* be discussed *is* usually set by the leader.

– So how do you get to be that leader?

See above list of points 1-10, be warned though that if you are not already a rich white man, you'd best do a bloody brilliant job at imitating one.

If we're really interested in creating a socially democratic model of leadership, we have a great opportunity to do so in Scotland right now. With all this energy and engagement coming from the usually 'invisible' women and minority group leaders, it's a timely moment to rewrite the governance models that underpin the systemic prejudice outlined above.

'Sounds a bit hopeless' you might say.

'Why would any woman want to be a leader if that's what you have to put up with?'

Or maybe you think, 'But we need to get things done! It's not like there's another way of doing things… is there?'

Yes. Another way is possible.

It's entirely achievable to create a high functioning culture if we begin as we mean to go on. We can reap the benefits of diverse knowledge by representing ALL of our talent in leadership roles, putting the best of our minds together. But to do this properly, we have to tackle this problem now, and to do that we have to see that the problem has at least four dimensions:

– It's systemic – the *way* we do things needs to change.

68

– Cultural – the way things have always been done has created a self-fulfilling prophecy that favours the same people over and over again. To re-programme this we need to actively select leaders on a positive bias from amongst those who are currently invisible.

– Behavioural – we need to set a new social contract about how we expect to conduct ourselves. We can't leave politeness only to the ladeeezzzz.

– Modelled on a pre-existing template of what 'success' looks like. So, we need to create new narratives and promote other models of success.

A four-dimensional proposal might be:

System
:

Based on a consensus model, big participation from many in small groups which allow quieter, diverse voices to present knowledge and feedback decisions and findings to the greater group. Decisions are taken by achieving consensus or as near to consensus as possible. Ensure questions are asked for clarity without jumping to stereotyped conclusions; then actually find a way to listen to the answers. Find a place to 'bank' suggestions and motions that are not for action 'right now' so that diverse ideas and voices are documented, even if they can't be achieved straight away.

Culture:

Quotas for representative / leadership positions and opportunities for development, will over time redress the cultural effect of one group having dominated the power and the narrative for so long

Behavioural:

Simply make the above list of points unacceptable behaviours, and set mutually agreed terms of engagement. If we feel that there's a time and a space where these behaviours are essential, only with the consent of others, demarcate a time-limited space which allows expression in those ways towards a specified goal. For example, it's not that head-to-head debate is *never* useful, but it should not be the day-to-day mode of leadership or persuasion.

Models:

Present and promote a range of possible templates for leadership, a range of flexible methods of working which admits the experience and processes of women, disabled people, people of diverse cultural backgrounds, ages and sexual identities. Transactional leadership processes replaced by transformational models.

BUT

That's jumping the gun.

We can't *decide* that's what we're going to do without the consent and participation of those who are invisible right now, because we need them to create and define our future constitution and processes. We need proportional numbers of women and people of protected characteristics to comprise our leaders and negotiators on the morning of September 19th.

This is going to mean some of these lovely rich white boys stepping aside and giving 'their' place to someone else on their team, OR making an extra place at the decision-making table for women and other missing voices.

I can't overstate the importance of this. Representation affects everything, not just the 'equalities bit' of the process. Representation is the foundation of governance.

We need to BE THE LEADERS DESIGNING THE ARCH-ITECTURE, not be told which safety net might catch us when we fall off it.

In Scotland we've all been changed by the great decision that we face on the 18th September. We've been changed by the discussions we have had, we've taken it upon ourselves to find the information we need to uncover the complexity of the issues and make our own choice. We've been changed by the way that we've led our own action, volleyed perspectives and possibilities with people we love, founded new allegiances and discovered new ways of working.

We have been changed because we have taken politics back into our own hands and we are representing ourselves and our communities.

We don't need to wait until we are 'allowed' to be leaders, we are doing it already. Shift your bum a bit and make space for us. We don't want to do the shitty jobs, we belong at the table.

We have a voice... now let us use it.

'It's Time': The Independence of Gough Whitlam

Meaghan Delahunt

One of my sisters' emails from Melbourne: It's like a death in the family. And when I heard the news last week, I wept, along with many other Australians. But we were not mourning a family member. We were mourning Former Prime Minister Gough Whitlam, the great, progressive politician of our youth. He died last week in Australia at the age of 98.

I was 12 when Gough came to power, ending 23 years of Liberal Party (Tory) rule. I was too young to vote, but old enough to know that change was coming, that we were living through something extraordinary. In 1972, the quiescent Australian suburbs were suddenly less quiescent: the Holden station wagons with 'It's Time' stickers, the badges, the posters, the T-shirts, the famous 'It's Time' theme song – rising to a gospel choir – all of this thrilled me as a kid. Australia was in the mood for something different. It was a great popular upsurge. And I realise that our recent experience here in Scotland – this sense that ideas have finally come of age and need expression – resonates with this childhood experience in Australia.

From 1972-1975, the Whitlam Government changed the face of Australia and altered its place in the world. As John Pilger puts it, 'Australia briefly became an independent state during the Whitlam years.' Of course, Whitlam made some mistakes (Timor, for example) but it's in the context of independence that I want to pay tribute. Within days of coming to office, Whitlam pulled Australian troops from Vietnam, abolished conscription and released draft resisters from jail. Equal pay and equal rights for women, free tertiary education, land rights, Medicare, public Arts funding, and anti-racism legislation were enacted. The White Australia policy was over: he oriented Australia towards Asia and the Pacific, refused to be a colonial power and granted independence to Papua New Guinea. The Whitlam government was anti-nuclear, challenged the legitimacy of the US spy base at Pine Gap and began to chart a foreign policy independent of Britain and America. His government sought to 'buy back the farm' – to have Australia's rich natural and mineral resources under Australian control and to use the funds to support its ambitious welfare programme. This is just one of the parallels with the Scottish Independence campaign – the desire for autonomy and control of our own resources. The desire to fund social justice. The spirit of the era was optimistic. As one of Whitlam's advisers later noted: '1972 was one of the really happy years in Australia...there was just an abundant air of good feeling.'

Whitlam was of his time. A generation radicalised and traumatised by the Vietnam War – over 60,000 Australians fought there, 521 were killed and 3,000 wounded – helped bring his government to power. Women's Liberation, Aboriginal Land Rights, Gay Rights were all coming to the fore. It was a movement of young people and the young-at-heart who wanted change after decades of conservative rule. This conservatism and accompanying cultural cringe had resulted in an exodus of talented artists, writers and scholars from Australia, something the Whitlam government wanted to reverse. Whitlam and his great wife Margaret were unashamedly literary and patrons of the Arts. As David Malouf wrote last week, the Whitlams regularly attended book launches, theatre and arts events and understood that the new Australian books they read, the new plays they saw, the new music they heard 'were essential to the excitement of the moment and what appeared to be a new national consciousness.' Artists and writers rallied to support the Whitlam government under attack in the same way that artists and writers overwhelmingly supported the 'Yes' campaign here.

I believe we can trace a direct cultural line between the election of the Whitlam government – its support for free tertiary education and public Arts funding, the injection of cultural self-confidence this gave the country – and Richard Flanagan's recent Booker Prize win. The fact that Australia has several Booker Prize winners at all is part of the legacy of that government. These days it's not surprising to see Australian artists up there on the international stage, but this was not always the case. The deep cultural reservoir Australian artists now freely draw upon – multiculturalism, internationalism and a colonial critique – found expression and encouragement during this period.

The 'Yes' campaign in Scotland, similarly fuelled by the young and young-at-heart: the T-shirts, the badges, the balloons, the wheelie bin stickers – I was reminded of the excitement of my 12 year old self in Melbourne so many years ago. I remember my parents so passionate about a Whitlam Labor victory – could it happen? Could we really change things in this country? Could we really aspire to be more than a British or an American outpost? It turned out that yes, for a brief, glorious period, we could.

It didn't last.

Too many forces lined up against it. As Graham Freudenberger, a key adviser to Whitlam said: 'The crisis of November 1975 began on the 2nd December 1972, the day Whitlam got elected.' The Liberals never accepted the legitimacy of a Labor government, it was an affront to their sense of entitlement, and they worked hard to undermine it. (Entitlement: the Labour Party in Scotland comes to mind.) The Australian Labor Party didn't have a majority in the Senate and the Liberals used this fact to block the money bills, forcing another election in 1974 and then the political crisis of 1975. Effectively, they starved the Labour government of funds. As it turned out, the enemies of the Whitlam government were not only at home. A progressive government, trying to chart its own course, enacting reforms at lightning pace: dispensing with 'God

Save the Queen' as the national anthem, dispensing with the Imperial honours system, drawing closer to the Non-Aligned Movement? Threatening to expose and possibly close American spy bases on Australian soil? It was the period of the Cold War, and this government, when viewed from the perspective of the White House and Westminster, seemed dangerously Red. Whitlam was no communist. But he was an ardent social democrat and reformer.

The 1960's and '70's were the heyday of CIA-backed coups and British complicity. Yet most people in the UK know more about what happened in Chile or Greece, for example, than the tumult in Australia. There are political reasons for this... Just last week, *The Guardian*'s slant on Whitlam was that he was 'ousted on a technicality.' The bigger story wasn't discussed. The bigger story puts the role of the Monarchy, Westminster and the White House under the spotlight. A more informed picture gives us cold, hard parallels with our recent Scottish Referendum experience.

I was 15 when Gough Whitlam was deposed by the Queen's Representative, the Governor General, Sir John Kerr. It was the defining political event of my childhood and I still find it shocking. John Kerr, of course, was not acting alone. He'd sought advice from Buckingham Palace on the 'reserve' powers of his position – and was advised that, yes, actually, the Queen's Man could dismiss a democratically elected government, if needed. It turns out that the Queen's Man also had very strong links to Anglo-American intelligence – referred to by the CIA as 'our man Kerr', he was also well acquainted with MI6 – who bugged Whitlam's cabinet meetings for the Americans. The full story of how the Brits and the Americans conspired to bring down the Whitlam government is still emerging. Wikileaks last year published diplomatic cables from the period disclosing that figures from both major Australian parties informed on Whitlam to Washington. These figures included a future Prime Minister and foreign minister. The coup left a deep psychic wound in a country founded on psychic wounds. It hammered home the fact that, despite our best efforts, Australia's colonial status had not altered. We were caught between Britain and the post-war imperium of the United States. We had exercised our democratic right in '72, again in '74 when Whitlam was re-elected, and been punished for it

From the buoyant technicolour of '72 to the black-and-white of the 'constitutional coup' in '75. This is truly how it felt. This period saw major demonstrations all over the country – 100,000 people on the streets of Melbourne, the army and navy on high alert in case of 'civil disturbance'. A month later, the forced election brought the Liberal Party and Malcolm Fraser to power. Almost overnight – a different set of stickers and posters appeared all over Australia: 'Shame, Fraser, Shame.'

What I remember in the final phase of Whitlam's government is the barrage of negativity and propaganda Australians endured. Again, very similar to our recent Referendum experience here. The powerful Murdoch Press and all the media turned against the government. Twelve months earlier, Murdoch had instructed his editors to 'Kill Whitlam.' Indeed, so great was his editorial interference that journalists from *The Australian* went on strike during the '75 election campaign. We were urged from radio, television, newspapers to say 'No' to change, to say 'No' to another progressive government – or suffer the consequences. Sound familiar? It should. The arguments are well worn: Our national security was at stake, our children's future was at stake. We needed American bases and spy facilities to keep us safe (Trident, anyone?). We were not ready or able to cut the apron ties to Britain. Not able to go it alone.

Britain and America have long experience in undermining independence movements. There are few countries which have broken completely free from Empire unscathed. Australia's attempt in 1975 and Scotland in 2014 are mere recent examples. Indeed, some of the same characters feature in both national stories: Henry Kissinger, for example. In the 1980's he admitted that 'The Whitlam government was one of President Nixon's pet hates.' In 2014 Kissinger emerged from the crypt to urge a 'No' vote in Scotland. The spectral face of Rupert Murdoch is another blast from the past. Indeed, a recent photo of Murdoch waving from the back window of a car in Aberdeen during the Referendum bears an uncanny resemblance to a photo of Murdoch waving from a car window in Australia after the 1975 coup.

One of the reasons so few people in the UK know about what happened in Australia is because it still raises so many awkward questions. 1975 exposed constitutional monarchy as an oxymoron scam. It raised questions about power, sovereignty and independence that still resonate. The Governor General used archaic 'reserve powers' to dismiss an elected government. British Intelligence worked with American intelligence, the ruling elites closed ranks to protect their own interests and preserve business as usual.

Fear and negativity won out in Australia after the coup. Again, that familiar tune. We learn from this that opponents of change will do anything. As we've seen here, they will play dirty, they will vow and pledge and undermine like there's no tomorrow. We cannot expect them to abide by democracy or decency. We can expect to be tripped up on 'technicalities.' We must be prepared. We must be more than prepared.

So. I've now lived through two great progressive upsurges – and two 'defeats'– in two different countries. The first as a child in Australia, the second as an adult in Scotland. How fortunate I am! I take heart from the fact that lessons learned young are lessons which endure. Through the Referendum in Scotland a whole new generation was politicised – just as I was during the Whitlam years. A whole new generation of artists and writers will come into their own, just as they did in Australia. We are still living through a revolutionary period in Scotland – nothing is settled, everything is up for grabs. How fortunate we are.

My brother texts me: 'We're all listening to 'It's Time'.' I get on YouTube and marvel at the hipsters and oldsters, the beards and miniskirts. I start singing along. I sing as if I'm twelve years old and it's summer in Melbourne; barefoot and joyous, impatient for change. "It's a choice between the habits and fears of the past and the opportunities and demands of the future' said Whitlam. I mourn his passing and the brief, wondrous time when Australia was, truly, in Noam Chomsky's words: 'the threat of a good example.'

Getting out of the Kitchen

Katie Gallogy Swan

Finger hovering over the 'send' button, I can't count the number of times I have been almost confident enough to offer an article for publication. At that moment, the piece stands on a cliff edge, waiting to be prodded gently into the 'real' world to be shared, interpreted and criticised on a bumpy nosedive into the abyss of online commentary. I hesitate, not because I lack confidence in my own capacities, but because the consequences of opining loom large in my mind.

The past few weeks have seen more than a stramash in the womenosphere of Planet Scotland.

The #GlasgowEffect saw a female artist lose days of sleep because of the abusive language on her Facebook page, while a regional newspaper published a picture of her home with no thoughts to her safety. A high profile twitter spat between J.K. Rowling and Natalie McGarry MP have seen both the object of twitter vilification. Scotland's ever-shrinking mainstream media lost respect in sacking Angela Haggerty at the behest of the Rangers' board—ironically less than a week after her article detailing the systematic misogyny and abuse she continues to receive from Rangers supporters as a result of her journalism. And in the latest instalment of why being a woman with a profile needs a health and safety protocol, anti-feminist supporters of Roosh V were encouraged to document details of women vocally opposing their network, in order to 'exact furious retribution' after an uproar about the 'gathering' of his supporters in Glasgow and Edinburgh this weekend.

For many women, publishing their work is a radical act. Barely a week goes by without a story about the alienation of women in media, whether in the reification of their role in society as sex objects who are only important insofar as the label or makeup they wear, or in more extreme cases of sexual harassment online. If we are to take equality seriously, our response needs to take account of the implicit and explicit mechanisms of this inequality.

For many women, publishing their work is a radical act. Barely a week goes by without a story about the alienation of women in media, whether in the reification of their role in society as sex objects who are only important insofar as the label or makeup they wear, or in more extreme cases of sexual harassment online. If we are to take equality seriously, our response needs to take account of the implicit and explicit mechanisms of this inequality.

I am immensely proud of every woman and man who has rebuked the ideology of Roosh V this week. However, I fear that in congratulating ourselves, we risk losing the opportunity to widen the net of discussion on the reality of everyday sexism in Scotland. While contentious figures like Roosh V can cause an isolated bubble of populist furore, it doesn't take very long for old habits to return. Just as a brief example, on one public Facebook page which declared it was 'never prouder' to be Glaswegian after Roosh V's tweet about vehement opposition to him in Glasgow, it only takes a few scrolls down to see previous posts which belittle and objectify women. Rape is easy to oppose, but what about body shaming?

This is not indeed to shame the admin of this page, since they too are victim and audience to the infrastructure of inequality hardwired into our system, but instead to recognise the gulf between the silos of self-identified feminists and the everyday experience of sexism which many are numb to. Sexism is insidious; the capacity to discern it is itself a privilege. All too often, possible allies are locked out of the discussion because they don't have the 'appropriate' vocabulary to bestow authority on their contribution.

This isn't helped by the popular expression of feminism as isolated crusades against a series of male antagonists. Daniel O'Reilly, Ched Evans, Julien Blanc, Tim Hunt—names whose banality conceal the heated and impassioned debate these personalities have initiated. In such circumstances, feminism gains recognition as people connect over the spectrum of stupidities uttered by these men, while simultaneously, the singular determination to crucify them leaves those who empathise with the men defensive.

Though some may bemoan the advertising the protests will afford Roosh V, perhaps inadvertently pushing more troubled men towards his ideology thusly, I believe he's also unwittingly handed feminists in Scotland an incredible opportunity—if we have the confidence and empathy to grasp it. This awareness raising campaign could be the gateway drug many need to connect a rape-apologist ideology with the everyday experiences of sexist subjugation. And while my patience for hand-holding men through the rationalisation of feminism wears thinner by the day, I want to match the fire in my belly with the radical strength of empathy and care.

Without the tools to perceive and translate structural inequality and its consequences, 'get back in the kitchen' jokes and 'stand against Roosh V' events will continue to coexist in the same warped timeline. What if we took this opportunity not to police one another, as we too often do, but to encourage more people to extend their passionate support of this protest to, for example, opposing the monstering and misogyny which stymies female voices? Thanks to Daryush Valizadeh, activists this week have propelled feminism into the timelines, feeds, and news pages of citizens across Scotland. The challenge is now in keeping it there.

Not Nationality but Language

Scott Hames

Like most people with an interest in 'the language question,' I welcome the sudden growth in awareness since the referendum. It's great that we're having debates about Scots in newspapers (and here on Bella) rather than specialist journals or thinly populated seminar rooms. The whole conversation feels more accessible and democratic, actually plugged into some of the vernacular energies it tends to champion.

But the fact that much of the new pro-Scots enthusiasm is fuelled by populist nationalism has its downside too. Alex Massie's column in *The Times* earlier this week is right about the current tendency to reduce language to just another front for political mobilisation. It's always been a shibboleth to some degree, but the question of Scots is now becoming hyper-politicised in crude and distorting ways. As the Edinburgh linguist Pavel Iosad remarked during the last Twitter-spat about this (when *The National* published its front page in Scots), it's as though language is just something to have opinions about, a source of ammunition for two entrenched 'sides' sniping at each other about something else. There are whole shelves of good books on the history of Scots, Gaelic and the standardisation of English, but they seldom feature in these debates.

The weightless and sometimes clueless quality of these arguments is not only depressing but potentially damaging, tending to shrink rather than expand the expressive possibilities at issue. (And yes, the very weak level of general knowledge about the history and development of Scots – and for that matter English – raises long-standing questions about the education system.) In the larger public arena to which the discussion has shifted, Scots is becoming reduced to a nationalist totem. This has as much to do with how Scots is passionately defended (broadly, as the embodiment of authentic Scottishness and cultural difference) as how it's attacked by disdainful commentators (as a deluded or sinister revivalism deeply out of touch with Scotland's overwhelmingly Anglophone reality). As it deepens, this dynamic begins to limit what the language can be made to do – or rather, what the reader/listener is prepared to allow it to do.

So it's becoming harder to recall that it's entirely possible to write a Unionist poem in Scots, and that English is by any sane standard a Scottish language too, not some Sassenach imposition from outside. (In case it needs saying, Polish and Urdu and Irish are also Scottish languages in this sense.) Douglas Dunn's gently polemical verse-treatise 'English, A Scottish Essay' has more to say to us than ever before ('English I'm not. As language, though, you're mine'), but struggles to gain a hearing when Scots and English are treated as a proxies for constitutional skirmishing. This is more than a shame. There are hugely interesting and inventive things happening in contemporary Scots writing – from Bill Herbert to Jenni Fagan to Matthew Fitt to Harry Giles – but in a 'literary' space which feels increasingly remote, and at times out of kilter, with the waving of linguistic flags on social media and in public life. Whatever it is, Scots is more than a badge of affiliation to be kissed or spat on.

All of this being said, 'literary' concerns are only one, arguably minor, part of this debate. This issue does not arouse fierce passions because Scotland is full of sticklers for not confusing Edwin Muir and Hugh MacDiarmid (who were famously on opposite sides of the Scots issue). Any number of textbooks or talking-heads can calmly insist that of course there's no linguistic basis for snobbery about accents, or that standard English is just another dialect of English – the one that ended up with all the institutional authority. The scholarly consensus doesn't, by itself, address the deeper problem.

I'm not a linguist but it's obvious that the heat generated by this topic has much less to do with spelling and grammar than with feelings of pride and contempt. As in other parts of the UK, many generations of Scottish schoolkids had it drummed (and if necessary strapped) into them that their way of speaking in the playground or at home was sub-standard, a sign of their inferiority. 'Linguistic insecurity' is a bad and baseless thing, but saying so doesn't instantly cure people's deeply engrained sense of inadequacy. A more human phrase for linguistic insecurity might be 'false shame', which is what the Hampshire lexicologist W.H. Cope called it in the 1880s, observing the first generation of children to come through universal primary education. Cope believed in the standardisation of English but was disturbed to see pupils freshly cleansed of their local speech wincing with embarrassment at the dialect of their parents. Blogs like this can briskly dismiss 'is Scots a dialect or a language?' as a tedious, largely irrelevant, borderline incoherent question, and point out that nearly all value-judgements about language are really aimed at its speakers, without ever laying a glove on false shame.

The history of that shame – and of resistance to it – has more to do with class than nationality. But it's true that 'improvers' and standardisers of the eighteenth and nineteenth centuries, many of them Scots, associated the spread of 'correct' English with achieving full acceptance as North Britons. In A Treatise on the Provincial Dialect of Scotland (1779), Sylvester Douglas (Lord Glenbervie) treats 'the idiom particular to Scotland' as 'a provincial and vicious dialect of English', and hence, as Lynda Mugglestone observes, 'particularly open … to the hegemonies of England in linguistic as well as political ways'. The legacy of these ideas persisted much later than we might expect. John E. Joseph cites a schoolroom primer on standard English published in Glasgow in 1960. Under the heading 'Barbarism' is listed 'The use of Scotticisms : – as gigot, sort (repair), the cold, canny'. As Joseph remarks, this 'amounts to the authors of the book telling its readers that, insofar as the language reflects who they are, insofar as it belongs to them, it is barbaric, and that if they do not want to be perceived as barbarians, they must do away with these features'.

So national identity is undoubtedly part of the picture; but it needn't be the whole picture. We should question how language is entangled in all dimensions of power, and attend to all the different ways living language can be sneered into silence. It isn't a stark choice between 'Scotland speaks English – get over it' and the dubious idea that the predominance of English-the-language proves Scotland's perennial victim-hood at the hands of England-the-country. Douglas Dunn captures the need to avoid this slippage, riffing on the awkward doubleness of 'English':

> Not nationality but language. So,
> What's odd or treacherous other than the name?
> Not that I like the name – all my bon mots
> In somewhere else's tongue! Why scourge and blame
> History for what had to happen in it
> When you can't cancel it, not by a minute,
> Not by a year, never mind an epoch?
> Go back, reclaim the past, to when we spoke
> Each one of us as quintessential Jock?

The quest for a kind of primordial Scottishness via linguistic revival is a dead-end, but we can cherish local and living language in other ways, for other reasons. With every other tongue spoken around us, we can celebrate Scots and Scottish forms of English without insisting that their value inheres in their Scottishness.

There is of course an opposing view. In an essay of 1970 the poet Tom Scott completely reverses Dunn's view, arguing that:

> "the English language is a record of the experience of the English people and is alien and largely antipathetic to that of the Scots. A writer using English is identifying himself with English experience, is governed and taken over by it, and ultimately not only frustrates his own true nature, but ends

up as at best a second-rate writer in that alien tradition. ...
If Scotland wins free of English power, but is still captive to
English literature and language, we have gained only the net
the fish has broken from. Our people will still be cut off
from their psychological depths by an alien consciousness,
still be essentially ruled from London."

This is 'language essentialism' in the service of cultural nationalism,
taken all the way to its rather chilling conclusion (whereby Scotland
can only become fully itself by somehow 'winning free' of a language
used by 99.82% of its population, according to the last census). This
extreme form of language nationalism is rooted in German
romantic thought, and an idealised conflation of national language,
community and consciousness. 'The mental individuality of a people
and the shape of its language', wrote Wilhelm von Humboldt, 'are
so intimately fused with one another, that if one were given, the
other would have to be completely derivable from it. ... Language
is, as it were, the outer appearance of the spirit of a people'. These
ideas have a very chequered history within nationalist movements,
and tend toward the condition Dunn's poem describes as a
'Balkanised brain': a hunger for ethno-linguistic boundaries that will
bring the political map into alignment with borders supposedly
already there in the souls and psyches of national subjects.

But borders and tongues seldom match up in this way, and we
should be careful not to mis-cast English as the red-coated enemy
and 'other' to Scots. (While we're at it, pause to notice that there is
no single 'Scots', but a patchwork of social and geographical
varieties.) As Pavel Iosad wrote in the *New Statesman*, 'the consensus
among academics, if maybe not among laypeople, is that historically
Scots is indisputably a sister language of English, sprung from the
same Old English root, with a liberal admixture of Scandinavian
speech, through the dialects of what is today the north of England'.

I don't suggest for a moment that we can or should separate
language from politics. But it's entirely possible to validate
marginalised language and fight 'false shame' without indulging in
ethno-national fantasies about English being 'alien and antipathetic'

to Scottish people. We have spectacular examples of how to refuse this choice – above all, in the work of Tom Leonard – but look also to the work of English-based poets such as Tony Harrison, Linton Kwesi Johnson, John Agard, Kate Tempest, Daljit Nagra. There are as many ways of creatively politicising language as there are varieties of language itself. Flag-waving language nationalism is one of the least interesting out there, and self-defeating to boot.

The trouble with the council tax is the sound your buzzer makes

Alistair Davidson

The trouble with the council tax is the sound your buzzer makes. Buzz. Buzz. Buzz.

The trouble with the council tax is that the top decile of the income distribution pay 2%, while...

No. The trouble with the council tax is the sound your buzzer makes.

The brilliant thing about council tax reform is that it is perfectly positioned, it can't be attacked, we'll win the election...

No. The trouble with the council tax is the sound your buzzer makes.

Buzz. Buzz. Buzz. It could be a friend, or your family – but it could be the man from Scott and Co, the bailiff. You opened the door to him before and he stuck his foot in the gap when you tried to close it. You opened the door to him before and the thought of doing so again fills you with dread, so although maybe it's your mum, or maybe it's a friend, and although you need them now more than ever, you stay still, as still as you can, quiet as you can, shaking, t-shirt drenched in sweat, waiting for the buzzing to stop, the footsteps to recede.

It's moments like that where you start thinking: I'm a child not a man, a coward, hiding from a doorbell; I'm a burden on this world, this world would be better without me and my cowardice and my shame and my sweat. Dangerous thoughts, for someone in your condition.

Buzz. Buzz. Buzz. As you try to breathe quietly you remember, you shouldn't even be paying council tax, but you missed one appointment and the buroo sanctioned you and the housing benefit say you have to prove you have no income. "If you have no income, how are you living?" "Overdraft." She looks shocked at that, but what can she do about it? Rules are rules.

So bills start coming with fantasy figures in them: £100, £200, £1000. Money you can't even imagine having spare. Soon, you stop answering the door.

Buzz. Buzz. Buzz. In this moment there's only the fear and the sweat. There's no party, no movement, no nation. No left or right. No ballot boxes. Just Buzz. Buzz. Buzz.

The pundits, the politicians and the strategists talk about the electoral maths, the newspaper headlines.

You don't hear them. You're just a coward, too ashamed and scared to answer the door to your own home. All you can hear is the buzzer. Buzz. Buzz. Buzz.

The trouble with the council tax is the sound your buzzer makes.

Scottish Independence and "PostCapitalism"

Pat Kane

I can't give a higher accolade to a book than to say it deserves reading three or four times – and that after that you should have it on hand for keyword reference, via whatever devices you possess.

Paul Mason's *PostCapitalism* connects our contemporary challenges – technological, socio-economic and planetary – to a very persuasive history, whose waves of change are explained by a powerful collection of theories. I expect that we'll be coming back to drink from this river again and again on the Scottish indy-left.

Yet the reader would do well to pay close attention to the subtlety of Paul's arguments about what might come after capitalism. He says explicitly that he is a "revolutionary reformist", and delights that this self-description annoys both the boss-class and the Occupy protester alike.

One of his most useful moves is to urge radical leftists to abandon the idea that capitalism can only be "overthrown" from the "outside" with an "entirely new plan" – and that instead, a postcapitalism can be "incubated" from within it. There's a number of reasons Mason gives for this. One of which is that Marx and Engels, for all their analytic power, got the collective mentality and experience of the worker (as a "proletariat") under capitalism quite wrong.

Marx pronounced that the proles were entirely alienated in their consciousness, brutalised cogs in the factory system – and thus would be desperate for enlightened vanguards to lead them to liberation.

However, over successive waves of capitalist development, the working-class found a way to "live alongside capitalism", as Mason puts it, by generating their own positive culture of liberation. They didn't just grimly press for better working conditions (which, by restoring demand to economies and improving workers' capabilities, enabled capitalism to renew itself).

They also created clubs, recreations, libraries, self-educations, entertainments – often themselves infused with utopian, humanistic visions, reaching way beyond the achievement of decent working conditions. (I once bought a "Socialist Sunday School Song Book" from a shop in Glasgow's Trongate: all those sentiments are in there, hymn by hymn).

The point Mason wants to make is that, historically, there has always been a zone of what you could call "complex liberty" in working-class lives. People have always had intense, lively reasons for wanting to push back the frontiers (and the hours) of societally-required labour, one way or another.

This was desired in order that rich and meaningful choices could be freely and consciously made – about the direction of one's life, or the relations with one's relatives, friends and neighbours, or one's attitude towards knowledge or skill.

In short, left politics should not always be just about defending the right to "labour", "jobs", "employment". It should also be about creating conditions where the maximum possible number of citizens can exert the greatest possible degree of autonomy and self-determination.

In pushing for as much free time as possible, as a benefit from increased productivity through technology, a modern left honours some of the best traditions of working-class life. The multitude itself has always contained multitudes.

So when Paul comes to tell us that digitalisation, enabled by computers and communication networks, opens up a realm of free products and services that threaten the very property rights and social arrangements of capitalism itself, he wants to be seen as drenched in workers' history, not some *Wired*-magazine neophile. (Though to be fair, the "New Digital Socialism" essay that founding Wired editor Kevin Kelly wrote in 2009 is fascinating to compare with Mason's work).

Friendly and mutual societies were the precursors of the achievements of the welfare state, public housing and mass education – all those wrested from the furious upheavals of capitalist development by the organised working-class.

In the same manner, suggests Mason, contemporary radicals and progressives should be even more ambitious for what current practices like open-source software, digital sharing practices and computer simulations could become, at the level of an entire society. What would be the postcapitalist equivalents of those great collective achievements?

My sense is that Mason wants these ambitions to be guided by this irrepressible historical desire – that is, to seek the resources to shape your life according to your sensibilities, in cooperation with others who have a similar openness and ambition.

Paul doesn't go exactly where I went in *The Play Ethic* in 2004, in trying to locate the source of this desire. I found it in the biological and evolved necessity of play and creativity to the development of the human animal.

The lives of most humans in history have been conducted under conditions of economic scarcity. Digitality and networks brought the spirit and practice of abundance into the socio-economic mainstream. For me, the digital revolution has felt like the platform that the creative principle in human beings has been long awaiting, over many millennia.

Ever since the first artwork on a cave wall, or the first consciously-formed social group, adult humans – themselves always forged through early childhood play – have sought to express their creative urges. Human imagination irrepressibly bubbles up through the cracks of brute survival. The current tumult of digital culture only hints at the kind of world we could forge if those exigencies of survival were radically reduced.

I know it's fun to tear strips off the "hipsters" and the "creatives" – and it's right to do so when they are just expressing their accumulated cultural capital, as a class privilege. But what is so valuable about Mason's PostCapitalism is that he makes us realise how propitious the general conditions are, in which we can make very significant redefinitions of the priorities of our lives.

Paul asks us to build the confidence that we can answer our complex needs with free, open and information-driven systems and practices – and to experiment like crazy in doing so. If we can do this, we might well be able to displace "work" from the centre of our societies, and replace it with "meaning" or "culture" or "purpose" or "creativity" or "care". Or any permutation of those.

Of course, who exactly the "we" is in those last few paragraphs – how big, how self-conscious, how clearly motivated to progress change – is the crucial question. In my *Guardian Live* discussion with Paul and others a fortnight ago, and in my recent column in The National, I flagged up a few potential problems.

Paul's chosen agent of change is the "universal educated person" that's coming to consciousness throughout the capitalist world system. These types are not just to be found in the developed world, but are also reacting to illiberalisms in China, the Middle-East, South America, the major African cities. All of them are empowered to dream bigger, and build or promote alternatives, by means of their networked devices.

Back in 2004, using an admittedly awkward neologism, I called them the "soulitariat" (the proletariat sold their physical power to the authorities; the soulitariat sell their mental and emotional power – but can never sell it entirely).

Back then, like Paul, I too hoped then that these digitally empowered "players" would become a majority class. And not just (to use the old Marxist language) a class "in" themselves, but a class "for" themselves – acutely aware of their own interests and agenda.

They've also been called "hackers", and then "makers" and "creatives", over these last ten or fifteen years.

But however many times we've described them, I'm not sure they've fully turned up yet – ready and willing to build the new society that their communication-driven lifestyles imply.

There may be deeper reasons why they haven't arrived. Paul and I both have quite a faith in the intrinsic, evolutionarily-rooted capacity for human creativity. He talks of an "adaptive left", ready to bring about "new kinds of human beings", whose eventual character traits cannot be predicted. "How will humans have to change in order for postcapitalism to emerge?"

But I wonder how strong the counter-tendency is: a desire for less change, for the conservation of things, for stability and security first?

...I wonder how strong the counter-tendency is: a desire for less change, for the conservation of things, for stability and security first?

We've no shortage of science-fiction in popular culture, imagining "new kinds of human beings" every week. The problem is, when it does, it usually reveals deep and enduring fears, rather than thrilling new possibilities.

I'm thinking about Channel Four's *Humans*, or Margaret Atwood's *MaddAddam* trilogy. The first is about humanoid robots, the second about bio-modification, both becoming an accepted fact of our coming lives. But both are predominantly cautionary – telling stories to prevent a future happening, rather than showing a pathway to it.

"What [we postcapitalists] are trying to build", says Mason, "should be even more complex, more autonomous and more unstable" than the flexible organism (or "adaptive system") that is capitalism. A capitalism whose ability to shift and mutate to changing conditions proved ultimately superior to the most meticulous Soviet planning.

But are there limits to how much "complexity, autonomy and instability" humans can cope with? For example, isn't one of the biggest forces in the contemporary world the kickback against the kind of incessant, transformative modernity that Paul celebrates? Whether that be militant religious identities, or hard-core environmental resistance, or more locally the four million odd votes on this island for UKIP, asking to "stop the world and get off"?

Mason has a tin ear for this philosophically conservative tendency (with a small "c"). At one point he writes about the travails of labour organisers in the global South, and the "social and ideological cobwebs" in the minds of locals that "they fail to overcome". Those cobwebs Mason defines as "ethnic rivalries, the village network, religious fundamentalism, organised crime".

For Paul to call these "cobwebs", presumably to be swept away by a confident ultramodern hand, isn't reckoning seriously with their shaping power. Take a young African-Muslim man's militant ethno-religious identity, fuelled by the meretricious quality (not to mention the lethal drone strikes) of Western civilisation. Would his head and heart be so easily "sublated" by the influence of his compatriots becoming "universal educated individuals" on their ever smarter phones?

Mason and I hugely admire the Catalan social thinker Manuel Castells, only glancingly referenced in this book. But I wonder whether a deeper engagement with his work might have helped here. In his trilogy on network society, Castells talked about the tension between "the Net" and "the Self" (I commissioned Castells on this topic for my E2 page in the Herald in 1997, and recently referenced this in an essay on Alasdair Gray's "settlers and colonists" controversy in 2012).

On one side, Castells posits the fluid experience of network society – the world at your digital fingertips, and the "multiple identities" you need to function properly in it. And on the other side, Castells concedes an equally strong impulse to have your feet planted somewhere, to lay down a collective anchor of identity in the global storm.

So yes yes yes, Paul, let's push forward new practices that both demand and forge "new humans". But shouldn't those interested in a good society also be trying to find a healthy balance between cosmopolitan complexity and traditional stability – or even more elemental, between risk and security?

One way to balance these poles is through a civic nationalism or constitutional patriotism – a vibrant national polity seeking to make its progressive, constructive mark on the affairs of the planet. This was summed up classically by the SNP pioneer Winnie Ewing's old 60s phrase, "stop the world, we want to get on".

Mason wrote a *Guardian* column recently which resisted mightily the idea of any kind of English identity, even while accepting that constitutional reform is coming to England. He wants Englishness itself to be like its language – a sprawling force for plurality, hybridity and worldliness. Something that could only be crudified by association with a flag or nation.

But couldn't that be expressed as a unity-in-diversity, an *e pluribus unum*, a national home whose framing of diversity and difference you could be proud of? That "green and pleasant land" implied by the recent invocations of William Blake's 'Jersusalem' – whether they be Jez Butterworth's, or Danny Boyle's?

"Don't try to burden me with yet another layer of bogus identity politics", says Paul in the Guardian article – and it's OK, Paul, I won't! But the national dimension brings me to the question of how Paul's PostCapitalism might inform the policy agenda of pro-independence parties and movements in Scotland – which I'll explore in my next Bella blog.

As you'd expect from a professional reporter, working for a respected global news organisation, Paul Mason's vision of a "PostCapitalism" – the title of his new book – doesn't shy away from uncomfortable facts.

The penultimate chapter, which is entitled "The Case For Rational Panic", is uncompromising and clear. Disruptive global warming, the demographic and pensions crisis, and the forces of migration responding to both of those, will deliver even more convulsive shocks and shudders to every country and region in the world – Scotland included.

As to the solution to these crisis, Mason is again refreshingly direct: a market-led approach to any of this – the default method recommended by the neo-liberal consensus for the last 30 years – is a busted flush. To a very large extent, his postcapitalist vision is an attempt to provide a comprehensive, structural solution to these deep challenges.

In this blog (a long one, but he's full of ideas) I'm going to go through Paul's strategies for dealing with these real-world challenges. And I hope to show how the pursuit (and realisation) of Scottish independence could be an ideal test-bed for his vision.

Yesterday I described how Mason is trying to make us all understand how transforming info-technology could be of our current socio-economic order. But it's worth thumbnailing his basic challenge once more.

Code + Copy = Revolution

A purely digital good, once made, can be reproduced and shared forever, at no extra cost. This is a direct challenge to the classic capitalist idea that goods and services can only be accessed through money and prices.

The more that other goods are shaped by digital processes – designs for manufacture of transport or houses, bio-formulas for drugs or food, machines that are ever more adaptive and even self-directing – the more the price-system for those goods begins to dissolve.

The baroque, often ludicrous structures of copyright and control which snake through our info-lives – suppressing a genuine potential for abundant services and products – could be halted and reversed. That is, if the "left" exerted enough "willpower, confidence and design" (in Mason's words) to create "projects" that proposed alternatives.

Who does Mason think could take these projects (of which more later) forward? In my previous blog, I charted Paul's attempt to cast the "universal educated person", or "networked individualist", as part of a longer history of the culture of the working-class. A culture which always surpassed, in its dreams and aspirations, any degrading or exploitative relation it had with the managers and bosses of capitalism.

Surely it's easy for Yessers to understand exactly what Mason is referring to, if they recall the everyday community flourishing unleashed by the Yes campaign during the indyref.

And in Scotland, that flourishing was amplified by the contagious, irrepressible use of network technologies – to organise and archive meetings, to distribute alternative news and counter-factual graphics, to raise cash for activist projects at cost price.

So Indy supporters should know, intuitively, what Mason means by the communicational and liberating power of digital computers and networks.

Networked activists used and built the web in order to prototype their future, "as if" it was already happening (or even "as if you were in the early days of a better nation"). But they aren't the only agents of change, for Mason, that could bring about a post-capitalism.

Mason spends a lot of his book berating old-style lefties for their lazy, managerialist assumptions – that all you do is take control of the state, by elections or other means, and the socialist dream is achievable.

So it's comforting to realise that, at the end, Paul does see the state – one with confidence in its regulatory and policy powers – as an essential player in the "transition phase" to post-capitalism. For Yessers, who directed their networked activism to the achievement of a Scottish nation-state, this part of Mason's vision should be of great interest.

How could the policy programme of a future Scottish Parliament respond to the already "post-capitalist" dimensions of the indy movement? Using whatever powers it can muster, short of and including full nation-statehood?

Helpfully, Mason closes his book with prescriptions – which he will be happy to see "torn apart and revised by the wisdom of angry crowds" – under the title of "Project Zero". This refers to three overall objectives:

    * a zero-carbon energy system

    * the production of machines, products and services with "zero marginal costs" (ie, too cheap and plentiful to price)

and the reduction of necessary labour time as close as possible to zero

    * Mason then outlines eight tasks in a project plan that might get us to this postcapitalist state.

A "Project Zero" for Scotland

The most pertinent thing to do, for Scottish readers, may be to briefly introduce each one, and then see where that fits into the Scottish policy landscape, whether historic, actual, prospective or hoped-for.

"Model first, act later." This is an intriguing suggestion from Mason, based on his investigation into how massively powerful computers can now model and simulate designs for reality.

His signature example is the aircraft jet engine, which in the old days was tested a couple of hundred times in real life, but has been tested a hundred million times by a computer simulation, before being actually constructed.

Simulations of climate change, or epidemics, or populations, or traffic flows take in thousands of different inputs, algorithmically calculated. But, Mason complains, when we model our economies, our inputs are pitiful: the European Central Bank uses only households, firms and the central bank.

Why can't we establish "a global institute or network for simulating the long-term transition beyond capitalism" – starting with "attempting to construct an accurate simulation of economies as they exist today"?

All the "big data" that surrounds us could feed into such a simulation, and allow us to eventually test out our post-capitalist notions to see what ones worked, or didn't, or needed tweaking.

There's a few obvious resonances with Scottish policy here. We already have a "Scotland Performs" website, which has scores of "national performance indicators" with arrows pointing up, down or both ways – yet it's hardly the Wikipedia-like interactive simulation that I think Mason anticipates.

We also have something of a legitimation-crisis when it comes to statistics that measure the performance of the Scottish economy, with claim and counter-claim coming from ScotGov, the Institute for Fiscal Studies, the Office of Budget Responsibility, and various other bodies.

Could a partnership of Scottish universities, government and the business sector take up Mason's suggestion – not just to use petaflop computers to model in real-time the Scottish economy, but to begin this process with global partners, and with a view to exporting and benchmarking this process? Why not do it here – the land of Clerk-Maxwell, Adam Smith and Red Clydeside?

"The Wiki-State"

If a state is like Wikipedia, it doesn't provide command-and-control from on high – but it does build a structure that enables much free and creative activity, often of great usefuless and relevance, and produced through diligent and respectful collaboration.

What stiffens Mason's spine is that such a state should be proactive in extending the zone of postcapitalist collaboration and free services. Which means both "switching off the neoliberal privatisation machine" (ie, don't cave in to the privatisation of public services ("the EU made me do it")), and actively using the power of procurement to "favour sustainable, collaborative and socially just outcome".

101

Do existing Scottish Governments accredit themselves well here? Not very – though there are enough flurries of protest (recently around the idea that the public service of CalMac Ferries could be passed over to Serco) to show that the Scottish public sphere understands how its state should act to benefit the commonweal.

But in recent legislation around community empowerment, and land reform, there is at least obesiance paid to the principle of pushing back against corporate imperatives in the name of the popular will.

However, it's not quite "clearing a space in the capitalist jungle", in Mason's words, to allow the "fragile new plants... of peer-to-peer projects, collaborative business models and non-profit activities" to grow.

A left-green electoral bloc in the May 2016 Holyrood elections seems like more and more a necessary component of a radical "independence" majority – at least to keep the possibilities open for something more than the SNP's boilerplate "fairness-and-prosperity" approach.

And in terms of what's coming, even a safety-first Scottish Parliament could be knocked off-course. Mason also ventures into how a "wiki-state" might stave off a deeper financial collapse, due to accumulating debts not just from botched austerity programmes, but also the looming pension payments crisis. At the very least, his projections should focus Yessers' minds on what form of Scottish national economic sovereignty could navigate through what looks like some very stormy waters to come – no matter what we do.

Again, here Mason takes a strong-minded view of the state's responsibility to exercise "law and regulation", in order to limit traditional enterprises' ability to "contribute to social injustice". These include start-ups incentivised by tax law to pay low-wages from the get-go, or large cheap-labour corporations that benefited from the space "ruthlessly carved out for them since the 90s" by the state.

What a state should also promote are businesses which produce free stuff in a collaborative way: he wants someone to set up an "Office of the Non-Market Economy" to nurture them all.

As I know from my board membership of the think-and-do-tank Common Weal, Scotland already has a deep historical tradition of co-ops, collectives, mutuals and credit unions. It's now being added to by cafes and bars, creative spaces, and most vibrantly news-and-views media platforms.

The latter – this blog, *Wings*, *CommonSpace*, *Newsnet*, *The Ferret*, *The National* and several others – are probably the best example of the kind of spontaneous networked organisations that can be generated from the combination of info-tech and social movement.

Though interestingly, online subscription and net-based crowdfunding – the latter of which doesn't even merit a mention in Mason's book – has been a vital, and even reliable way of ensuring sustainability (sometimes even sanity) for those who run these platforms. Yet these are literally gifts to valued figures, granted money by the community in a similar way to the elite employees of high-performance info-capitalist enterprise – who as Mason says, "are basically paid to exist" (or more likely, for the cybernats, post more than a few times a day).

But the idea of an "Office of the Non-Market Economy" sounds like a slam-dunk offer, if the Scottish Government was vaguely interested in Mason's analysis.

"Suppress or socialise monopolies"

Faced with the tendency to abundance and freedom of informational and information-shaped goods, info-capitalism's primary response is to try and establish a monopoly (the posterboys being Google and Apple). Mason is bracingly militant about the state's response: break 'em up. And if you can't break 'em up, take them into public ownership.

103

Paul is also very clear about the impact of public provision of items like water, energy, housing, transport, healthcare, telecom infrastructure and education. If they were delivered at close to cost price, the price of basic necessities would cheapen, labour time could be reduced, and the free production zone increase. It would be a "strategic act of redistribution, vastly more effective than raising real wages".

In Scotland – and I would love to know how this phrase made it into the First Ministerial vocabulary – we actually have a policy beachhead for all this. The concept of the "social wage" has been part of SNP policy for several years now.

It is usually represented by the eight year freeze in council tax; free prescriptions; elderly personal care; free school meals; a commitment to the Living Wage for all public sector workers under Scottish Government pay policy; the roll out of 600 hours of free childcare for all three, four and vulnerable two-year-olds; the Scots students saving up to £9,000 per year with fee-free tuition.

As Salmond wrote in the *Guardian* in 2012: "We have made a conscious decision to provide certain core universal services, rights and benefits, some of which are no longer prioritised by political leaders elsewhere in the UK… We do this because we believe such services benefit the common weal. They provide a sense of security, well-being and equity within communities. Such a sense of security is vital to a sense of confidence – and as we have seen over the last three years, confidence is essential to economic growth."

The last line slides into orthodoxy. But the overall principle is clear – however tough it may prove to use Scottish sovereign power to defend its application (from EU regulators and the like). There is an overall Scots consensus for using public services to counter the atomising and fear-inducing impact of neoliberal marketisation on everyday communities.

What Mason can add to this defensive argument is a positive opportunity. A "social wage" (along with a citizen's basic income – see below) can support a steady growth of non-market mutual provision, driven by the sharing, copying and modelling digital technologies he champions.

Even short of full independence, wouldn't it be possible for a Scottish government to open up and support these possibilities? Does this not go with the very grain of the "commonweal" so often invoked by ScotGov ministers?

"Let market forces disappear"

This is a slightly misleading header, as Mason concedes that "networked individuals" have a strong consumer identity, and that markets – as a way that producers and makers can respond to complex desires – should still have their place. But if the private sector seeks profit, it must do so from "entrepreneurship, rather than rent".

What that means for information goods is that you don't just keep extending copyright and controlled-usage for ever – which provides you with rent, forever – but you deliberately make those copyrights "taper away quickly", after the short-term gains from innovation (new clothing style, hit record) fade away. The way to make more money is to then come up with something new again!

Thus a "commons" of intellectual property grows and grows, providing a necessary resource for non-profit/free labours and enterprises. This would be further enriched by ensuring that state-funded research results, generated by from universities and other institutions, were "free at the point of use".

Again, in the context of the Yes campaign, Scots have recently had the experience of playing fast and loose with copyright – of people getting themselves together around projects and worrying (or forgetting) about who "owns" it afterwards.

I've often thought there could be a much bigger infrastructural responsibility invested in something like "Creative Scotland". Because if creativity and innovation is "becoming exponential", as Mason phrases it, shouldn't the macro-institutions which sustain that be of an appropriate scale?

And again, what is to stop a Scottish Government experimenting with support systems for postcapitalist artists, creatives and entrepreneurs – involving not just open cultural rights, but different forms of communal living, different kinds of community contribution?

Interestingly (for so-called "statist" independistas like myself) Mason isn't afraid to bat for the state interest when he perceives it to be urgent. Around energy, he's forceful about the need to take the grid and its carbon-based suppliers into public ownership. (As they can't burn their reserves without burning the planet, he quips, "these corporations are toast anyway").

So far, each of Mason's project goals has consequences for how Yessers think of Scottish sovereign state power – and this is just one of the more acute. If a future Scottish government were to conduct these nationalisations – and it's certainly not on the SNP-majority ticket at the moment – could this happen within the framework of EU competition law, in its current, neo-liberally punitive form?

The more that Mason specifies the state policies that will help the transition to a postcapitalist society, the more militant it looks like the next Scottish assertion of sovereign independence will need to be, to get anywhere near this state of affairs. The SNP's indy-lite policy prospectus for 2014 ("independence in the UK", as Iain Macwhirter once waspishly called it) seems like a proper dead-end, as a model for the next heave (whenever it happens).

"Socialise the finance system." This is a complex section, and it's perhaps easier to begin by quoting Paul's ambition:

"In the short-term, the intention is not to reduce complexity – as the money fundamentalists want – nor simply to stabilize banking, but to promote the most complex form of capitalist finance compatible with progressing the economy towards high automation, low work, and abundant cheap or free goods and services".

His range of measures to ensure this are pretty familiar to those who have engaged deeply with the Scottish policy debate over the last ten years. Firstly, a nationalised central bank, targeted at sustainability (see notions like a Green or a People's Quantitative Easing, flagged up in the Corbyn campaign in the last weeks).

Secondly, a much more regionalised and regulated banking sector, with credit unions, peer-to-peer lenders and the like given greater status. And thirdly, a re-regulation of complex global financial activities, emphasising investment for production, and hunting down tax havens.

But let me keep coming back to the Scottish indy context. To take these measures forward would require a general popular confidence in the ability of one's state to conduct sovereign reforms of its macro-financial systems.

We just didn't have enough of that on September 18th, due in part to the terrifying psychological bombardments of the media-establishment complex (though it was touch and go for them). And the spectacle of the Greek Syriza government being pummelled this way and that by their Euro "partners" might have boosted the resolve of the already-engaged, but perhaps has worried even more those older, pensioned, tremulous Nos.

Yet again, Mason's challenge to any potential postcapitalist state, and its confidence in its agency and sovereignty, is considerable. Are we up to it, and up for it?

"Pay everyone a basic income"

This relates to a pillar of Mason's overall historic argument. The organised working classes and their militant demands for better terms and conditions, as a wave of capitalist expansion crests, actually helps the whole system thrive in the long run.

The new social measures they force (from public housing to universal education) improve the capabilities of the worker; and the expensiveness of the labour compel companies to develop more efficient and innovative production technologies.

But neo-liberalism smashed the power of labour over the last 30 years – which meant that, even as the startling powers of info-tech have bedded in, stagnation has been the result. This is because neo-liberalism's control freakery is essentially happy with the majority of its populations working in low-skill, low-wage, "bullshit" jobs. A basic income is an attempt to kickstart the "workers" end of systemic development again – by removing the opportunity to make a business from bullshit jobs.

Basic income is also a future-oriented response to the prospect of postcapitalist enterprise being much more about non-market behaviours and relations. We will have to start valuing this kind of activity, because the necessary hours of labour in society are due to start rapidly declining, due to automation – which threatens to remove 40% of existing jobs by 2040.

In Mason's vision, basic income (his levels are £6000 for the BI, with a minimum wage at £18,000) provides a basis on which the techno-mutual society can flourish. It gives people a high economic floor, from which they can strike a new mix – between their jobs (which are now tending towards high-wage, high-skill occupations, employers pushed their by the basic income), and their lives (and loves).

The Scottish pathway towards this is, actually, pretty clear. The late feminist economist Ailsa McKay is perhaps best known in the country for persuading Alex Salmond that a massive investment in childcare would serve a number of positive outcomes – both supporting women's autonomy, and paying for itself by bringing more women into the labour market.

But it's not as well known that Ailsa's next policy horizon was the introduction of a "citizen's basic income" (CBI) in Scotland (see her Royal Society of Edinburgh policy paper). She's worth quoting in full:

"In contrast to current social security measures, a CBI does not explicitly link income provision with work. In this sense it can be regarded as an emancipatory measure in that it serves to free individuals from the economic necessity of toil and provides the basis to support a range of welfare enhancing activity undertaken outwith the confines of market based exchanges. A CBI is not merely an alternative to existing social security provision but rather a philosophy aimed at enhancing individual freedom and promoting social justice. In essence providing the basis for securing 'real freedom for all'."

Certainly, welfare powers are coming piecemeal to Scotland under devolution, and we can't get the integrating powers required short of independence. But the Utrecht experiment in basic income seems to be happening at the level of a city or municipality. Are there "Yes" towns, with the required cohesion, patience and municipal vision, that would be willing to take on an experiment – Coatbridge? Dundee? Inverness?

"The network unleashed"

You gotta love Paul Mason for paragraphs like this:

> "There is no reason other than exploitation why world-class techniques of automation cannot be applied, for example, to the labour of the sandwich factory or the meat-packing plant. In fact, it is only the availability of cheap, unorganised labour, supported by in-work benefits, that permits these business models to exist. In many industries old disciplines of work – time, obedience, attendance, hierarchy – are enforced only because neoliberalism is suppressing innovation. But they are technologically unnecessary"

Mason performs a crucial service in the *PostCapitalism* book – in that he continually smacks you upside your head, and jolts you from the consensus view about how our modern, producing-and-consuming lives should be.

But as I wrote in my first piece on the book in *The National* a few weeks ago, I think Paul underestimates just how brilliantly seductive those info-capitalists are. The Zuckerberg's, the Ive's and Jobs's, Larry and Sergey and Jeff Bezos and all devote billions designing ways to corral us back into a passive, orderly space with our daily techno-structures.

How we keep mentally and imaginatively escaping from those comfort zones into more dynamic, active visions of our coming society – think the closing credits of Wall-E, where the blobby humans work with their robots to rebuild their world – is a question perhaps for artists most of all. (Pause to mourn the passing of National Collective, now probably more needed than ever).

Luckily, Scotland is not short of what Disney called "imagineering" or "imagineers". From conceptual artists to science-fiction writers, from games-makers to hard-core researchers, from SF blockbuster scripters to open-source coder communities, we have an embarrassment of future-oriented riches.

I facilitated an encouraging conference on Scottish innovation a month ago in Edinburgh – and by far the most exciting contribution came from Glasgow School of Art's head of design, Irene McAra-McWilliams.

Irene actually suggested a new verb to us all – "to studio". Meaning that the vibrancy of creative practitioners in Scotland was suggesting new organisational forms that we could begin to scale up across Scotland. A studio (as opposed to a a lab) is about a collective display of work, a space of explicit mutual inspiration and soft prototyping.

From everything that Paul has suggested in his extraordinary, mobilising book, what would a "postcapitalist studio" scene look like in Scotland? Who can build them? From what elements? What would they do?

And BTW, dear Yesser: Do you remember what it felt like, to have the energy to ask all these questions, and find the people around you who might help you answer them – or ask better ones?

You do? OK. So there's one idea – "modular, self-managed, granular", as Paul might approvingly say – for the Scottish future. Get his book, read carefully (and with pleasure), and come with a fistful of your own.

The Sinking of the Whale

Maxwell Macleod

On the nature of faith, the effect of the lingering horror of war and the dynamics of father-son relationship.

"Maxie, Maxie, Maxie, wake up. Wake up! Wake up! I've got stories to tell you."

It's 4.30 on a summer's morning in a bedroom of the Manse on the Hebridean island of Iona. The year is 1960. There is an old man and a young child in the room.

The old aged pensioner is sixty-five, his son, this writer, eight. My mother sleeps next door, writhing in the early part of her pregnancy.

"Wake up, Maxie, wake up,"The old man would whisper in my tiny ear. He had a soft and sexy voice. I can hear it yet. They make an odd couple, these two. The old man looks half mad. He is wearing a torn dressing gown, blue and white striped. The hair an explosion of white. The oyster eyes juggly, the collapsed mouth stale with dried froth, snot on the moustache. The eyes like lasers.

Meet my dear dad, The Very Rev Lord Dr Captain Professor George MacLeod of Fuinary. Military Cross, Croix de Guerre,

Doctor of Divinity and, at this moment, quite possibly certifiably insane.

George is tall and was once elegant, though perhaps not so much now as he hasn't got his teeth in.

Beside him the slugabed child is just a tight little bundle of red curls, milky skin and 'go-away-I'm- sleeping, Daddy'.

The old man hasn't slept for thirty-six hours and for six of those hours has probably been too drunk to legally drive a car, a state he prefers when he is writing about his belief in a living God.

He is now so tired he hardly knows his own name. Luckily many others do. Indeed, he is quite famous, or perhaps notorious, for he has many enemies.

All night long he has been pacing around the downstairs room with a paraffin pump lamp hissing out a warm yellow bubble of light.

He lights another Capstan (Full-Strength) cigarette, draws deeply on its giddying smoke and drums his fingers hard and fast on the table. He's writing a three-minute prayer for the early morning Service he will soon conduct in the half-ruined Iona Cathedral lying a few hundred yards from here, his home in the Cathedral Manse. His congregation at that service will be his team for the most exciting project to have taken place in the Church of Scotland for a century.

Sitting at the front of the draughty church in their blue denim overalls will be half a dozen Gaelic masons who will soon be out working, on the rebuilding of the Cathedral walls. With them will be perhaps six clumsy volunteers, mostly young ministers drawn to George's crazy dream of rebuilding the Cathedral as a symbol of hope for the world. It's a project that has been born of the horrors he had witnessed in the First World War.

Alongside them in the pews will be fifty visitors who have paid to come to week-long conferences in the half-completed Cathedral.

His clan of followers may have little money but they are rich in dreams, their day being often jump-started by the sheer electricity of their leader's morning prayers.

And so in preparation George will hustle and fuss, sometimes all night, to make those prayers pin perfect. Fine-tuning the music within the words, fiddling with the micro pauses, adding just a hint of vibrato… until the prayer moves along like a little red boat that scarcely troubles the water with its passing.

George doesn't really know why he believes in God; he accepts it's irrational but still believes. Why? Three reasons.

Firstly, he sees it as being a better option for the kind of world he wants to live in. He wants people to be Christian in their dealings with him and so is prepared to enter a contract to be Christian in his dealings with them. The thought of the world spinning senselessly through space while all mankind simply scramble over each other trying to get the biggest slice of the pie is so instinctively awful to him that he dismisses its reality as being improbable.

Secondly, he is culturally a Christian. His family has always been Christian and they have lived lives he has admired, so he wants to believe.

It's the third element, the mystical part of his faith that keeps him worrying away at his prayers in the long watches of the night.

He feels that there is a radio frequency obtainable in everything that is somehow right, somehow perfect. You only have to work at the fine-tuning handle until the reception is so crystal clear that the voice of God can be heard. Sometimes he will get near to that perfection in a sentence, in a sermon, in an action.

And he clings to this madness as a possible rebuttal to the awfulness of a Godless world.

Then there is Nature. Again and again he will see something so sublime that he sees it as being in that frequency of perfection. He recognises the irrationality of assuming that just because his human mind judges a soaring bird to be perfect does not necessarily mean that the bird has been created by God, or indeed that God exists. But living on Iona with its strange energy pulsating out of the rocks and seeing what may possibly be flashes of the divine in the beauty of Nature, well it's enough to give him permission to take the leap of faith to which those first two elements of his faith push him.

During four years of the First World War, he had been a Captain in the Argyll & Sutherland Highlanders, leading hordes of Gaelic-speaking youngsters to their deaths and had grown to love them for their mysterious naturality.

On one day alone he had led four hundred forwards over the top and returned with eighty. They had given him a medal.

"A Military Cross!" He had once told me. "My God maybe if I had killed a thousand Germans perhaps they would have given me a Victoria one!"

Ho ho ho; he had laughed at the joke. It was a safer option than starting to cry; perhaps if he had ever started he wouldn't have been able to stop.

His experience in that first world war had been so horrific that even then lying in that bed, forty-two years after the event, he would still hear the cries of the youngsters he had had to lead out of muddy trenches, into cold rain sown with stinging bullets that in his own words would, "Unzip their tummies and leave them wide-eyed running forward with strings of warm sausages overflowing their soft young hands…or crack open their knee caps so that they would scream for their Mothers for all of the few minutes until they bled to death."

He was twenty-two years old, when he witnessed such scenes. Not once but hundreds of times. In one period of three weeks in that war more than six thousand highlanders were killed, and he was in the thick of such fighting for month after month after month.

On one such day his men had seen him jinking and jumping across a dangerous patch of ground until he had joined them in a muddy trench laughing with delight; "Well at least it's not raining!" he had joked to their astonishment.

Later some of them were to submit him to a mock court-martial under the charge of being "Aggressively optimistic." It was in December 1917, the place, Arras.

He often dismisses the Gaels as being feckless dreamers, and yet their culture haunts him … There had been something about how they lived, something about how they were prepared to die for each other that had been superior to the English culture he had learnt at Winchester and Oxford.

George has an almost manic focus on whatever job is to hand, and is never more obsessive than when he is writing prayers. During the night this focus is often targeted on getting into the mental groove in which he can get on to the right frequency. He knows the recipe to get to that groove all too well.

First make loads of black, heavily sugared coffee, add a little whisky, some Capstans (full strength), plus some doubt and guilt; and then throw in a profound sense that there really ought to be a God.

After getting into this state, his spinning mind is usually able to drill a peephole through the thick door of his objectivity into a misty world that might not only exist, but also be eternal. He scarcely dares to believe in this other invisible world, but is even more frightened of not believing in it. So, he kneels and believes and is then able to believe and kneel.

Once he has seen what any scientist would regard as invisible, he will mix a few well-tried ecclesiastical flavourings into his prayers. Using colourful images of the sea, sky, sex and soul he will conjure up a cocktail not only to shake sleepy minds awake, but also stir up their energy for harsh days on high scaffolds, working as they do with heavy granite blocks in the driving rain.

He's a good man, George. A good man now exhausted. He had been dog-tired when he had started the practising of the prayers and that was now seven hours earlier.

Upstairs, his young wife of 32 lies waiting in her warm bed. Her body yearns to spoon to his warmth, but he grips instead to his older and safer lovers; God and duty.

The Abbey restoration project is constantly with him. He has dedicated his life, his money and almost his entire fevered mind to restoring it. Now he must keep the volunteers motivated to get the thing finished. He must, he must, must...

The completed building, he tells himself, will be half of Nature and half of Man, a bridge between the material and the spiritual; on Iona too, an island where only a veil as thin as gossamer divides the spiritual from the material. The holiest place in Scotland will send out a radio beam in perfect frequency with the divine.

Nature incarnate on a wind-ripped island ... Yes that's on frequency.

A megaphone for God's still small voice. That isn't... He practises such phrases out loud, watching the sound as it flies through the air like a wild bird, tasting it as a chef might taste a sauce. Then, if he likes the sound and the flight he will snatch at the beautiful butterfly he has created, pinning it to the ink-splattered paper before him.

It had all been easy enough fifteen years earlier. After the Second World War, former soldiers had flocked to his newly hatched Iona Cathedral restoration project. Such fun then. Such japes. It was just like the war, though with fewer young bellies being unzipped by the machine guns.

The men had lived like campers in garden sheds beneath the ruined walls of the Cathedral, dozens of them, swimming naked in the freezing sea at dawn to charge up their enthusiasm. But then, aged 53, he had fallen in love with a 27-year-old youth camp leader and now there were two slugabed children in the Manse beside the Cathedral.

How many years of work did he have left? Time seems to be speeding up, Christmas comes once a month, and the Abbey lies uncompleted. Oh my God! The child stirs in his bed.

"Oh Daddy leave me alone! I don't want to come swimming with you before breakfast. I'll go tomorrow I promise. Go to bed. Mummy will wake you up in time for the Service. Don't be afraid, she won't let you sleep in. Go to sleep Daddy; go to sleep."

The old man falls onto the bed beside the child, his body dropping on to the cheap mattress like a felled ox, the mind trying to will the eyes not to close. The child can feel his collapsed father's desperation and puts out a tiny hand and prods at the slobber of his Dad's mouth with baby fingers. He can smell his Dad. It's a blood warm stew of juicy body stench. The snot, the saliva, the sweet sweat in his greasy arm pits.

But there is salt there too. Salt dust from yesterday's dreadful douche in the dawn sea, crusted in crevices of skin and held fast on hair. God's seasoning of the seasoned in the great cauldron of cold reality that is the freezing sea. The child buries his nose in a towelled shoulder and lies floating on an ocean of sleepy odour and utter adoration. The monster that is his father explodes from the blue depths of sleep, aghast at what had nearly happened.

"Maxie Maxie Maxie, get up now, get up. Get up now!" Then George plays his joker,

"It's still dark. If you get up now you may see the dream moment…"

The child smiles and stretches. The 'dream moment' riff's a-coming. How nice; how very nice.

The phrase has hauled him from sleep. Soon he will rise, but first he must hear his Father's mysterious tale about the dream moment and the sinking grey whale and taste a spoonful of the sweetness of Nature that awaits him on his barefoot walk in the ice-cold dew.

He hasn't a clue what his Father's tale means, he only knows that its poetry is like summer honey to his hungry soul. The one-boy congregation responds to his priest according to their shared secret prayer-book.

"What do you mean by 'dream moment' Daddy?" And then the minister will say,

"Well, my darling one; here we lie on Iona, God's own perfect place and you well know that when we watch the sun go down we sometimes see tiny green flashes." The boy sighs, floating,

"And so it is at dawn, except it is only those who hear the voice of God like tiny thunder on distant mountains who will know of it . . . the children don't know it, they are of it, in it, by it, for God is in their innocent faith. At the dream moment God places all the dreams into all the heads of those little children lying safe in their little linen envelopes, and they smile as they wake and sigh as the wind sings the quiet song of Iona.'

'Sings the quiet song of Iona.'

What a medicine man the old fool was. What a magician.
And then the little boy will say,

"And how will I know when the dream moment comes
Daddy?" And his priest will reply,

"Why, the lamb, Maxie. That lamb will become as still as a rock
in that moment. And the seal turning in the wave will pause; the
gannet, broad as a man is tall, will not have to move his wings as he
slides down the back of the wind, for the very rhythm of life he will
be feeling."

"And the whale Daddy. Tell me about the falling whale…"

What does it mean to be mad? What does it mean to be sane?

The Very Reverend Lord Captain Doctor Sir Prof George
MacLeod of Fuinary M.C., Croix de Guerre, was either totally mad
or utterly sane when he would come to the answer of that final
request.

For the medicine man would be taking his leap of faith, floating
on his own sea of either self-delusion or incisive exposition, dancing
with the white lambs, sliding down the banister of the wind to a
place where the existence of God was perhaps proven by the
perfection of Nature and his whole cultural being would make
sense, and all those young kilted children would not have died in
vain.

His reply to my call for the falling of the whale would be a
raising of his own weary body. Sometimes he would sit up, eyes shut,
the hands grasping the sheets for comfort. My own hand might
perhaps be on his towelled leg, trying to be with him in his moment
of almost physical passion, the final words squeezed out of the
orgasmic cleric in a rainbow of glory.

Utterly exhausted, on fire with nicotine, coffee and whisky, his
mind would be flailing around looking for something to grip onto
and all that he could find that made any kind of sense would be the
nonsense of God and he would reach out to the heavens,
aggressively optimistic that God existed, and that there was a
difference between right and wrong and that all the kilted children
hadn't died without reason.

"And the great whale, Maxie, oh my Lord, that great grey whale, falling through the white to the blue to the green to the black will turn on its side and it's empty eye, that eye that has seen the free falling of time, for it is all eyes, that empty eye will gaze upwards and at that moment, at that dream moment, it will both see and be of God."

Sometimes I would have to hug him as he rid himself of his doubt. Hold him tight in the agony of his brave choice of uncomprehending faith. Sometimes I would laugh, sometimes gasp.

Always I would love him. Always.

And after that? Well after that the old man and the small boy would go swimming before breakfast.

Donald Trump and the Second Sight

Alastair McIntosh

Alastair McIntosh on the psychopathology that the American election has set loose upon the world.

I was driving through Tong on the Isle of Lewis. I was with an old school friend from Leurbost village of my childhood on the island.

"Wonder which is Trump's house?" I said, though not intending to veer off and go a-gawking. It was just a passing point of conversation, the way you do when driving round the island with folks who know it intimately, exchanging stories, retelling history, and whatever else comes from the free association that springs up along the route.

"I know which one," he said. Then preemptively, just in case I was going to make a detour, "But I'm not showing anybody."

In a nutshell, that sums up the island view of Trump. Partly because he so much doesn't represent the island's values that they're at a loss to explain it. And equally, partly out of the respect for the privacy of the family. Trump is dirty washing that the island would rather not hang out, and not just on Sundays.

"Trump is dirty washing that the island would rather not hang out, and not just on Sundays."

Donald John, or Dòmhnall Iain, is one of the most common island names. It translates, from the Latin and Norse roots, dom and val, as The Ruler of the World.

Far be it for me to apply the Second Sight as to the American election outcome. Ironically, however, the island's traditions of the Second Sight – *an dà shealladh* or "the two sights" – might shed a little light on just how The Donald should have turned out so very wayward, or "prodigal".

In his acclaimed biography of a way of life, *Isolation Shepherd*, Iain Thomson of Loch Monar remarks: "No Highlander has any doubt about the existence of the second sight or indeed simple prognostication."

Such a statement still holds true of most indigenous Hebrideans to this day. It is based on ongoing experience. Experience that characterises tight knit communities where empathy remains profound. Where it does so because the deeper levels of the psyches of individuals are not as disconnected from one another as they become in highly competitive metropolitan settings.

I found myself reflecting on this after hitting on some correspondence about the Second Sight that took place in the late 1600s. It was between Lord Tarbett and Sir Robert Boyle.

"Donald John, or Dòmhnall Iain, is one of the most common island names. It translates, from the Latin and Norse roots, dom and val, as The Ruler of the World."

Tarbett was one of the Mackenzies of Kintail and Seaforth, the Anglicised clan that had connived to own the Isle of Lewis from the 17th to the 19th centuries. Sir Robert Boyle was the Anglo-Irish physicist who gave us Boyle's Law – the one stating that the volume of a gas varies directly according to its temperature.

Their correspondence is quoted at some length by the Rev Robert Kirk of Aberfoyle, writing around 1690. His posthumously published book is called *The Secret Commonwealth of Elves, Fauns and Fairies*. Ethnographers consider it to be probably the most important early statement of Gaelic metaphysical beliefs.

In response to Boyle's interest in the paranormal, Tarbett says: "There were more of these seers in the Isles of Lewis, Harris, and Uist than in any other place."

Tarbett took a business interest in "the African Trade," as he called black slavery. A later family owner of Lewis, Colonel Francis Humberston Mackenzie, governor of Barbados in the twilight years of British slavery. His daughter, Mary Elizabeth Frederica, inherited Lewis in 1815 and used her power of landed patronage to introduce the new breed of hard-line evangelical clergy to the island.

Tarbett tells Boyle about an observation made by a gentleman friend of his who been to the Barbados. Of islanders, who went abroad, "Several of those that did see with the Second Sight when in the Highlands or Isles, when transported to live in other countries, especially in America, they quite lost this quality."

That fascinated me. It suggests that when the bonds of community are broken, the capacity for deepest intimacy goes too.

In recent articles, it has emerged that Donald Trump's mother did not leave the island to go for a holiday in New York. As one island writer has it, the idea that anybody went from Lewis to New York for a holiday in the 1930s "is so unlikely it's almost laughable."

The Macleod family daughters who went to America were economic migrants who "made good". There appears to have been a family difficulty involving Mary's elder sister having a child out of wedlock, but in the backdrop, large numbers of the island's youth were at that time emigrating to America.

Why? Because they lacked land, the prerequisite for livelihood.

Why did they lack land?

Because during the first half of the 19th century, the proto-capitalist speculative Mackenzie landlords evicted people from southern and western Lewis (Pairc and Uig). Their ancestral land was rented out for commercial sheep farming. These Hebridean expressions of the Highland Clearances started with the need Francis Humbertson to pay off his gambling debts run up in the Barbados. The first clearance orders were issued from that distant outpost of the Empire.

At the same time as Mary Elizabeth Frederica was evangelising the islanders with hellfire preaching, her second husband, James Alexander Stewart-Mackenzie was clearing them to maintain himself in the lifestyle to which he aspired. In Uig, land was even cleared of families specifically to make way for the minister's greed for grazings.

CNN Politics put it all in perspective this past week. It reported, from local genealogical evidence: "Two branches of Trump's family were forced from their homes in this way, becoming refugees in their own country – the Macauleys forced from their homes in the west of the isle, the Smiths further south."

When I look at Donald Trump – his colossal egotism, his grandiosity, his disconnect from empathy – I see a man who nurses a narcissistic wound, a wound to his primal integrity from places that he probably doesn't even know about. And that's just on his mother's side. Like those plantation managers in the African trade of whom Lord Tarbett spoke, his capacity to be and inwardly see – his capacity even to have an inner life as distinct from it all being on the outside – has been cut off by his deracination, his uprooting, from holding in his community.

"When I look at Donald Trump – his colossal egotism, his grandiosity, his disconnect from empathy – I see a man who nurses a narcissistic wound, a wound to his primal integrity from places that he probably doesn't even know about."

Such is the tragic dynamic by which – not inevitably, but very often – the oppressed turn oppressor. It is why Paulo Freire said that the great task of the oppressed is to liberate their oppressor as well, otherwise there can be no lasting freedom.

Such a background also speaks to The Donald's appeal to poor white American voters, many of whom share a similar psychohistory. Their ancestral hearts, similarly, had metaphorically been buried at Wounded Knee, long before they and their kind perpetrated such massacres as Wounded Knee.

Such is the psychopathology that the American election has set loose upon the world. It is in part fuelled by a binary division in fundamentalist religion between the Damned and the Elect; a division by which the oppressed, held in a kind of Stockholm syndrome, take solace in the notion that at least there'll be comeuppance for those who have humiliated them in the afterlife.

Tragically, this too easily plays out into the world as the binary politics of good state / bad state, with us / against us, and the black / white racism not just of America, but previously of Apartheid South Africa that drew explicitly on such sorry theology.

Irrespective of whether Trump wins or loses, roughly half of America will have voted for him. It's time to understand such psychohistory. Time to call our prodigals home. Even a Donald Trump is still the island's son.

A Toxic Culture

AL Kennedy

AL Kennedy was yesterday awarded the Heine Prize in Dusseldorf, Germany. The prize is "to personalities who serve by their intellectual heritage in terms of fundamental human rights, for which Heinrich Heine used, to promote social and political progress, international understanding or the realisation of the unity of people". The Heine Prize jury said: "The Heinrich Heine Prize of the City Dusseldorf 2016 is awarded to the excellent AL Kennedy, well known for her idiosyncratic literary work, which plumbs the limits of the human soul. Her views on political and social conditions sharpen social discussions about the Iraq war and the proposed referendum on the United Kingdom's membership of the European Union in the tradition of Heinrich Heine. AL Kennedy is a great literary figure and European". This is her acceptance speech.

I would like to thank the judges of the Heine Preis for allowing me to receive this honour, to be thought of as a good writer by people of intellectual rigour and good judgement is always a kind surprise. To be thought of as in any way worthy of a prize which also seeks to celebrate the promise of humanity and the role of writing within the ongoing project which is human civilisation is very moving. To be associated with the spirit of Heine's writing, his compassion, his imagination, his daring, his mourning and his outrage – this is beyond what I would have hoped for myself, or my work.

So, thank you all.

But, as you know, the arts today cannot simply be about maybe some happy press releases and a congenial event where we congratulate each other on knowing about values. We are all aware that the values which keep us all safe, promise us the best possible opportunities to fulfil our humanity and to see and cherish what is human in others – those values are currently being forgotten, derided, or quietly buried alive.

As Germany clings to the lessons it learned about cultural toxicity long ago, I speak to you as a citizen of the UK, a country where books do not have to be burned – epidemic library closures and a massively compressed literary culture quietly prevent books ever being read or even born. Mine is a country which would rather leave traumatised and undefended children in the Calais mud, or now who knows where, than offer them the welcome we once extended to the kinder transports and to 100's of thousands of refugees before and after World War II. This is a country where the availability of the arts has narrowed shockingly in the last decades and where community arts are especially under threat. This is a country – a wealthy country – where around 130,000 of our own children are homeless.

This is a country which tortures in black sites abroad and police stations at home, which incarcerates citizens without trial. This is a country with a wrecked education system for the masses based on monetisation and testing and an emotionally traumatising and entitling education for the elite. This is a country where there is less and less mass media arts coverage. This is a country where the public discourse is a hell's broth of gossip, malign invention, racism, rabble-rousing hatred and smut. This is a country where civil servants despair, where politicians base decisions on faith and feeling which does not include faith in our species or fellow feeling, where any attempt to rise above the gutter is reframed as smugness, or otherworldly insanity. This is a country where – as the UN recently pointed out, our government's treatment of the disabled contravenes their human rights and where there is no need for an equivalent of Aktion T4 to organise the extinction of human beings with disabilities. We have simply withdrawn all their means of support, subjected them to official harassment and mass-media demonisation and waited for them to die in their tens of thousands – of stress, starvation, or else driven to suicide by their pain and despair. Make no mistake; we have been lost for some time – long before Brexit advertised that fact to the world. There is no morning when I could not wake up and say, like Max Liebermann – who once illustrated an edition of Der Rabbi Von Bacherach – *"Ich kann gar nicht soviel fressen, wie ich kotzen mochte."* [There's no way I could eat enough to vomit as much as I would like to.']

"This is a country where the public discourse is a hell's broth of gossip, malign invention, racism, rabble-rousing hatred and smut. This is a country where civil servants despair, where politicians base decisions on faith and feeling which does not include faith in our species or fellow feeling, where any attempt to rise above the gutter is reframed as smugness, or otherworldly insanity."

And this lack of art and this lack of humanity – they are connected. You know it, I know it, we have known it all along, but we have allowed the dominant discourse to forget. But as Franklin Delano Roosevelt said, *"Democracy cannot succeed unless those who express their choice are prepared to choose wisely. The real safeguard of democracy, therefore, is education."*

The practice of arts, contact with the arts, is our lifelong education – right here – it prepares us to choose wisely. It exercises our imagination, the force that allows us to visualise any change, all consequences, to empathise with each other. Without it, hope is a form of delusion. Art is at the heart of democracy. If we doubt ourselves, if we feel we may simply be making ourselves feel important because we are artists, then we can look to science, we can read about situation pressure and its massive power – what is culture but situational pressure. We can read about empathy, about compassion – how diminish it and how to enlarge it – by doing what art does. We can study history, we can learn all over again the beautiful and terrible truth of Heine's words from the play

Almansor, *"Das war ein Vorspiel nur, dort wo man Bucher verbrennt, verbrennt man auch am Ende Moonstone"* [*That was just a prelude, where books Are burnt, people will eventually burn too*].

We can look at the work of Raphael Lemkin, the man who invented the term Genocide before that crime had a name and who studied many culture's progressions into genocide – and see that the *vorspiel* is always the same – first the art is murdered, then the people. Always. Always.

And speaking now for myself – I'm 51 years old and my life a writer has failed. For something like 35 years I have produced work and I have loved the process of that and I have earned my living – I have been paid to dream aloud, there could be no better life for me – and I have a nice home and I've won some prizes and I have – from time to time – worked with writers in prisons, or community centres, or hospitals, worked with new writers, with children, written in the media – and I have learned from that, but I haven't talked enough about what I have learned. I have seen art light up lives, because that is what art does. But I haven't done enough. I haven't told enough people how precious that is, I haven't fought to make a space within which that could be heard. Like many of us, perhaps, in comfortable, apparently stable democracies I have forgotten that the price of freedom is eternal vigilance and I have mistaken lazy silence, cowardice, for truly loving tolerance. Love tells the whole truth – when something is wrong there is no love in being silent and nodding as if it were right. And I haven't said – at the start of every workshop – we will now make a part of culture – the thing which tells us to be cruel or to be kind, alone or united, ignorant and frightened, or endlessly learning and brave. And this matters – always – so we will now break our hearts to be extraordinary because anything else, anything imperfect, anything simply self-obsessed, weak and "conceptual" diminishes the place of art amongst us, wastes perhaps the only chance that art will have to improve and awaken and even save a life. This is life and death.

Whenever we see reality TV shows that diminish humanity, articles that lie in a way fiction wouldn't dare to, words used to rob them of their sense, or cynical website pieces that feed off outrage, while creating more, I haven't said often enough – There cannot ever be a place for this amongst us. It is not elitist to want the best for our fellow-man – it is insulting to stand by while other human beings are fed manure, are shown, over and over, only how low humanity can go. It cannot be that only our cars and electrical goods are aspirational. It must be that our dramas, or novels, songs, photographs, paintings, cartoons, poems, ballets, operas and all the rest are extraordinary, diverse, unexpected and things of life. If we have no money, then we have no money – art can be cheap without being bad, toxic, hateful. This is a necessary truth.

And I owe my career, my artisan's satisfaction and any morality I might lay claim to as a person to art, to writing, to – for example – a single scene in a drama that haunted me in my childhood and has ever since. In the drama a man who was not a torturer, but who was weak, stood in a torture chamber and was handed a pair of pliers – and there was the torture victim and there was the torturer and there were the pliers and there was the unspoken assurance that if the weak man did not torture he would be tortured and there was the pause. And that drama, by German screenwriter Lukas Heller who was born in Kiel in 1930 – asked me and still asks me – and what would you do? How weak are you? How best can you control your weakness and your desire for self-preservation – how do you prevent your fall and keep yourself and others truly safe?

And the how is what art always tells us – amongst everything else that it shows us and tells us. And it makes me think of lines from Heine's poem – *Allnächtlich im Traume* – which is large enough to be about more than one kind of love...

> *Du sagst mir heimlich ein leises Wort,*
> *Und gibst mir den Strauß von Zypressen*
> *Ich wache auf, und der Strauß ist fort,*
> *Und das Wort hab ich vergessen.*
>
> *You say to me secretly a soft word,*
> *and give me a garland of cypress.*
> *I wake up, and the garland is gone,*
> *and the word I have forgotten.*

As writers and artists we keep hold of the cypress that reminds us we all die and that we should be merciful and we serve the dreams that come to us to be expressed. We make them articulate and let them join the larger dreams that others make for us, the dreams that form our culture. Our culture makes the reality we inhabit. As artists, as writers, we are paid to dream awake and that is very nice for us. As human beings, which is more important, we have a duty never to forget those secret words we hear in darkness and to guard each other from the worst of who we can be, the worst of worlds that we can make and to do better. And we can love that, we can love that loudly. I would thank Heine and the Heine Preis for being part of what I love.

Automation

Irvine Welsh

Irvine Welsh on the automation of work and what this means for our social relationships.

The media and politicians will often blandly inform us that we are living in unprecedented times, usually without any real explanation of what this actually means. The basic answer, that we are approaching a technologically driven end of capitalism, doesn't on its own suffice. We have to look at the changing relationships between key factors that characterise this inchoate era. One of the most important of these is automation, and its recently altered association with productivity and employment.

That capitalism, in its post-industrial phase, has evolved into a very different beast from its depiction in the oft-idealised pin factory of Adam Smith, is now universally accepted. It's also becoming widely consensual that this economic system of production, distribution and exchange has a technologically determined life-cycle. Industrial capitalism, which manufactured physical goods, explicitly supported the development of a market system. Now human activity produces mainly information, often counter-intuitive to private profit. Monopolistic corporations,

133

which owe their strength to economies of scale, increasingly produce the remaining tangible goods and services. This corporate pre-eminence is both progressed and cemented by defensive, statist and supranational legal strategies, rather than being the outcome of any successful competition in the market place.

So the end of capitalism's natural life has been promoted by neoliberalism, which has exacerbated technology-led deindustrialization. Technology cannot be un-invented. But its development can be phased in for the social good of the community, rather than the rapacious desire for bigger profits. This wasn't done; in the 1980's and 90's, neoliberals seized every aspect of the state, including the media and the main political parties, in order to promote the shift of wealth from the broader community to the already rich. In Britain, the Conservative and Labour governments of the 80,'s 90's and 2000's saw it as 'modernising' to erode the traditional blue-collar unionised basis of socialism. But this approach now seems based on a misunderstanding of what the state and free market actually constituted within a capitalist society.

It used to be fashionable to think of capitalism and socialism as two antagonistic forces: battling for supremacy in a pluralist democracy. The neoliberal ascendancy of 1984-2008 established the notion that capitalism (or at least a warped facsimile of it) had triumphed in this struggle. It could therefore do nothing more than impose a hegemony of ideas and practices, which circumvented and negated a democracy that had come to be covertly regarded as inefficient and wasteful by elites, with its potential to produce outcomes beneficial to citizens but detrimental to profit margins. All of progressive post-war institutions, from the BBC to the Labour Party to the Universities, were co-opted into this dominant paradigm.

"Our awe of the latest technological advances, with robots like Baxter, Watson and Kiva being given the C3PO/R2D2 media treatment, bizarrely means that the notion of 'machines taking our jobs' still retains a sci-fi extravagance in our imaginations. However, this is simply the historical reality of industrialisation. What is totally unprecedented is the scale and speed at which this is happening. In

Britain, Deloitte and the University of Oxford have predicted that 10 million unskilled jobs could be taken over by robots."

But having an ascendant end-of-history 'there is no alternative' mode of thought, encompassing all political parties, the media and the education system, isn't just intellectually limiting. In a more practical sense, it's also disastrous. Economist Steve Keen recounts the Queen calling outraged bullshit on Britain's sheepish top economic experts at a meeting at the London School of Economics, where they meekly argued that nobody could have predicted the 2008 crash. In fact, a substantial number of them (including Keen himself) had done exactly that over the years. The truth is that only those classical, neo-liberal economists, hopelessly trapped by the prevailing wisdom and their groupthink, had marginalised their more critical colleagues over the years. Of course, they themselves proved to be as useful as chocolate fireguards when the crash came along, simply because their self-regulating schematic model of capitalism permitted no room for such crisis.

But the underlying reality is that capitalism and socialism were always complimentary as well as competing forces. Both are the children of industrialisation, and both are now in secular decline in face of a relentless technology, which is destroying the paid employment offered to labour, and the profit awarded to capital. Neoliberalism's 'solution' to this problem was privatisation, the transfer of state assets to the rich, and financialisation, the transfer of the middle-classes assets to the same elite, in exchange for debt, and of course, the steady reduction of worker's wages through the erosion of union power, in order to bring them down to the levels of the emerging economies.

The ironic truth that neoliberalism has not only destroyed industrial socialism, but in its rapacious greed, failed to protect an ailing capitalism, is a hard one for many to swallow. The right-wing's more libertarian advocates of full-throttle privatisation and attacks on union power, failed to recognise that that the system had scientifically developed into a monopolistic, global, corporate concern. Therefore, dreaming of returning to the pin factory of Smith and perfect competition is Pol Pot style nostalgia. By 'deregulating' capital and 'regulating' the labour market (by putting constraints on the personal freedom of workers to assemble), far from increasing competition and making the market function more efficiently, the ascendant right-wing were helping to erode it, by building a transnational corporate state of the superrich. Milton Friedman himself gave the game away, when he described monopoly as a 'reward for efficiency.' It was this reward that paved the way for the mergers and acquisitions fever of the Thatcher and Reagan era, where profits were boosted, not by increasing competition in the market place, but by eliminating it through the development of monopoly power, and solidifying this through the co-opting of democracy by the lobby system and the transnational bodies like the IMF and the World Bank. While such elites would prefer to use these globalist institutions to maintain their power, the bailout of 2008, a response to their failed policies of financialization, illustrates how much they see national taxpayer's money as their own.

As citizens, we justly mistrust the 'unprecedented times' mantra. After all, it would seem to give implicit emergency powers to elites whose behaviour has precipitated such crisis. Most people, justifiably, want to simply get on with life and make progress without being burdened by external threats and upheavals. Indeed, much of Conservatism's power as a political creed is that it taps into the compelling illusion of this possibility. But in an era where we face species-threatening imperatives on population, climate, a broken financial system, flatlining growth and real wage reductions, it's fanciful to imagine that we can sustain this delusion.

These factors, in conjuncture with our information technology revolution, are pushing us towards a different set of social relationships and a new type of society. Now the dispassionate view is one that used to be reserved for neo-Marxists; it sees Western capitalism in technologically driven decline, with its ability to provide economic growth and employment prospects for its citizens rapidly receding.

Our awe of the latest technological advances, with robots like Baxter, Watson and Kiva being given the C3PO/R2D2 media treatment, bizarrely means that the notion of 'machines taking our jobs' still retains a sci-fi extravagance in our imaginations. However, this is simply the historical reality of industrialisation. What is totally unprecedented is the scale and speed at which this is happening. In Britain, Deloitte and the University of Oxford have predicted that 10 million unskilled jobs could be taken over by robots.

Automation, the reduction of the need for people in jobs, was once seen as a positive process, liberating us from backbreaking, mind-numbing routine work. We could enjoy more leisure and holidays, make love and write poetry, go canoeing and abseiling. Karl Marx, despite the grim Soviet experience of communism, and the relentless distortion of his ideas, was primarily interested in human freedom: the removal of external dictates by other individuals and systems. The principal flaw in Marx's analysis of industrial capitalism was the belief that the urban proletariat had to be the agents of political and social revolution. In fact they were beneficiaries of capitalism's superiority over central planning in solving problems of economic scarcity. Yes, capitalism did promote obscene inequities, wars, conflict and poverty, and it was an unfair lottery that cemented advantages of birth. Yet it also gave a majority of working people in the western world a better shot at leisure and comfort than anything that had preceded it, or would rise to challenge it. Marx saw that the automation, which was the foundation of this wealth, was alienating, but part of a process that would eventually lead to revolution. In the heady 60's there was great interest in automation and alienation, when the studies of writers like Robert Blauner gained prominence. Now automation, once identified as both the route to a possible anarchist utopia and the destruction of the worker's consciousness and psychological well-being, is increasingly associated with a future of stagnant income and worsening inequality under a crumbling capitalism.

"As citizens, we justly mistrust the 'unprecedented times' mantra. After all, it would seem to give implicit emergency powers to elites whose behaviour has precipitated such crisis. Most people, justifiably, want to simply get on with life and make progress without being burdened by external threats and upheavals. Indeed, much of Conservatism's power as a political creed is that it taps into the compelling illusion of this possibility. But in an era where we face species-threatening imperatives on population, climate, a broken financial system, flatlining growth and real wage reductions, it's fanciful to imagine that we can sustain this delusion."

Advanced automation has been common in many types of manufacturing for decades. It has now developed to a level of flexibility and cost where it's viable to have industrial robots, like Baxter of Rethink Robotics, perform manual jobs for small manufacturers in a variety of sectors. What goes for modest companies is even more expressed in big ones. The orange Kiva robot scurries across the hanger-like warehouses of its parent company, Amazon, and other e-commerce enterprises, grabbing racks of goods for the clerks who package the orders. Now super-Kiva's have already made thousands of their poor old prototypes redundant. High profile sensations like Google's driverless car, suggest what automation soon might be able to accomplish. As I write this, Amsterdam is introducing the unmanned 'roboat' onto its network of canals.

Until recently blue-collar jobs took the brunt of the personnel decimation, as technology relentlessly automated assembly-line work. Now artificial intelligence, robotics and new disruptive technology are having a devastating impact on previously inviolable white-collar professions. IBM's Watson, best known for its dazzling performance in a TV game show (Jeopardy!) has already shown a much more accurate diagnosis rate for certain cancers than human consultants: 90 percent versus 50 percent in some tests. Watson's diagnostic edge comes from the robot's voracious assimilation of newly released medical data, which would take a Doctor up to 160 hours a week to match.

Automated systems are already in use to aid surgeons in low-invasive procedures. In more complex operations, the doctor remains in control, but we've already seen demonstrations of how a robotic system can remove a tumour from tissue. And at least one hair transplant robot is on the market, allowing a solitary surgeon to oversee multiple procedures on a group of pop stars, or even an entire team of footballers.

Reviewing the thousands of documents required in big legal cases was traditionally one of the lower-level tasks lawyers or paralegals could face. Now this can be done by new software systems, which comb through emails, texts, databases, and scanned documents, sourcing the relevant material using syntactic analysis and keyword recognition. In the near future a legally-trained Watson will be able to construct a system with a vast store of cases and precedent, creating drafts of briefs, the sort of work usually handled by associates in law firms. Even senior lawyers, highly paid for knowing which arguments are most salient to win a particular case, assessing past court rulings and even the peculiarities of a judge, are potentially under threat as quantitative legal prediction is another virgin territory that information technology is now encroaching on. The main difference between the present and previous periods of technological advance is that now there are no signs of this trend reversing. As technology is evolving faster than ever before and with almost zero regulation, the likelihood of more jobs being replaced by new tech is at an all-time high. An Oxford University study in 2013 concluded that some 47% of present jobs in the US could be computerised in the next 10 to 20 years.

The crux of the argument is a straightforward one. In economics, productivity (the amount of value created by any given unit of input, such as an hour of labour) is a crucial indicator of growth and wealth creation – a measure of progress, if you will. For years after World War II, productivity and jobs closely tracked each other, with increases in one corresponding to rises in the other. As businesses generated more value from their workers, the country as a whole became richer, fuelling further economic activity and creating even more jobs.

In 2000, divergence started to occur; despite a robust rise in productivity, employment had started to wane. By 2011, the "great decoupling", as described by Erik Brynjolfsson and Andrew McAfee from MIT's Sloan School of Management, had taken place. We now have a significant and increasing gap between productivity and employment, with economic growth resulting in no parallel increase in job creation.

A view as to the permanence (or otherwise) of this phenomenon is dependent on how one sees the development of capitalism. Since the Industrial Revolution began in the 1700s, improvements in technology have changed the nature of work, in the process destroying certain types of jobs. Agriculture employed 41% of all Americans in 1900, but by 2000, this had shrunk to a meagre 2%. The proportion employed in manufacturing decreased from 30% after World War II to around 10% today, mainly because of increased automation. The biggest increases were recorded in the Reagan years of 1980's wrecking ball neoliberalism, a trend mirrored in the UK under Thatcher.

Structural changes can obviously destroy the livelihood of citizens whose skills no longer match the needs of employers, and the communities on which a traditional industry is based. But will 'technological unemployment' ease over time? Harvard economic historian Lawrence Katz, takes the orthodox line that no long-term historical pattern indicates that such changes lead to a net decrease in jobs. Indeed, Katz's research on how technological advances have affected patterns of work over the last few centuries is a testimony to the adaptive powers of capitalism. While it may take decades for workers to acquire the expertise needed for new types of employment, Katz argues that in the long-term we never have run out of jobs.

But even Katz won't dismiss the notion that there is a different quality to today's digital technologies; features that might adversely influence a much broader range of work. The question he posits is whether past evidence will serve as a useful guide. As a discipline, economic history is, and has to be, largely the narrative of feudalism and capitalism. Can its extrapolations be applied to the conceptualist society, where the prime activity of production is intangible information? Can capitalism, in its risk-averse era, where entrepreneurs have been replaced by corporate elites who use monopoly power, manage to adapt to encompass the technological (to say nothing of social, climatic and demographic) changes, within a private profit system, or is it near the end of the line?

Wendell Wallach, from Yale University's Interdisciplinary Centre for Bioethics, claims that robotics, 3D printing, and other emerging technologies are fuelling technological unemployment, (the concept of technology killing more jobs than it produces) and promoting global wealth disparity. Wallach offers the example of how, in 1990, GM, Ford, and Chrysler generated $36 billion in annual revenue and hired over a million workers in America. The present day big three of Apple, Facebook and Google, bring in over a trillion dollars but employ around only 137,000 staff. Such social changes, taking place under neoliberal regimes where wealth redistribution remains a taboo concept, have ironically created a revival in Marxist ideas, as capital increasingly concentrates in the hands of a smaller percentage of the population. According to Wallach, the USA is approaching 70% of stock ownership owned by 5% of the population. "When people no longer receive the money from wages they need to support their families, it is hard to know what they will do, but in the past and in other countries this has been thought of as a situation ripe for a revolution."

Against this background, simple pragmatism dictates that we prepare for a world without paid work. But this means that those who enjoy great power and wealth will have no hold over the populace. This partly explains the existential rage of the rich and privileged classes. Despite having everything in terms of wealth and power flowing relentlessly in their direction for the last thirty odd years, they remain as angry as the former 'aristocrats of labour'; the skilled white workers in post-industrial regions of the west, who have been lain to waste by the same technology and politics that has so benefited their masters. This angst of the elites and their cheerleaders comes from the sense that nobody will listen to their vainglorious, self-aggrandising nonsense, when they can no longer pay wages. The problem for them becomes: how can you control people and maintain dominance over them when you can't offer them anything? It's not easy to relinquish long-held power, especially when you can divide citizens by appealing to the tawdry status that racism, nativism and imperialistic nationalism offer. Moreover, politicians are creatures of the present, and few votes are available in stating the basic truths; you are not going to have a job, and if you do, you are going to be paid next to nothing for doing it. In such an environment, we are inclined to turn to the elites reserve figureheads of loud-mouthed ignoramuses peddling their false certainties, from the arrogance and stupidity of minds unfettered by abstraction.

The crunch for the elites may come when it dawns that these technological developments are, in the long-run, against profit too; that the workers late capitalism grinds into debt-dust are also the consumers it needs to buy its products and sustain the profits of its corporate enterprises, the tax base of its co-opted states and the legitimacy of its governments and supranational institutions. The concentration of wealth has created a post-democratic caste of business and political elites whose primary interest is their own welfare and perpetuation. They have been and are becoming increasingly irrelevant to the needs of the rest of us. If citizens want the benefits of the liberation that technology offers, it's incumbent on us all to wise up and start mapping out the kind of world we want to live in. You can rest assured that those who have no interest in these freedoms are doing just that. The alternatives that elites and other power seekers offer, as supported by history, and clearly visible in the weeds sprouting through the increasing cracks of a failing neoliberalism, are fascism and war.

In Defence of Nostalgia

Paul Tritschler

Paul Tritschler considers that remarkable attribute of memory — nostalgia.

School and childhood were complicated, and I got out of both as fast as I could. Aged fifteen — that seems quite young to me now — I found a labouring job in a boat shed along the Clyde. The days of good apprenticeships in the Glasgow shipyards, or anywhere else for that matter, were fading fast, and I settled for poor pay and prospects in a badly ventilated box buffing fibreglass boats.

My hair, clothes and sandwiches were each day covered in a fine white powdery dust; I brought it home with me, and often expelled it as a gluey muck into my handkerchief or coughed it up to the point of vomiting. We were not issued overalls, boots, masks or safety instructions, and accidents were not uncommon — cuts, chemical burns and eye injuries — though they were minor against those at the yards: sometimes men were carried out whilst others in the line were still clocking in.

Some way into the future, as part of research on behalf of the Scottish Labour History Society, I interviewed retired miners at their home and recorded memories of their time in the pits. Accounts varied. Most recalled a blend of campaigns, camaraderie, and colliery catastrophes, but others would talk only of the best of times. Among them was JL, an eighty-something from Tranent who, despite having only one lung, filled my reel-to-reel with hilarious accounts and bursts of wheezing laughter. He said he was fortunate in that he had never encountered much by way of major accidents. I was claustrophobic in those days – imagining the descent into the pits made me uneasy – but 'working conditions' was a prompt on my open-ended questionnaire and I probed into the darkest corners of pit life – areas into which this ex-miner from Tranent was perhaps reluctant to go. 'It's not that there were no accidents,' he conceded, on being pressed: 'I saw men lose a foot or a finger, and there were fatalities over the years – caught in the blades or under a fall – but I never saw anything on the scale of what you might call a pit disaster. Mind you, it was never far from our thoughts.'

There was no talking during work time in the boat shed, but workers could listen to the mindless oblivion that was Radio One, and for all but myself, this seemed to make the day go by faster. The Hollies sang a song, repeatedly, about the air that they breathed, and I longed for some of that. And so, despite the pleas of my parents, when I turned sixteen I entered one of life's major transitions: I boarded an overnight bus destined for London, and after a week in youth hostels found a room in Talbot Road and a job in a factory putting rubber knobs on the legs of dish racks. It took months to find even the most rubbish work in Glasgow, but in London I managed it in a week – how much easier it was to get on in London!

It seemed everyone in Notting Hill lived in squats at that time: bohemian communes, clusters of nonconformity, arty types campaigning against everything all at once. And in a stucco-fronted house stuck in the centre and yet the periphery of this village, I paid rent to a shady landlord of the boat-shed-boss mindset in exchange for a dimly-lit room with mice, metered gas, and a tabletop electric cooker that took an hour to bring a can of tomato soup to bubbling point. It was the dreariest place in W11, the batteries in my cassette player drained constantly, I went to bed early to stay warm, I was lonely, hungry and homesick, I read Tolstoy over and over – how much harder it was to get on in London.

The Spanish squatters who lived opposite ran a stall around the corner in Portobello Road, and by way of 'Hola' I bought two large scented candles from them as a Christmas present for my parents. The candles arrived on the day their electricity was disconnected. 'What a happy coincidence', they said. They were told that if they paid the bill immediately, even though it was late, they would not be plunged into darkness over the festive period, and so they did but they were – the spirit of Christmas conveyed by the South of Scotland Electricity Board.

My dad moved the lifeless tree back from the bay window and closed the curtains to give the neighbours less to talk about. I rang from the corner phone box on Christmas Eve. Back to the blackouts, said my mother, but it wasn't, really: that was something shared communally. Wartime reminiscences flooded back nonetheless and, like JL, the ex-miner in Tranent, they would steer clear of dead ends. I suppose that was something my parents got through, and they were getting through it again. The candles lit the room and my parents relived their past until the night and the memories blended with sleep. They had said they were happy. It was the sort of happiness that had something to do with making the best of it, and the sort of cheerfulness that made me sad, but a sadness that, even yet, I want to hold on to.

'All happy families are alike; each unhappy family is unhappy in its own way.' I wonder if I am at last beginning to understand Tolstoy's double bind – I wonder if we were a gloriously unhappy family.

Dwelling on the past was once linked to depressive states, but there is today a growing body of research that suggests nostalgia is a unique asset that enables us to make sense of our existence, to improve psychological health, and to reduce fears about death. Regardless of age or culture, nostalgia narratives are never absent from our lives. They might be tinged with sadness and triggered by negative thoughts or loneliness, but in the end they are always positive experiences, and frequently socially oriented.

The universality of nostalgia as a discrete aspect of memory suggests it evolved as part of selective pressures in our environment;

it appears as an adaptive neurological protection system that strengthens neural pathways and builds resilience and motivation by reminding us who we are and where we are coming from.

According to research conducted by psychologists Constantine Sedikides and Tim Wildschut, nostalgia has three main functions: it increases positive (but not negative) mood, it defends our sense of self, and it reinforces social connectedness. Their empirical studies also suggest the centrality of its place in increasing relationship satisfaction, of strengthening belongingness and empathy, and of preserving a sense of meaning in life. It does this, says Wildschut, by connecting the past with the present to point optimistically to the future, and not surprisingly there are now multidisciplinary teams looking at ways of developing nostalgia narratives as therapeutic interventions for post-traumatic stress, depression and early stage Alzheimer's.

Far from being a dark, depressive indulgence, nostalgia is a remarkable attribute of memory that helps dissolve barriers and give structure and meaning to our life. Just as the brain is set up for metaphor, nostalgic experiences, as my parents could attest, operate as an emergency generator when the power is cut. I see them clearly now in the flickering shadows alone together on Christmas Eve. I don't suppose they said all that much. I don't suppose they had to.

The Theatre of Humiliation

George Gunn

The Theatre of Humiliation: From 'The Province of The Cat' by George Gunn

As the ungainly farce of Brexit blathers to its inevitable conclusion, now that Theresa May has set the date for leaving the EU – 29th March 2019 – and bowed low to the inevitable cash settlement for the European divorce bill which will be £50 million (although it could rise to £90 billion or more, as it is an ongoing negotiation) – it is timely that the Scottish theatre community is in full panto-mode, to set the scene for January next year when Creative Scotland will announce just how the financial wheels are coming off the cultural wagon. To conflate arts funding and the cliff cascading exercise that is Brexit may seem to many to be flippant, if not downright perverse, but I think the two are intrinsically linked. Both these things are unnecessary, and both are tragedies for Scotland.

It was the Irish poet Patrick Kavanagh who claimed that all tragedy consisted of was underdeveloped comedy. The comedy of Brexit is ever realised in the antics of Boris Johnson, Theresa May, David Davis Michael Gove and co and their ham-fisted impersonations of politicians, negotiators and democrats. They are

147

the cast of a new kind of comedy: the theatre of humiliation. Their singular joke is that they, apparently, represent the people of the UK, when they so obviously have only the interests of their own class in mind. Oh yes, they do! As John S. Warren has repeatedly pointed out on Bella, the shambles that is the Tory negotiations with the EU is the plan. These people know what they are doing even if they give off the appearance that they do not. What they want the mass of people to think is one thing, what they are actually up to is another. Look out, they're behind you!

In his book, *The Anatomy of Fascism* (Knopf, NYC. 204) the American historian Robert O. Paxton persuasively defined fascism as a form of political behaviour marked "by obsessive preoccupation with community decline, humiliation, or victimhood", in which "a mass-based party of committed nationalist militants, working in uneasy but effective collaboration with traditional elites, abandons democratic liberties and pursues with redemptive violence and without ethical or legal constraints goals of internal cleansing and external expansion".

That is closer to a definition of the US than the UK. However, as a former powerful state, now in decline, the UK does excel in humiliation and victimhood. The core ethos of Universal Credit is the personalisation of the poverty of the individual and a denial that it is systemic of a crumbling economy. We have moved from decrying "rights without responsibilities" to accepting "responsibilities without rights". The clarion call of the Leave campaign during the EU referendum was the threat posed to "British" workers by European "immigrants". Fear was used as a smokescreen for the desires of the elite. The "redemptive violence" engaged on these islands, I would argue, is the UK state's heavy metal fetish for the twin brothers of nuclear weapons and nuclear power and its addiction to its seat on the UN Security Council. These are dangerous dreams and totally at odds with the reality of the UK's real place in the world's economic and military pecking order. But as long as the UK allies itself so unthinkingly to US foreign policy and Scotland is constitutionally attached to the UK the "goals ... of external expansion" can be applied to us, no matter how much we declare that we are different from "Conservative Britain". In truth, as long as all the parties in Holyrood concern themselves with the mediocre politics of managing the crisis that is the economy, then we can demonstrate little real difference.

In Scotland we have few real defences against the "obsessive preoccupations" of the big state. The devolved parliament and the current SNP government only offers us partial protection from the "internal cleansing" which lurks at the back of the Brexit madness and permeates the thinking of Tory immigration policy. Throughout the dark days of Margaret Thatcher's government and during the years of the Iraq war it was to our creative community that the Scots looked for energy and imagination to resist Thatcher's bullying and to believe in a better world. Our writers, artists, theatre and film makers were the ones who had the big ideas, who articulated what the people believed, who were maddened with frustration, by what the French call *ressentiment*. They wrote, sang and painted the shape of our political consciousness. They offered us through imagination a hope for the future. Come January next year, after what Ruth Wishart has called the "cultural carnage" that is coming, who is to say whom or what will be left standing in Scotland's artistic community, able to muster anything, never mind *ressentiment*? We will be forced to attend the theatre of humiliation, with the likes of Bo-jo and the Govester, and witness performances charting our own decline. Oh, how we will laugh! Humiliation and decline were two of Professor Paxton's signifiers of the political behaviour of a fascist state.

The development of theatre in ancient Athens was paralleled by the development of democracy: they were mutually enhancing and one depended upon the other. They were like two vines which wrapped themselves around the civic pillar of the Polis to ensure that it weathered the storms of history. If we cut our cultural sector in Scotland we are diminishing our hard-won democratic rights. That the majority of people do not make this connection and think it unimportant if they do, only shows how successful the ruling elite have been in disenfranchising us from our cultural history, from our imagination. Fascism is an extremely ugly word, but at the moment there is no other nomenclature that fits or definition for the way of political travel in the UK. By limiting people's cultural life you limit their future possibilities. That is another form of internal cleansing.

In Scotland the theatre has always been a public forum. It is, by its nature, passionate, poetic and political. It has also been accessible, portable and has concerned itself with the cry of life, rather than indulged the dolorous chorus of death. The theatre brings people together in order to speak freely, one to another, one with all. It is the last public place where we can truly be free. I have believed this all my life and I am not about to change my mind because some political managers find it necessary to savagely cut the creative sector which amounts to less than 0.01% of the GDP. To what end? Without art and artists we are less well placed to counter the chronic self-harmers of the present Tory administration. If we erode our civic imagination how can we put forth alternatives to Moray councillors, for example, who every fiscal year decide that shutting public libraries is the way to alleviate the reduction to their block grant. "Mechty, ye'll nae be needin tae read ony oh they books noo that the hospitals hed tae close!" What alternative narratives can we offer our children who are constantly bombarded by digital messaging and the mind-numbing fodder of flat screen tv's. If they have no idea of who they are, where they are and how they got there, how are they supposed to form a pathway to the future? If our children are not exposed to the imaginative fabric of Scotland, in all its many colours, how can they be expected to believe in their own dreams? This covers ever aspect of our cultural inheritance.

This is what the architect Ian Begg wrote in the Japanese *a+u* *(Architecture and Urbanism)* magazine in 1997:

"Where do I see architecture featuring in Scotland? What do I want to see happening and what am I doing about it? It is a big subject; but I want to see the people in Scotland becoming more aware of our history including our architectural history because through that we can more easily understand who we are, what the problems have been in the past and how we have coped with them, and with this appreciation build up confidence and courage which are to me essential if we are going to progress. Teaching children comes first, but we must do more. I want our museums and the countless modern heritage centres to shift emphasis and focus more on the future while teaching the past story of Scotland. History is primarily a story and it never stops. It is part of the continuity of all life. It is strange that as we lose our traditions we, ordinary people, also lose control of our future."

When Creative Scotland, in association with the Scottish government, under licence from Westminster, cut the budgets of our arts organisations to the bone they are ensuring that we in Scotland are losing "control of our future", as articulated by Ian Begg. They are diminishing the possibilities of that future. They are making the gaining of the independence of our country just that bit harder. They are funnelling us into the theatre of humiliation. The laughter is fading and when the clowns have left the stage the lights will go out. One joke doesn't get you very far, except on the charabanc of corruption which keeps rolling on.

The revelations of the Paradise Papers shows the extent of the corporate deceit and of how the people are being swindled. The UK government has shown little enthusiasm to do anything about. The Scottish government can do very little, even if it wanted to and I'm not convinced it does. Oil companies now have the ability to sell assets to new companies who would then inherit the big companies tax write-offs, thanks to the Chancellor Philip Hammond's recent budget. This effectively declared the North Sea a tax-free zone and reduced Scottish oil revenues for years to come just in time to banjax the next independence referendum. In the House of Commons the hypnotised SNP actually thanked him for it. There are, as currently estimated, 20 billion barrels of oil in reserve in the Scottish North Sea. The price, as of last month, was $60 a barrel.

Meanwhile over in the land "of committed nationalist militants" which, as defined by Robert O. Paxton, is the US, the national debt is about to double to $50 trillion in the next few years. The US is by far the worlds biggest debtor. Meanwhile China, with cities with names unheard of in the West which have GDP's bigger than many European countries, is the worlds biggest creditor. Very soon China will become America's landlord. What will the world look like then? Will the resulting regime be the one that finally cements modern 21st century fascism and, again to quote Professor Paxton, be the one to continue "working in uneasy but effective collaboration with traditional elites, (and which) abandons democratic liberties"? Or has that happened already?

The goat song of Brexit pales into insignificance compared to that prospect. "History is primarily a story and it never stops." as Ian Begg wrote in 1997. Increasingly, it will be more difficult to maintain our national moral and to construct an alternative narrative when Creative Scotland have silenced all the storytellers. Maybe that is why they are doing it? The theatre of humiliation will stand stark, cold and empty. We deserve better than this.

For Ian Begg (1925 – 2017)

Means and Ends

Caitlin Logan

As someone who has never been comfortable being described as a 'nationalist', who is suspicious of excessive enthusiasm about flags, and who mostly views the concept of patriotism as a tool of states to control their populace, I'm not an obvious cheerleader for 'Scottish exceptionalism'.

I'm one of those people who a certain subsection of independence supporters may well view as harmful to 'the cause': one of those who will happily admit they see independence as a means to an end, and who recoils in horror at the sight of people lashing out with paranoid fervour against any criticism of a pro-independence person, organisation or political party.

(By which I mean criticism against people, organisations or political parties they actually like – because if we don't like you, you don't really support independence anyway. That's how logic works, didn't you know?).

And yet, this is exactly why I'm here to make the case that the only way independence can, or even should be achieved is through striving for exceptionalism, and that a failure to recognise the ways in which Scotland has already managed to do and be 'better' will surely be the road to another lost referendum.

I've been amazed (in the "I'm amazed that there's a significant audience for people I've never heard of eating bugs on TV" kind of way) to find that the 'independence-must-be-ideologically-neutral' contingent seem not only to be holding strong, but getting louder – at least within the echo chamber of social media.

Never mind the fact that there is no such thing as ideological neutrality, for me, the whole 'means to an end' business is just common sense: to convince someone who something is a good idea, you need to show them what it would mean for them. And I'm firmly of the belief that people can and will be persuaded by a vision for a more socially just and equal Scotland.

I am proud to be able to say that Scotland's campaign for a major shift in the balance of power in 2014 was predominately progressive and distinctly inclusive, and that our Scottish Government, while presenting itself in stark opposition to the Westminster establishment, has maintained a clear pro-immigration and pro-equality stance.

This may seem a small achievement if not viewed in the international context: where a vote for the UK to leave the EU was won by stirring up xenophobic sentiment; where an unintelligent, narcissistic millionaire was elected US President on the back of a campaign of hate and division; and where support for far right parties has grown across Europe, from Sweden to Germany, Austria to the Netherlands, France to Greece.

All of these trends have something in common with the movement for Scottish independence – they have been fuelled by years of alienation from existing power structures which have failed to represent large sections of the population, all while propping up an increasingly cutthroat capitalist economy in which inequality and antipathy are on the rise.

Yet Scotland truly has achieved something unusual by seeking to fulfil that thirst for change from the left, and not, as so many have, by cashing in on humans' basest instincts to exclude and vilify others. By boldly building on this momentum in the next referendum (because I have to believe at this point that there will be a next time) Scotland has the chance to show the world that it is possible to avert pressure to be driven to the right and to win popular support at the same time.

When the referendum was announced back in March 2013, support for independence sat at around 28 per cent. By September 2014, 45 per cent of the highest turnout in decades voted Yes, and two Survation polls in the last month have identified independence support at 46- 47 per cent. From where I'm sitting, that looks like a pretty enduringly convincing campaign – just imagine what could happen if we tried that again?

In light of this rare feeling of optimism that I can just about muster when I put my mind to it, it is both disheartening and puzzling to see some in the 'Yes Movement' resist attempts to push for more equal representation or attention to issues of equality, instead arguing that we should focus solely on independence until such time as an independent Scotland comes into being.

This is not only an unfair request to make of anyone who might actually be affected by any number of other issues on a daily basis, it also unrealistically treats the achievement of national independence as a single event which can take place within a bubble, as opposed to forming part of a wider and ongoing movement for political and social change. People will never compartmentalise issues that cleanly in the real world, so suggesting they do is a lost cause from the outset.

What is true is that some people will never be appealed to by the idea of a fairer, more re-distributive society, or one which takes seriously the concerns of women and minorities – and if those are the people we're going to base our politics around, we've already lost. But it's also true that there are people who can be won over to new ideas through considered conversation, information, and persuasion – or, as some like to call it, 'campaigning'.

What I think is more likely to drive people away is an attitude that these conversations can't be permitted, that no self-improvement is necessary, and that the movement is closing ranks and closing the door on anyone who dares to question it – because, hey, we don't need you anyway. Except, we really, really do.

We need the numbers — that's just a fact — but we also need to hold on for dear life to the ideals that drove so many of us to vote for independence in the first place. These ideals are easy to lose sight of at the best of times — we know that, because we've seen how almost the entirety of political history has played out — so if we can't hold on to them even in the pre-campaign stage, what chance do we have of creating a country around them?

And this has as much to do with the 'how' as the 'what' we want to achieve — it seems to me that much of the problem with Westminster politics is its centralised, unrepresentative nature, its tendency towards politics as performance, of adversary for adversary's sake, and of a lack of transparency on the matters of real substance.

If we hope for an independent Scotland to represent something genuinely different, it won't do to replicate the same structures, systems and dynamics which have failed us in the past. When discussion and debate within and around the independence movement so frequently descends into tribalism, suspicion, and outright hostility, it becomes hard to imagine that we are "living in the early days of a better nation".

It would be far too easy, but tragically unwise, to take for granted that we can offer that hopeful vision to people without first embodying it ourselves.

Audre Lorde was quoted a little over two weeks ago in Bella Caledonia in aid of similar sentiments, and the relevance was striking enough that I think I can allow myself to present a few more of Lorde's words of wisdom: "The master's tools will never dismantle the master's house. They may allow us to temporarily beat him at his own game, but they will never enable us to bring about genuine change."

As it is, we are standing on the precipice of the future and we have a serious choice to make about the tools we want to use, and the nation we want to build.

A Song for Europe – Lost in Translation on a Grand Tour

Neil Cooper

On March 25th 1972, the Eurovision Song Contest was held at the Usher Hall in Edinburgh. The then sixteen-year-old international competition was hosted by Dunfermline-born Moira Shearer, the dancing queen from Powell and Pressburger's ballet based 1948 blockbuster, *The Red Shoes*.

The Eurovision Song Contest was founded in 1956 by the alliance of public service broadcasters that made up the European Broadcasting Union, and was based on the Sanremo Music festival, which had been running in Italy since 1951.

The first Eurovision saw fourteen countries showing off their wares in Lugano, Switzerland. There was no entry from the UK, who wouldn't join in until the following year. The Edinburgh event was the fourth time the contest had been held in the UK since it was first hosted at London's Royal Festival Hall in 1960. The 1972 event was also the first in the UK to be programmed outside London, and, to date, the only Eurovision held in Scotland.

In Edinburgh, the UK's entry was 'Beg, Steal or Borrow', performed by The New Seekers. This was a band put together by Keith Potger, after Australian folk-pop quintet, The Seekers, of whom Potger was a member, broke up. The similarly styled male/

female vocal line up of The New Seekers featured 'Perth's own Eve Graham', as partisan Eurovision commentators would have it.

At that time, the group was probably best known for their hit with 'I'd Like to Teach the World to Sing' (1970), a song based on a Coca Cola jingle, and preaching a suitably saccharine sounding form of global unity.

There were high hopes for The New Seekers and 'Beg, Steal or Borrow' in Edinburgh. The song had been co-written by Australian singer/songwriter Tony Cole with Steve Wolfe and Graeme Hall. Another of Cole's songs, 'The King is Dead' (1972), would later be adapted into French by Long Chris and Patrick Larue. Under the title, 'Gabrielle' (1976), Gallic pop sensation Johnny Hallyday would take it to number one in the French charts.

Back in the Usher, The New Seekers and 'Beg, Steal or Borrow' came second, with 114 points, while Ireland's entry, the Gaelic language 'Ceol An Ghra', sung by the Welsh sounding Sandie Jones, came fifteenth out of eighteen acts, with 72 points.

Overall winner of the 1972 Eurovision Song Contest with a world beating 128 points was Vicky Leandros, representing Luxembourg with 'Après toi'. Leandros was a Greek singer who lived in Germany, and who sang in French. The song's original lyrics were penned by German composer Klaus Munro and French lyricist Yves Dessca, with music by Munro and Leandros' father, Leo Leandros, writing under his pseudonym, Mario Panas.

Under the management of her father since she was thirteen, Leandros had previous Eurovision form. Five years earlier, when she was seventeen, Leandros had represented Luxembourg a first time, singing 'L'amour est bleu', French composer Andre Popp's collaboration with lyricist and fellow countryman Pierre Cour.

While that song's jaunty melancholy acquired a form of period chic, by the time Leandros represented Luxembourg a second time, in 'Après toi', she was tackling some pretty grown up stuff. Opening with a flourish of package tour horns, 'Après toi', which translates as 'After You', is a first person melodrama in which the song's narrator tells her departing lover the consequences of him leaving her. 'After you,' the chorus goes with overwrought abandon in its literal translation, 'I will be nothing but the shadow of your shadow.'

As delivered by Leandros in a frock that on black and white TV bordered on arthouse funereal, Après toi's already stirring paean to heartbreak and betrayal became a captivating masterclass in how to deliver a song. Leandros was still only twenty-two, but, like a Miss Havisham in waiting, she seemed to inhabit what was effectively an existential hymn to emotional defeat and the path of wilful and perhaps self-destructive aloneness that follows. Even if you didn't understand a word of French, as many of the millions of British viewers watching it undoubtedly didn't, you believed everything Leandros sang.

A Very British Coup

By the time the English language version of 'Après toi' was released on the back of Leandros' Eurovision success, however, something had clearly been lost in translation. The new English lyrics came care of Norman Newell, aka David West, the Essex born songwriter and producer, who was something of a specialist in Anglicising songs from abroad. In 1961, he gave Shirley Bassey a number one with Reach for the Stars, taken from the Italian. He did likewise for Petula Clark the same year with Sailor, adapted from a German schlager song.

Like Leandros, Newell had also done Eurovision before, having penned the words to the UK's 1963 entry, 'Say Wonderful Things'. The song was performed by Northern Irish crooner Ronnie Carroll, himself a Eurovision veteran, having also represented the UK the previous year singing an upbeat ditty called 'Ring-a-Ding Girl'. Whether composer Syd Carroll and lyricist Stan Butcher's number had been influenced by an episode of American sci-fi based anthology series The Twilight Zone from four years earlier that bore the same name is lost in the mists of time.

In Newell's version of 'Après toi', now titled 'Come What May', what had once been a lovelorn existential psycho-drama appeared to have had its troubled heart ripped out. Leandros'

159

character seems to have been replaced by a hopelessly devoted Stepford Wife-like doppelganger singing the praises of what one can only presume to be a similarly domesticated spouse.

It may have had the same tune, but where 'Après toi' spoke of how its about-to-be jilted confessor 'will be nothing but the shadow of your shadow', the one time party girl in 'Come What May' tells how 'I will love you forever/ And forever my heart belongs to you.' She goes on to say how 'Come what may, for as long as I'm livin'/I'll be living only for you.'

None of this seemed to matter much to Leandros, who belted it out on record and TV with the same unabashed gusto she displayed at the Usher Hall. Maybe Leandros herself didn't understand the words she was singing? But for English listeners at least, something had been lost, even if they didn't know it.

Either way, 'Après toi' seemed to have fallen prey to a very English form of imperialism, which preferred its songs to swear undying allegiance to the tongue-tied patriarchs at their centre. The UK might have been taking part in Eurovision on equal footing with its international neighbours, but showbiz microcosm of little Britain was a place where the songs remained the same, even if they were originally written in French.

Despite the watered down passivity of Newell's English lyric, 'Come What May' reached number two in the UK charts, and made the same position in Ireland. In South Africa it went to number one.

Leandros also recorded the song in Italian (as 'Dop Te'), German ('dann kamst du'), Spanish ('Y Despues'), Greek ('Mono Esi') and Japanese ('Omoide Ni Ikiru'). With a host of writers from each country changing the song to suit their linguistic needs, it is the original French version sung by Leandros in Edinburgh that remains the most powerful.

Despite the disappointment of 'Come What May''s English lyrics putting feminism back several years, having a Greek singer who lived in Germany winning Eurovision on a Scottish stage for Luxembourg with a song sung in French that would subsequently be translated into several languages nevertheless implied something exotic and cosmopolitan. There was a sense of liberation and easy movement at play – a freedom of movement, even. For many, be it 'Après Toi' or 'Come What May', Leandros' Edinburgh performance was possibly the most magnificently European thing they'd ever heard.

In real life, in terms of joining the international jet-set, the rise of cheap holidays abroad in a pre Easyjet and Ryanair era opened the door to Majorca, Benidorm and, eventually, Ibiza, where the international language of electronic based club culture would travel the world on the back of it. The sky truly was the limit

Luxembourg

Prior to 'Après toi', Luxembourg had won Eurovision twice before. The country's first victory came in 1961, with 'Nous Les Amoureux', performed by French singer, Jean-Claude Pascal. This made up for the previous year, when Camillo Fegen's rendition of So Laang We's 'Du Do Bast' for Luxembourg at the Royal Festival Hall event came bottom of thirteen entries with a humiliating one point.

Luxembourg hosted the event in 1962, prior to another presentation in London the following year. The big one for Luxembourg came in 1965, when French *ingénue* France Gall sang 'Poupée de cire, poupée de son', penned by her equally French god-father, Serge Gainsbourg.

Four years later, Gainsbourg would become notorious in the UK for his French language duet with English actress Jane Birkin on 'Je t'aime... mois non plus'. With the title translating as 'I Love You... Me Neither', the song was originally recorded by Gainsbourg and French actress Brigitte Bardot in 1967. In the UK, the Birkin version went to number one. This was despite a ban on it being played on the radio being enforced. The record was also banned in Italy, Spain, Sweden, Portugal and Brazil. Even liberated France stopped it being broadcast before 11pm.

The Observer newspaper later described 'Je t'aime... mois non plus' as 'the pop equivalent of an Emmanuelle movie', referring to the French soft porn film franchise that packed British cinemas throughout the 1970s. In 2004, Birkin told the Observer she didn't know what all the fuss was about. "The English just didn't understand it," she said of the song. "I'm still not sure they know what it means."

Brighton, Stockholm, Dennistoun

In 1963 in London, while Ronnie Carroll sang 'Say Wonderful Things', Luxembourg was represented by Greek singer Nana Mouskouri singing 'A Force De Prier'. Luxembourg duly hosted the 1966 contest, won by 'Merci Cherie', sung by Udo Jurgens for Austria. That year's event was also notable for Norway's entry being performed by an acoustic guitar wielding Åse Maria Kleveland, who ended up becoming the country's mister of culture. The UK, meanwhile, was represented by a kilt clad Kenneth McKellar singing 'A Man Without Love'.

The UK's first Eurovision victory came the following year, when a barefoot Sandie Shaw sang 'Puppet on a String', co-written by Govan born Bill Martin with Derry composer Phil Coulter. Leandros' rendition of 'L'amour est bleu' came fourth.

Simply billed as Vicky, despite not winning the contest, Leandros had a worldwide hit with French composer Popp and Cour's song, which she recorded in French, English, German, Italian and Dutch. In the hands of French conductor Paul Mariat, an orchestral instrumental version of the song as 'Love is Blue' became an American number one. Now regarded as an easy listening classic, Mariat's version has popped up on the soundtracks of *Mad Men* and *The Simpsons*, and was used by *X-Files* creator Chris Carter in an episode of his series, 'Millennium', in which the song is used by a kidnapper to brainwash a group of youths.

Popp and Cour had previously scored a Eurovision winner at the 1960 London event, when their song, 'Tom Pillibi', sung by Jacqueline Boyer, won the competition for France.

Given the reach of 'L'amour bleu', Leandros's presence in Vienna, where the 1967 contest took place, can be looked on as something of a reconnaissance expedition for greater things to come.

Also destined for a second Eurovision life were Martin and Coulter. They would go on to write the 1968 UK entry, 'Congratulations', for Cliff Richard. At the Royal Albert Hall in London, the song came second to Spain, who enlisted Maria de los Angeles Santamaria – aka Massiel – to belt out the cunningly titled 'La La La'.

Future triumphs for Martin and Coulter, incidentally, included 'Saturday Night' (1973), for the Bay City Rollers. A re-recorded version of the song gave the Bay City Rollers an American number one in 1975. As posited in a BBC TV documentary a couple of years ago, the song's foot-stomping opening terrace chant was said to have been heard by bratty American proto-punks The Ramones, who promptly wrote the similarly styled Blitzkrieg Bop, and helped kick-start a cultural revolution.

Martin and Coulter also penned the England football squad's 1970 World Cup song, Back Home. While that too went to number one, the 1966 international football tournament winners were beaten by West Germany in the quarter-finals, and didn't qualify for the competition again until 1982.

1969's Eurovision event was a four-way tie between Spain, the UK, Netherlands and France. Back in Blighty, however, as far as British pop pickers were concerned, it was Lennoxtown born former Dennistoun resident Lulu's rendition of 'Boom Bang-A-Bang' that was the winner. The song's lyricist Peter Warne had penned the English version of 'La La La' the previous year, though the chorus somewhat understandably remained intact. This was also the case for the German, Italian and French versions of the song.

While the school of international songwriting favoured such infectiously alliterative simplicity, 'Boom Bang-A-Bang' ended up being blacklisted by the BBC in 1991 during the Gulf War, lest anyone be inspired to pull the pin on explosions of a different kind.

In 1970, future Irish politician Dana won Eurovision with 'All Kinds of Everything'. 1971 saw a victory for Monaco, with Severine singing 'Un banc, un arbre, une rue'. Neither of these came close, however, to Leandros' Edinburgh performance of 'Après toi'. A year after Leandros' win, Luxembourg made it a double whammy with

'Tu te reconnaitras', a song by Claude Morgan and Vline Buggy performed by French singer Anne-Marie David. The UK came third, with Cliff Richard singing 'Power to All Our Friends'.

If Luxembourg's open-minded pluralist internationalism seemed to have conquered Europe, it didn't last long. In 1974, a bunch of Swedish insurgents turned up in Brighton, where the contest was held, and blew pop music out the water with a song that used the Battle of Waterloo as a metaphor for laying down your arms and surrendering on the eternal battlefield of romance. Luxembourg had set the tone. Now Europe – and the world – was opening up even more.

London Calling

The UK may have taken part in Eurovision since 1957, but it wouldn't become officially part of what was then being lauded as the Common Market until January 1st 1973. By the time Vicky Leandros and 'Après toi' went global in Edinburgh, however, the wheels were already in motion for the UK to become part of the European Economic Community.

Conservative Prime Minister Ted Heath had signed the Treaty of Accession on January 22nd 1972, with Denmark, Ireland and Norway applying alongside the United Kingdom of Great Britain and Northern Ireland. The Treaty was also signed by the then 'inner six' founding states, including the Grand Duchy of Luxembourg.

The UK had first applied to become part of the EC back in 1960, the same year as the UK first hosted Eurovision. The UK's application followed the fallout of the 1956 Suez crisis, but was vetoed by France, whose president Charles de Gaulle saw Britain as a Trojan horse for American interests.

The UK resubmitted its application in 1967, the same year Sandie Shaw won Eurovision in Vienna with 'Puppet on a String', with Vicky coming fourth for Luxembourg with 'L'amour est bleu.'

By March 1972, Leandros and 'Après toi' were fanfaring in a new era, in which those involved promised themselves to each other seemingly forever. One probably shouldn't read too much in the way of symbolism regarding the UK's entry being called Beg, Steal or Borrow. In 'Après toi's laying bare the disastrous consequences of walking out on someone, however, the personal and the political joined hands in what had inadvertently become an anthem of European unity.

The 1975 referendum that asked the Great British Public if they should continue to be part of Europe was purely academic. By now, ABBA ruled the airwaves, and pretty much everything else besides.

Paris The First Time – It's All Greek to Me

The first time I went to Europe, I accidentally ended up on an anti immigration demo. That was in Paris almost a quarter of a century ago. I'd been packed off to interview Romanian theatre director Silviu Purcarete about his production of Ancient Greek epic, *Les Danaïdes*, which was visiting Scotland for dates at Tramway in Glasgow

It was my first press trip abroad, and, high on Situationist slogans, Jean Luc Godard films and May '68 romance, I was a free man in Paris, and the revolution would be mine. Without a mobile phone, a map or a word of French to my name, I intended to follow Guy Debord's maxim of the *dérive*, and explore the city at random.

I watched the matinee of *Les Danaïdes* not understanding a word. Coming from a climate where putting as few as half a dozen performers on a stage was likely to bankrupt a theatre company, I was nevertheless impressed by the spectacle of some 120 people moving in formation in a vast modern arena.

Les Danaïdes was drawn mainly from *The Suppliants*, the only surviving play of a tetralogy by Aeschylus. The play tells the tale of the fifty daughters of Danaus, who flee Egypt after rejecting the advances of fifty male cousins determined to have their way with them. The play ends with the men thwarted and the women saved from their fate.

Reconstructions of the remaining plays see the women double bluff their assailants with a plan to slaughter their new husbands on their wedding night. Forty-nine of them oblige. Spoiler alert, only one is let off the hook, and the surviving couple go off to found a new dynasty.

All of which makes the high drama of 'Après toi' appear tame by comparison. Nevertheless, as a Greek songwriter, with his country's rich, world-changing mythology to hand, you can perhaps understand where Leo Leandros drew his inspiration. His daughter, meanwhile, was cast as an amalgam of every tragic heroine going, relating her father's yarn in a musical monologue that could have been taken from the opening play of Aeschylus' state of the nation trilogy, *The Oresteia*,

In *Agamemnon*, the first play of *The Oresteia*, stay at home queen Clytemnestra exacts bloody revenge on her returning war hero husband who gives the play its title. Like Leandros' character in 'Après toi', Clytemnestra too is betrayed. This prompts her to kill the king, though not before she's told him in no uncertain terms the damage he's done, both to her and their country.

Purcarete had inserted lines from *Agamemnon* into his take on *Les Danaïdes*, as well as others from *Seven Against Thebes*, from Aeschylus' *Oedipodea* trilogy, and from another of his plays, *Prometheus Bound*. Not that I was any the wiser. Like 'Après toi', *Les Danaïdes* was performed in French. Given that we were in Paris, there were understandably no surtitles, which wouldn't be necessary until the show arrived in the largely mono-lingual UK. Perhaps unsurprisingly, Purcarete would go on to direct *The Oresteia* in full a couple of years later. I expect it was as huge as *Les Danaides*.

If Clytemnestra's act of vengeance on Agamemnon was something Leandros' character in 'Après toi' might be considering, the happy ever after of the lost Danaid tetralogy more resembles Norman Newell's take on things in 'Come What May'.

If such comparisons seem fanciful, twenty years after Purcarete did *Les Danaides* and *The Oresteia*, Edinburgh based writer Zinnie Harris wrote her version of the latter. Presented at Glasgow's Citizens Theatre, renowned for decades for its European attributes, the three plays of Harris' woman-centred *Oresteia* were initially presented under the banner of *This Restless House*.

The first play opened with a microphone wielding Clytemnestra doing a turn in what looked like an unreconstructed cabaret club, where would be chanteuses might break into cover versions of 'Après toi' – or 'Come What May' if we must – any second.

Not that I had a clue about any of this that Saturday afternoon in Paris. As with Newell's reconfiguration of 'Après toi' that made 'Come What May' more resemble the reconciliation scene in a suburban rom-com than the Greek tragedy in miniature of the original, I misinterpreted the plot of *Les Danaides* wildly. I certainly hadn't spotted what the play had to say about migrants fleeing oppressive regimes and seeking amnesty elsewhere.

This probably didn't help much with my interview with Purcarete afterwards. Done through an awkward alliance of broken English and the presence of a translator, on my part, at least, the international language of European theatre was lost on me.

But a Romanian director reinventing a Greek epic in French in an international co-production between festivals in Holland, France and Romania that was about to take the UK by storm? Purcarete and Leandros had more in common than they might think.

Paris (Mis) Match – Mind Your Language

If I jumped on the Metro, the bohemian revolution I was seeking would surely be easy to find. Once there, I'd be embraced by intellectuals and drink too much wine while the wildly gesticulatory conversation flipped between dialectical discourse and existential despair.

But which stop? Republique. That sounded about right. The name alone felt alive with possibilities. 'Be Realistic! – Demand the Impossible!' as the Situationist slogans in '68 declared.

I could hear impassioned voices shouting through megaphones in French before I made it onto Place de la Republique, named to commemorate the first, second and third French republics that existed at various points in the eighteenth, nineteenth and twentieth centuries. It wasn't a big demo, a couple of hundred, maybe, gathered round the speaker in the square, occasionally erupting into equally impassioned chants of support. Support for what, I didn't know, but I couldn't believe my luck, landing in Paris in the midst of some kind of mini insurrection.

This was how it was done, waving flags and shouting slogans about something or other that continued in earnest once the demo set off to march in a rag-tag rabble through the Parisian streets. I decided to tag along, not knowing where I was, where I was going or what anyone was getting so het up about. Just another Brit abroad with nothing to declare, basking in my own blissful ignorance like I'd brought it as a gift.

I'm not sure when alarm bells started to ring about what I was taking part in, nor when the penny finally dropped that, far from jumping some mythical revolutionary barricades of my imagination, I'd actually joined in an anti-immigration march.

It might have been at the end of the march, when everyone dispersed, and I suddenly found myself alone, not knowing where I was. Or it might have been on the 24 hour TV news back at my cheap chain hotel, which I eventually found after four hours wandering around in the dark, trying to find my way home.

To clutch at straws to try and justify my mistake, in my mind, at least, it hadn't been obvious what the march was about. There was no one there who looked even vaguely like the crazed yobs off the leash of a latter day EDL march, say. Everybody appeared to be quite ordinary, and who were simply exercising their freedom of speech in a language I couldn't understand. But I guess that's where it starts.

What those gathered in Republique actually were, I see now, was the sort of everyday bigots who wouldn't have let the fifty women in *Les Danaïdes* into their back yard if they'd been paid for it. This, despite knowing that if they forced the women to go back to their own land, they risked rape, murder or both on their return. Of course, it could never happen here.

Wherever I'd ended up, like Bonnie Tyler's 1976 hit, I was lost in France. As I marched blindly along ever darkening boulevards, my solution was to accost passing strangers and regale them with my secondary school standard knowledge of their presumably native tongue.

"Excusez-moi?" I proffered umpteen times with hopeful desperation. "Anglais?"

This lame attempt at bi-lingual solidarity was greeted in various ways. There were those who simply ignored this mad foreigner and walked on. Others were initially polite, until they heard the word "Anglais", and their politesse turned to contempt. One man simply shrugged and shook his head, firing back with a terse "Francais!" Which was fair enough. It was his country, after all, where his language reigned supreme. Me, I was defeated, he'd won the war.

I eventually stumbled on what I thought was the cheap chain hotel I was staying at, only to discover from the concierge at reception who spoke perfect English that they had four branches across various parts of Paris. As he pointed out on a map, mine was several miles away. Words somewhere between *Merde!* and *Sacre bleu!* raced through my mind with cartoon consternation as I channelled my inner Inspector Clouseau. Why I didn't just get a taxi, I don't know, but I probably hadn't brought any money with me either.

It was after midnight when I finally did get back to my hotel, starving and exhausted. Taking stock of the act of international stupidity I'd just inflicted on myself, for not recognising the small-minded ideological bullies on the anti-immigration march I'd accidentally gatecrashed by itself, I should have been deported. Yet, as shocked as I was at mistaking such small-mindedness for the spirit of *Liberté, égalité* and *fraternité*, I was as bad as any of them. Especially given what had followed.

My presumption that every Parisian passer-by would be able to speak English and guide me home was the equivalent of every lobster-boiled British ex-pat in Benidorm, who started the day with a full English breakfast and ended it in a pseudo Irish pub, with a daring visit to a tapas bar where they inexplicably call the waiters 'garkon' in between.

Like watching Vicky Leandros sing 'Après toi' on TV live from Edinburgh a quarter of a century earlier, I hadn't understood a word, just as I hadn't understood a word of *Les Danaïdes* earlier that afternoon. This time, however, ignorance had consequences, and I'd ended up lost in every way.

Liverpool

But, like David Byrne in the Talking Heads song, 'Once in a Lifetime', my God, how did I get here? I was hip to all things European, or so I thought. I'd come of age in an era when Europe was all the rage, and was considerably more than old enough to know better.

My education had come through subtitled films on BBC 2 and then Channel 4 in a three and four channel TV age. It was through seasons of films by Godard – *Breathless/À bout de souffle* and *Sympathy for the Devil/One on One* – Fassbinder, Wim Wenders and all the rest. It was Luis Bunuel and the Surrealists, provocateurs all. Later, it was all the cult classics, like *Diva*, *Subway* and *Betty Blue*, and all the actresses, like Anna Karina, Catherine Deneuve, Emmanuelle Beart and Beatrice Dalle. Isabelle Huppert, especially, had shown me what French film could be, from *The Lacemaker* to *Violette Noziere* and beyond.

It was the Penguin Modern Classics section in the tiny Liverpool John Smith's bookshop, packed with grey-spined editions of Camus, Genet, Sartre and all the gang, each announcing themselves with a reproduction of a painting on the cover, and not knowing where to start. For years, I pronounced the 't' of Albert and the 's' of Camus to myself, not knowing any better, because I'd never had a conversation about him to hear his name said out loud.

There is a possibly apocryphal story about a Scottish pop star who apparently had a complete collection of Penguin Modern Classics, and who read just the first and last page of each. Knowing the beginning and the end was enough, they reckoned, to get them by in bookish circles. As for the middle, Jean Luc Godard might have a few ideas.

Berlin

As with many earnest young men of my generation, I had an earnest obsession with the Berlin Wall, that icon of East-West division that set capitalism and communism as polar opposites. My idea of all this Cold War world of conspiracy and intrigue was gleaned, not from history books, but from ice-cool '60s films peopled with stern but glamorous spies defecting and double crossing their way to perceived freedom to a John Barry soundtrack.

It was gleaned too, from David Bowie's Berlin trilogy of albums; *Low* (1977), *Heroes* (1977) and *Lodger* (1979), and the image of him recording Heroes, co-written with Brian Eno, in Hansa Studios beside the Wall. Heroes draws its title from 'Hero', by German *kosmiche* duo, Neu! Michael Rother and Klaus Dinger of Neu! had both been early members of Kraftwerk, whose own synthesised contributions to forward-moving machine music came through the prism of Trans Europe Express and the melancholy of Europe Endless.

Bowie's *Heroes* is a poignant romance that charts a love affair across the barricades, and captures all the strung-out pain and passion that entails with an anthemic grandeur.

When Bowie performed the song during a concert in front of the Reichstag In 1987, close to the Wall enough for those on the other side to hear it, its inspirational intent sounded like a call to arms. Following Bowie's death in 2016, as detailed on the fotostrasse.com website, the German Foreign Office tweeted how Bowie's concert had helped bring down the Berlin Wall. They were probably too diplomatic to mention it, but they could have also advised not to let David Hasselhoff tell you any different.

Whichever David pointed the way towards the future, little did they know that theirs was a clarion call that would end up, not with international revolutionary socialism as some might have imagined, but with global capitalism on the grandest of scales. Once the Berlin Wall fell, it felt like we'd been shot by both sides.

Over the Wall

At one stage in my early teens, despite never having been to either side of Berlin, I hit upon the idea of building a cardboard model of the Berlin Wall. This despite a cack-handed boyhood making gluey messes of Airfix Messerschmitts and Fokkers which, on sticky completion, looked like the result of an act of pro-Brit sabotage that seemed unlikely to win any war.

Of course, the idea never got beyond looking at as few photographs of a bleak terrain looming either side of Checkpoint Charlie, and realising this was a wall of my own making I was never going to get over, no matter how insignificant.

By the time I eventually made it to Berlin for real a decade and more after the Wall had fallen, I considered myself a seasoned traveller and a proper European, even if I maintained a complete lack of direction. Despite this, and armed with at least two maps and a carefully plotted itinerary, I determined to make the most of my downtime and explore a city, which, like Paris, I only knew from films.

I'd seen Fassbinder's mini series, *Berlin Alexanderplatz*, which eventually trickled down to Channel 4 five years after the German *enfant terrible* had first directed it, and two years after his death. Alexanderplatz itself wasn't far from where I was staying, and I headed there, just to see a street sign saying 'Alexanderplatz' as much as anything.

Walking along its expanse, I spotted a glass case on one side of the pavement. Inside, to my surprise and delight, was a hand made scale model of the Berlin Wall. Here, toy cars were held up at barriers as plastic grey painted border guards peered on from miniature watchtowers. Elsewhere, tiny pieces of barbed wire shrouded dolls house sized cardboard and plastic walls, with further obstacles beyond designed to prevent anyone from getting any further.

A sign on the plinth the glass case containing the model was set on announced the model was from the Checkpoint Charlie museum, close to where the real crossing point from East to West Berlin during the Cold War had stood.

It took a good hour to walk there along Alexanderplatz. Inside what looked like a private DIY venue on Friedrichstrasse was a living archive of the Wall and those who struggled to get to the other side, where the freedom they imagined lay beyond their own divided, closed off world. The museum had opened in 1963, two years after the Wall had gone up. It followed a first exhibition held the year before in a tiny apartment by human rights activists opposing the Wall's construction.

I still have a postcard of a photograph I bought at the Museum taken beside Checkpoint Charlie, of a woman hitching up her stockings besides a sign reading 'YOU ARE LEAVING THE AMERICAN SECTOR'. I wasn't the only one to see the fascination of the Checkpoint Charlie Museum. Since the Wall fell in 1989, it has become one of the most visited museums in Berlin, with some 850,000 annual visitors. It remains an essential reminder of what happens when countries attempt to cut themselves off from the rest of the world.

Oh, Vienna

Someone once told me another, possibly even more apocryphal yarn than the one about the Scottish pop star and the Penguin Modern Classics. This one was about how 'Vienna', the 1981 hit single by Midge Ure era Ultravox!, had originally been called 'Dunfermline'.

Whether there is any truth in such a claim, I've no idea, and have never heard anyone else ever suggest it. In the unlikely event it is true, one wonders if it might have been in honour of Moira Shearer's success in making it from the most heavily populated town in Fife to *The Red Shoes* and presenting the Eurovision Song Contest at the Usher Hall in Edinburgh.

And yet, however nonsensical both this and the Penguin Modern Classics story might be, their presence nevertheless points to a certain sense of healthy ambition, whereby lads and lasses with ideas above their station aspire to conquer the world.

'Vienna' in particular was epic in intent. Released as a single in 1981 taken from Ultravox!'s fourth album, also called *Vienna*, and released the previous summer, the song marked the band's crossover into the mainstream. It also cemented the presence of Cambuslang born former Slik and Rich Kids frontman Ure as the band's singer following the departure of original vocalist John Foxx after a 1979 tour in support of the release of the band's third album, *Systems of Romance*, released in late 1978.

Featuring acoustic piano married to a slow pulsing electronic backdrop, *Vienna* tells vaguely of a lost love affair of ambiguous significance, presumably having taken place in the Austrian city of the song's title. Despite some press spin about it being inspired by *The Third Man*, Carol Reed's 1949 film of Graham Greene's post World War Two Vienna set Cold War novella, Ure's lyric is more a sketchy sense memory scaled up into something anthem.

This sensibility was amplified even more in the accompanying video. Partly shot in moody black and white, the clip features a raincoat clad band led by a pencil moustached Ure walking meaningfully besides sacred looking monuments and statues. The video then switches to colour for what looks like a nineteenth century ball in an ornate mansion house.

The record was co-produced by Conny Plank, the German producer who had worked on records by the likes of Can, Neu! and Kraftwerk, as well as with Brian Eno. Despite appearances, the video was only partly filmed on location in Vienna, with record company budgets not stretching much further than Covent Garden. No Dunfermline landmarks are known to have been filmed.

Ultravox had previously dallied with European sensibilities with 'Hiroshima Mon Amour'. Penned by Foxx with fellow band members Warren Cann and Billy Currie, *Hiroshima Mon Amour* took its title from Alan Resnais' 1959 film, written by French novelist, playwright and film director Marguerite Duras.

The film follows the fleeting relationship between a French actress and a Japanese architect. This is done through an extended series of conversations between the two punctuated by mini flashbacks that mark out their inevitable parting in the aftermath of destruction. Duras was Oscar nominated for her script, which set the tone for much of France's *nouvelle vague* to come.

'Hiroshima Mon Amour' appeared on *Ha!-Ha!-Ha*, Ultravox's second album, released at the end of 1977. Heavily influenced by Berlin era David Bowie's work, *Ha!-Ha!-Ha*, also saw Ultravox fleetingly become Ultravox!, with the exclamation mark in honour of Neu!, It also pointed to the band's own new, synthesiser-led future. They weren't alone in their ambitions. Nor would Foxx and co be the last of post punk's own avant-garde new wave to pay homage to Duras.

From Brussels with Love

In an anything goes post-punk climate, Europe was trickling outwards all over. There were exotic sounding record labels like Les Disques du Crepuscule, which was based in Belgium, and put out elaborate compilations that included contributions by artists from the Factory and Postcard labels in Manchester and Glasgow respectively. These nestled next to piano based instrumentals and spoken word abstractions by artists from all over the world.

The first of these was called *From Brussels with Love*, and came out in 1980 on an elaborately packaged cassette. The Durutti Column, Kevin Hewick and A Certain Ratio from Factory were there, as was a now solo John Foxx, who book-ended the cassette with a pair of instrumental jingles.

There were compositions by Harold Budd, Michael Nyman and Gavin Bryars, who had all recorded for Brian Eno's Obscure record label. There was poetry by Skids vocalist Richard Jobson, and an atmospheric instrumental by Bill Nelson, formerly of Be Bop Deluxe, but who by now was releasing solo work on his own tellingly named Cocteau label. There were contributions too from German band Der Plan and Belgian ensembles, Repetition and The Names.

Breaking up the music on either side of the cassette was a pair of interviews. One of these was with Eno, who, over the previous decade, had moved from providing *avant-garde* squiggles as a founder member of Roxy Music, to ambient explorations at home and abroad, to producing fourth world funk with American CBGBs graduates, Talking Heads.

On the other side, there was a substantial interview – in French – with actress Jeanne Moreau, star of Louis Malle's *Lift to the Scaffold* and *The 400 Blows*, and *Jules et Jim*, directed by Francois Truffaut. *From Brussels With Love* wasn't just a record. It was an aural salon that acted as a gateway to European culture of all kinds.

The presence of Jobson, Foxx, Kevin Hewick, A Certain Ration and The Durutti Column suggested that culture existed on our own doorstep too, and that it was part of something. A movement, maybe. Was this what Glasgow Beat *émigré* Alexander Trocchi had in mind when he wrote of his proposed 'invisible insurrection of a million minds' and Project Sigma? Either way, *From Brussels With Love* was Art. An expanded 2CD fortieth anniversary edition featuring even more elaborate packaging made this even clearer when it was issued by Les Disques du Crepuscule in November 2020.

Another Crepuscule compilation, *The Fruit of the Original Sin*, followed a year later. This double LP basked in its own myth-making, describing itself on the cover as 'a collection of after hours preoccupations…' The inside cover trailed the record's contents as being 'news from home, deserted islands, Scotland, Manchester, America the brave, Belgium' and 'comprising forgotten dreams, wasted blood, tyranny and more tyranny'.

What this meant in actuality was more from the likes of The Durutti Column and The Names, plus contributions from Arthur Russell and DNA. There was a cover of Francis Lai's theme to Claude Lelouch's 1966 film, *Un homme et une femme*, by Belgian band, Marine, and fellow Belgian pianist Cecile Bruynoghe playing Debussy's 'Clair de Lune'. There was a live recording of William Burroughs reading in San Francisco, and an interview – in French – with Marguerite Duras.

In terms of Scotland's *entente cordiale*, there was a live cut from Orange Juice, and an instrumental by Paul Haig, vocalist with Franz Kafka inspired Edinburgh band Josef K. The Fruit of the Original Sin also featured the recorded debut of Malcolm Fisher's evocatively named French Impressionists, featuring future Bourgie Bourgie singer Paul Quinn and members of Aztec Camera. Richard Jobson was here again too, declaiming poems in praise of Duras, and her 1975 film adapted from her then unperformed play, India Song.

In terms of his poetic homage to India Song, Jobson was ahead of the game. Only the English sensibilities of the National Theatre in London, it seems, were unable to embrace Duras' European aesthetic.

India Song

Duras had originally been commissioned to write *India Song* in 1972 for the National by the company's then artistic director, Peter Hall. The play and the film are focused on the character of Anne-Marie Stretter, the bored and promiscuous wife of the French ambassador in India.

Duras had only visited India once in her teens when she wrote the play, and, rather than refer to source material, preferred to imagine what it was like. Just as Ultravox's video for 'Vienna' saw a London town-house double up for the Austrian city, Duras' film was made, not in India, but in a mansion on the outskirts of Paris.

In the film, Anne-Marie is played by Lebanese born French actress, Delphine Seyrig. Like the rest of the cast, Seyrig doesn't say a word onscreen. As the characters mill about the house with studied languor, all dialogue is spoken in voiceover by a series of narrators. Perhaps this was why Hall and the National never took the commission on to full production. Maybe such a device was simply not British enough for the South Bank.

It took several years for *India Song* to reach the stage. This was thanks to Belgian director Ivo van Hove, who brought his 1998 Holland Festival production to Edinburgh International Festival the following year after originally directing it in 1984. With the audience sat onstage close to the action, as with the film, the play used recorded voices. To complete the sensurround style experience, live musicians played on stage alongside the actors, while the piped-in smells of colonial India wafted around the theatre.

Since then, Van Hove has become a major international director. In 2015, he brought his production of *Antigone* to Edinburgh, with French actress Juliette Binoche in the title role. Two years later, he returned, with his production of nineteenth century Norwegian writer Henrik Ibsen's tragedy, Hedda Gabler. Produced by what by now was the Royal National Theatre in London, Van Hove used a new version of the play by English writer Patrick Marber. Amongst his many international credits, Van Hove directed Lazarus, the play co-written by Irish writer Enda Walsh and the late David Bowie.

A Song for Europe

Duras was possibly writing 'India Song' as Vicky Leandros heralded in Britain's forthcoming entry into Europe at the Usher Hall in Edinburgh with 'Après toi'. Meanwhile, a new British band called Roxy Music, who already sounded like the future, were about to record a song that arguably remains as current as it did when it was first released. Then again, as with Après toi, maybe a Song for Europe is just one more everyday tragedy about being dumped.

Roxy Music were formed in 1970 by singer Bryan Ferry, who recruited core members Andy Mackay on sax and oboe, guitarist Phil Manzanera, electronicist Brian Eno and drummer Paul Thompson. Together, they created an audacious fusion of pop-art glam Eurotrash that sounded like it had been beamed down from outer space.

In just over a year between June 1972 and November 1973, Roxy Music released an astonishing three albums of salacious retro-futuristic sci-fi glamorama. In the strung-out '60s hangover that prevailed over much of British music at the time, Roxy were alive to life beyond. On the pop chart calling card of their debut single, 'Virginia Plain', which notably and wilfully wasn't originally on their self-titled debut album, released two months earlier, they were sophisticated, experimental and knowingly cocksure. On the album,

'Re-Make/Re-model' and 'Ladytron' had already set down their template.

A mere nine months later, the urgency continued on *For Your Pleasure*, with 'Do the Strand' strutting its stylish way onto the coolest catwalk in town. The slow-burning Ballardian salaciousness of 'In Every Dream Home a Heartache', meanwhile, was an alluringly kinky riff on the loneliness of the long distance pop star.

By the time of Roxy's third album, *Stranded*, towards the end of 1973, the world and the band had changed. Eno was gone, and even though it was made without him, Eno reckoned Stranded was one of Roxy Music's best albums. He may have been right

Despite such magnanimity, the absence of the off-kilter experimentation Eno provided on the two previous albums was a major loss. *Stranded* makes up for it, however, in high drama and a seriousness in both form and content that goes beyond the opening thrust of 'Street Life's deceptively brash scene-setter.

Everything, then, that could be applied to an outsider's idea of what a European pop sensibility might be. Coming at the end of the year after the UK joined the European union, this was probably to be expected of such an art-conscious combo.

A Song for Europe is central to this perception. Knowingly drawing its title from the name of the televised competition to find a UK representative for Eurovision, one might expect a song so named to serve up some kind of sing-a-long *joie de vivre*. As it turned out, the funereal pomp and circumstance of Roxy Music's 'A Song for Europe' ached with an abandon that suggested Ferry and co were already in mourning for an endlessly collapsing continent.

'A Song for Europe' is an internal monologue dredged from the poetic embers of a love affair's end. As Ferry's character sits alone reflecting on his loss, each verse cuts between Paris and Venice like scenes from a mini arthouse film Marguerite Duras might have made, relishing the intimacy of the song's sombre emotional offloading.

As Ferry relays his character's sense of abandonment over a solitary cigarette, after singing in English, he relates his loss twice more, first in Latin, then in French, imbuing the song with a universal weight that crosses all imaginary borders. Being chucked never sounded so profound.

When Ferry breaks into a final impassioned refrain of 'Jamais, jamais, jamais, jamais, jamais, jamais', the urgent desperation of his Lear-like repetition is a shocking declamation. But of what? As the lyric stands, Ferry is saying 'Jamais' as in 'Never' or 'Never again' in defiant protest. Is he putting up the barriers to the possibility of love, like Leandros' character – part Miss Havisham, part Clytemnestra – on 'Après toi?' Or is he co-opting an anti fascist slogan of resistance for something even greater?

But in the spluttering bloodrush of inarticulate despair, the clarity of Ferry's pronunciation might easily get lost, so his anguished howl might be heard as 'J'aimais', as in 'I loved'. This grand poetic gesture isn't putting a full stop on the apparent end of the affair, but leaves things hanging, so in terms of what might happen next, the door remains open to reconciliation. In the end, it could be both.

Either way, the yearning in the sentiment of the delivery – and it is sentiment – isn't that far from those in 'Après toi'. Unlike 'Come What May', in 'Never again', there is nothing lost in translation. Once again, however, the French is more evocative, allowing Ferry to indulge himself as a martyred torch singer prepared to die for the cause while the world collapses around him. And yes, I have brushed up my French.

A fan-made video for 'A Song for Europe' on YouTube opens with the old logo that introduced the show it was named after, before opening out to a series of black and white still images of European cities captured in their faded splendour. It looks a lovely place to visit, but you wouldn't want to live there.

Jeux sans frontieres – Playing the Joker

All of this, of course, is purely academic. Had not one word of any of all I'd been listening to and reading and watching for decades sunk in enough for me to avoid playing the bad tourist that time in Paris?

Or was it all superficial and about some mythical image of an idea of Europe rather than what it actually was?

Maybe that was how I'd absorbed it, second-hand, through a screen, or in the artfully black and white pages of some vintage magazine. Or perhaps it was some half-digested, misunderstood paperback by some writer whose name I couldn't pronounce because I'd never had a conversation about them?

In truth, my early exposure to Europe came, not just through Eurovision, but the international editions of self-consciously madcap TV game show, *It's a Knockout!*

Running between 1966 and 1982, *It's a Knockout!* was adapted from French comedy game show, *Intervilles*, and was part of the *Jeux sans frontieres* franchise. Done on the cheaper than cheap, the show promoted a kind of cartoon civic pride, as teams from assorted towns dressed in outlandish oversize costumes were pitted against each other. The games they took part in usually involved buckets of water, custard pies and foam filled plastic swimming pools. To add insult to injury, this was often filmed under floodlights in pouring rain at the local park or recreation ground.

The international edition of *Jeux sans frontieres* upped the ante, with teams from assorted European countries embracing their national stereotype by way of an excess of flag-waving, as each country attempted to navigate even more ridiculous games. These invariably meant team members getting soaked in the process as they attempted to navigate assorted obstacles that included their opponents' invariably brutal efforts to shove them out the way.

To double their points, each team could play a Joker. This didn't always go well, and, as with the best and worst of comedy japes, the joke sometimes backfired, and nul points were had by all.

The collective humiliation of each team was brought home even more by the guffawing laughter of the commentators. Sports day for grown-ups was the original premise of what resembled a cross between an absurdist play and a fun pub day out. In truth, this was war.

Perhaps it should come as no surprise, then, that the brains behind *Jeux sans frontieres* was Charles de Gaulle, the President of

France for a decade from 1959, who in terms of historical greatness as a French leader, is regarded by historians on a par with Napoleon – Waterloo notwithstanding. The same Charles de Gaulle who vetoed the UK becoming a member of Europe back in 1960, then, thought *Jeux sans frontieres* would be a great way for French and German young people to bond.

De Gaulle's idea caught on, and Belgium and Italy signed up for what was initially called the Inter Nations Games, run, as with Eurovision, by the European Broadcasting Union. Perhaps President de Gaulle saw *Jeux sans frontieres* as a dry run for the events of May '68. 'Be Realistic! Demand the Impossible!' would have made a great slogan for the show.

Arriving typically late to the party, the UK joined in the fun in 1967, the same year the country's second application to join Europe was finally accepted.

Since then, the UK hosted *Jeux sans frontieres* twice, in 1969 and 1976,. Both occasions were held in sunny Blackpool, whose team won the competition in 1971. Other UK winners were Shrewsbury in 1969, Ely (1973) and Dartmouth, who were joint winners with Lisbon in 1981. As with Eurovision's four-way in 1969 that included Lulu singing 'Boom Bang-a-Bang', Lisbon probably doesn't get a mention over here.

Other than the involvement of President De Gaulle, possibly the best thing to come out of *It's a Knockout* and *Jeux sans frontieres* was Peter Gabriel's 1980 hit single, 'Games Without Frontiers'. This was an anti war song of sorts that used children's' games as a metaphor for those played by grown up types on international battlefields. The record was worth the ticket price alone just to hear guest backing vocalist Kate Bush punctuate each verse with a typical fusion of the strident and the ethereal as she cooed a suitably game 'Jeux sans frontieres'

Paris The Last Time

The last time I went to Europe, I went back to Republique, but I went further. I was in Paris with a group of Edinburgh based circus and street artists from the Circus Alba and PyroCeltica companies, who were collaborating with French street spectacle auteurs, Compagnie Remue Ménage on a show for Edinburgh's Hogmanay.

It was a Bank holiday, and we were staying in a hotel that was part of the same budget chain as I'd stayed in a quarter of a century earlier. I've no idea if it was the same one, though I'd hopefully learnt a bit since then, and was armed with a map and some Euros. More significantly, my knowledge of the French language now recognised that the word 'anglais' was not a passport to anywhere. Given the ongoing Brexit fiasco still had more than an exasperating year to go before reaching anything resembling endgame, I suspect anything even remotely 'anglais' was likely to provoke the sort of violence only previously seen on *Jeux sans frontieres*.

We were heading out to a circus school on the outskirts of the city, set in a network of big tops in grounds next to University Paris Nanterre. This was where the companies could train together, working out their own international language of circus skills.

En route, we fleetingly alighted at Republique. As with much of Paris that day, the square was largely deserted, and free of protests of any kind. I breathed a sigh of relief.

The circus school was tucked away on a large piece of land behind the university's ordered complex of 1960s buildings. If you didn't know what you were looking for, you wouldn't know they were there. Nor is there a hint of University Paris Nanterre's past as the starting point of the May 1968 uprising that ignited the series of seismic events that followed.

This was the place that sparked all the revolutionary spirit I'd romanticised all those years ago. I'd love to claim you could still feel that spirit beneath the pavement of University Paris Nanterre's clean-lined boulevard. On a wet Bank Holiday Monday morning in November, however, it was as deserted and as eerily desolate as an urban landscape in a Michelangelo Antonioni film set in another part of Europe entirely.

Whether I'll ever get to go back to find out if the sprit of '68 still exists or not remains to be seen. I left renewing my 10-year passport until the last minute, so I could have one bearing the words

'European Union' right up to 2029. Whether I ever get to use it or not is a different matter.

Europe After the Reign

In the meantime, a once musically thriving Luxembourg hasn't taken part in Eurovision since 1993. Future generations who have never experienced free movement will likely get their idea of Europe, not from Godard or Duras. They probably won't even get it from *It's a Knockout!* or the Eurovision Song Contest, but from Emily in Paris, the glossy Netflix hit from the makers of *Sex and the City*.

Come what may, then, we'll always have the myth of Paris, at least. And if Vicky Leandros understood the value of defiance when she sang Après toi in the Usher Hall all those years ago, Europe is still endless, and will remain so. As for where we are now; *jamais. Jamais. J'aimais.*

The 40th anniversary edition of From Brussels with Love *is available on Les Disques du Crepuscule. lesdisquesducrepuscule.com.*

Invaluable information was purloined from The Complete Eurovision Song Contest Companion – Paul Gambaccini, Tim Rice, Jonathan Rice, Tony Brown (Pavilion) (1998).

From Paris to Nantes, State Violence 1968 - 2018

Chloé Farand

As part of our series reflecting on the 50th anniversary of May 1968, Chloe Farand looks at the destruction of the ZAD protest community, and what it tells us about Macron and Macronism.

When a journalist called out French President Emmanuel Macron in a televised interview last month for misnaming his centrist party *En Marche* [Onwards] rather than *En Force* [In Force], he was accused of a brash interview style.

But among many French voters, his comment resonated strongly.

Since the day of his election nearly a year ago, Macron's spectacle appearances on the world stage have seen France's youngest President since Napoléon win over the global liberal elite.

The moment he walked through the courtyard of the Louvre Palace in Paris – alone and solemn – in a long black coat to the tune of the European anthem Ode to Joy will remain a defining moment of his Republican rule.

Sharp, eloquent and self-assured, 12 months after taking office, Macron ploughs ahead with his ideas and vision.

A former philosophy student and avid reader, Macron is no doubt familiar with Machiavelli's reflections on how to be ruler and "whether it be better to be loved than feared or feared than loved?".

Machiavelli's concludes "it is much safer to be feared than loved" and Macron seems to have taken on the advice.

With less than a quarter of the votes in the first round of last year's election, Macron yet used ordinances to speed up the legislative process to reform and "modernised" the country's Labour laws – a long-standing contentious issue.

The social movement which has gripped the country over the last few weeks – embodied by the rail workers – is another symbol of France's confrontational political style: on the one hand, Macron's government imposing new legislation with little parliamentary scrutiny and on the other, immediate calls for protest from still powerful and organised unions.

In Macron's Republic there is so far little space for dialogue.

But the most poignant example of Macron's forceful presidential style are the images of violent clashes between riot police and anti-capitalist and eco-warriors protesters at the illegally occupied site of Notre-Dame-des Landes, in western France, also known as a Zone to Defend (ZAD).

In 2008, environmental activists joined a few farmers on the site and set up a protest camp against plans to build a new airport.

In January, following a decade of opposition, the government abandoned plans for the airport and gave an ultimatum to the two to three hundred zadists (ZAD residents) on the site to regularise their status by registering for individual farming projects or face eviction.

For the state, the zadists are illegally occupying land to which they have no rights. For its eclectic group of residents, the ZAD is more than a contested piece of land but a home in an organised community living on the margin of society and which advocates an alternative way of life, away from the mass consumerism destroying the planet and worsening inequality.

The zadists built homes in bricks and wood and over the years a bakery, a brewery, a radio station, an online newspaper and a weekly vegetable market were also created.

This was a social experiment. Some may say it was a success. Others will point out to a divided movement of people opposing state authority.

Either way, the ZAD became known as a safe space to carry the voices of those who reject the individualist liberal economy and refuse to play by the rules of a capitalist system in which they don't believe they have a place.

The ZAD was a thriving parallel world to Macron's own reality as a former Rothschild banker. But under French law this utopian project remains illegal and despite the government's ultimatum, many zadists refused to leave.

Early April, the government sent 2,500 police officers to evict the zadists. The operation turned violent and soon images of police throwing tear gas to protesters in wellies went viral on social media.

But the violence came from both sides. Footage also showed young people in balaclava throwing what is believed to have been petrol bombs to the police, which accused radical left groups to have used the movement to spread disorder.

The images were shocking. It looked just like civil war. The zadists have estimated up to 300 people have been injured, some seriously. Among the police, dozens of officers are reportedly injured.

A group of zadists is now preparing to take a case to the Défenseur des Droits, an independent rights mediator which is responsible to investigate reported claims of police misconduct.

Luce Fournier, a spokesperson for the group VigiZAD, told independent French media Mediapart the complaint included allegations the police used offensive GLIF 4 grenades which contains TNT explosives on protesters.

Fournier added the group was considering further court action against the French state over its abuse of force and violence.

"This is a first step and it will help us gain support for future court actions," she told Mediapart. "Given the level of violence which took place, we must respond with all available options and we do not exclude any legal challenges," she added.

The operation to evict the ZAD is reported to have cost €300,000 a day of taxpayers' money – reaching an estimated total of €3m.

Authorities say 29 of the 97 structures on the site have been destroyed and according to French newspaper Liberation, a delegation of zadists have since registered 40 "mutually dependent and collective" projects with the authorities.

This was not the first time French authorities attempted to take back control of the ZAD. In 2012, a similar operation failed to clear the site after the government u-turned following public outrage over the violent scenes.

But unlike his predecessor, Macron made the choice of an authoritarian crackdown on the ZAD – choosing to be feared rather than loved.

In an interview with French television channel France 3, Macron said he had kept his promise to restore "the Republican order" on the site, denouncing "those who are there to cause disorder".

"The people who are protesting are people who are illegally occupying public and private land. But they no longer have a reason for their protest since they will not be an airport. So we are doing what citizens are expecting from the state – we are restoring the Republican order," he said.

The incident stirred up a bags of mixed emotions among the French population.

Some local residents have long resented the ZAD and its residents for appropriating the land without paying their dues. Others have continued to bring their support towards a community which for a decade has ardently tried to live a much simpler life closer to the earth – sometimes on the edge of outright poverty.

But above all, the force and scale of the police operation on the ZAD has brought back other memories of a different time when groups in society decided to defy the authority of the state.

This was the biggest police operation for a public order matter since the student revolution of May 1968, which 50th anniversary is being commemorated this month.

Back then, public opinion was shocked and divided over the pictures of students firing cobblestones from behind barricades blocking the streets of Paris in response to police tear gas and truncheons. These pictures now form part of a collective memory.

The student movement carried the ideals of a generation rejecting the conservative morality, customs and values of traditional society. May '68 was a generalised strike action but it is the students which remain the most symbolic aspect of what commentators at the time called a "revolution".

Critics saw the student movement as little else than a violent attempt to spread disorder and chaos. In this respect, parallels can be drawn between the way the events of May' 68 and what happened at the ZAD were perceived by an unsympathetic part of society.

In both instances, the heavy-handed actions of the police to stifle public disobedience has divided opinions.

But in all other ways, there is little to compare between the isolated incident at the ZAD and the movement which swept across the whole of France 50 years ago and which legacy in liberating customs and ideas continues to resonate today.

What was once seen as radical in May' 68 is now perceived as a keystone moment in the construction of modern France.

The rejection of authority in the name of utopian ideals have played important roles in fostering communities and challenging societies. But what happened at the ZAD was not an all-embracing movement to change the system at its root. In many ways, it was a self-centred initiative of a few carrying out an alternative experiment.

What legacy the ZAD will bring to France's anti-capitalist movement is yet to be seen.

A year into his presidency, Macron has asserted his strong presidential style, powering through a string of promised reforms — fearless.

His zealous attitude fascinates political experts and commentators who invented a new word to describe Macron's ruling style: Macronism.

Macronism is not a defined concept but rather a way of continuing to ask the question who is Macron?

A young and ambitious minister in the year ahead of the vote, he suddenly rose through the ranks and unexpectedly announced his candidacy to the presidency. Often compared to Jupiter and Napoleon for his commanding behaviour, he is a staunch European and a great believer of a more integrated EU.

Macron has seduced widely on the world stage – thanks in parts to his knowledge of English – and in line with Machiavelli's advice that "one should wish to be both" feared and loved.

One person who appears to appreciate him dearly is no other than US President Donald Trump.

The pair's "bromance" reached a new high during Macron's visit to Washington – the French President being the first head of state to attend an official state visit to the US.

They were kisses and hand shakes, tree planting and compliments all around. But when it came down to business, Macron delivered nothing less than what the liberal elite expected of him.

Strong words on the importance of the Iranian nuclear deal and the urgency to tackle climate change may have irritated Trump but not enough to break his strongest relationship with any European leader.

Meanwhile, Macron used his special relationship with Trump to act as an indispensable bridge between the US President and the rest of the western world watching.

Even Macron's critics will have to admit that the French President is a master in diplomatic and foreign relations, which have won him what seems like unconditional support from some parts of the British press.

Macron may be loved abroad but back in France there are fewer distractions from the fact his authoritarian stance at home is inspiring both fear and distrust.

Macron's two faces – one feared and one loved – may provide some insight into what his Macronism ruling style may hold in the future.

While he struts on the world stage, his term in office will ultimately be judged on domestic issues by French voters.

Learning Gaelic, Learning Scotland: Normalising Language

Ali Lightbody

I'm sitting in an entirely empty train carriage at Glasgow Queen Street Station on my way to Mallaig. Two older ladies board and start speaking to each other in Gaelic, believing they won't be understood. They are discussing how I am sitting in one of their booked seats and how young people these days have no respect or regard for the rules. I politely reply, in Gaelic, that they could have their booked seat and I was just trying to find a better view for the journey. I said that I was more than happy to move and I hoped that they would enjoy their trip.

I often tell people this story and say that the reaction on the ladies faces when they realised I had understood every word made learning Gaelic worthwhile. However, this is only the start of a large list of experiences that have made learning Gaelic one of the best things I have ever done.

Na Luinn – "shimmering, glitter-like appearance in grass during an especially hot summer."

I started my degree at the University of Glasgow in 2010 and chose Gaelic as my third subject. Coming from Stirlingshire there was no opportunity to learn Gaelic in my Primary or Secondary School and so attending the University was my first chance. I think I could just about stumble through a ciamar a tha thu and maybe even a slàinte, but that was pretty much it. It became clear to me very quickly that I was going to stay in the Gaelic department for the rest of my time at the University and it soon became my priority.

My decision to learn Gaelic came from many years travelling in the Outer Hebrides with my parents and attending the Hebridean Celtic Festival. It is hard to imagine now, but I remember a time when our family would be the only people camping on Horgabost beach on Harris. It always seemed strange to me that I had no understanding of a language that was so commonly used in parts of my own country. I still find this strange. Only recently at Murrayfield watching Scotland play rugby did it occur to me how many patriotic Scots, while singing along to Runrig's Loch Lomond, fall silent when it comes to Ho, ho mo leannan, ho mo leannan bhòidheach. Is even this too much of a stretch?

Glasgow University has a Gaelic Initiative which creates opportunities for Gaelic speakers to use it daily on campus. It also, as I discovered, helps introduce learners to the fluent speakers and the culture of Gaelic in Glasgow. We had ceilidhs and events and weekly meet ups and I quickly got to know all the Gaelic speakers in the department and realised that, dare I say it, Gaelic was… cool? Vibrant? No, just normal. A completely normal part of these young Scots' day to day lives.'

Driùchcainn – 'chaffing between the toes caused by walking barefoot in warm sand.'

I have had so many different opportunities since strolling into the Celtic and Gaelic Department back in 2010. Performing Gaelic songs at Celtic Connections gigs with fellow students, attending the Sabhal Mòr Ostaig college in Skye for workshops and summer schools, appearing on television shows filmed in Glasgow and in Skye, doing interviews on Radio nan Gàidheal and recently taking part in some extra work for the 4th series of Outlander. All of this is in addition to teaching Gaelic classes to adults and children and also my current job.

I work for the Digital Archive of Scottish Gaelic (dasg.ac.uk) and we currently have a team of 15 people. We speak Gaelic to each other every single day. In meetings, during our lunch breaks, organising work schedules, and in the pub on a Friday evening, Gaelic is our language of communication. I am part of the Glasgow Gaelic Choir where, again, Gaelic is used commonly. It is normal. For this reason the recent negativity in the press and on social media goes over my head, as it is so far removed from my own experiences that, if it wasn't so concerning, would be laughable.

When people say nobody speaks Gaelic, I say, I speak it every day. My best friends speak it. My work colleagues speak it. My bosses speak it. Those two ladies on the train slagged me off in it. I text in it. I write Facebook messages in it. To say that nobody speaks it is untrue, and nothing but ignorance. Of course people speak Gaelic.

I have heard it claimed (mostly by monoglot English speakers) that Gaelic is insular and restrictive. Again, this is not something that I recognise to be true. I have met people with not only a tolerance of but huge interest in other cultures. This could be down to the understanding of speaking a minority language and being regarded as 'other', even in a country that you call home. Mine is not the place to lecture on the benefits of bilingualism, but only to observe the skill and talent with language of my Gaelic speaking friends.

Meuran nan daoine sìthich – 'foxglove' (lit. 'the thimble of the fairy people')

As an adult learner of Gaelic I am in the position to remember my life without it. To say that Gaelic opens up your country to you feels cliché but it's what I've found to be the case. Place names are an obvious example. I think there is sometimes an acceptance among non-Gaelic speakers in Scotland that place names just are what they are without questioning why. Before learning, I didn't think much about them. Now I see them as descriptions of the land and sometimes what the land was used for. They shape my vision of place and many Scots are missing out on this, which is a massive shame.

It is an absolute privilege to be able to consider myself even a small part of the Gaelic community. I put down my love of Gaelic not only to the language itself, but down to the wonderful people I have met along the way, fluent speakers and learners alike who have been nothing but welcoming and supportive.

If you are even considering giving Gaelic a go, siuthad! Do not underestimate the opportunities and richness of culture that will open up to you once you begin. You don't need to become fully fluent to gain a better understanding of the culture and language that surrounds us in (all areas of) Scotland. The next time I'm at Murrayfield, I hope to hear you singing as well...

Ho, ho mo leannan, ho mo leannan bhòidheach.

Racism, The New Right and Media Failure

Amna Saleem

The New Yorker 'festival of ideas', having now disinvited Steve Bannon, is facing his ire – despite the fact that he knows he's won either way. Invited, he gets to peddle his half-truths and dog whistles; uninvited, and he's the victim of PC culture.

A Newsnight segment featuring, of all people, Laurie Penny and Ella Whelan highlights the problem of Bannon's influence. Whelan is determined that his "bad politics" be heard on account of free speech while throwing millions of minorities under the bus just for the sake of playing devil's advocate. She has fallen hook, line and sinker for the belief that lives like mine are acceptable to debate, yet has the audacity to present it as a concern for balance, despite the fact that he is a well known white supremacist who encourages others to wear accusations of racism as a badge of honour.

Minorities are overly-familiar with this game, and while we see through it, the media seem to keep falling at the first hurdle – which is differentiating between free speech and hate speech. Inciting genocide or a civil war is not a right. Everything said in the name of free speech is not free from repercussion. It's not a magic phrase that when uttered instantly absolves the person of all responsibility. Steve Bannon, however, goes one further. He plays the master

197

manipulator and the victim effortlessly. He cries about being denied his right to free speech while shouting from an incredibly large platform. And the media falls for it. Every. Single. Time.

Steve Bannon doesn't even have to work that hard because the news outlets do all the work for him. If we could trust those with power to hold him to account I could perhaps be compelled to see things differently but on the occasions where he has been invited on TV or radio he is never adequately challenged, leaving him to spout his nonsense with minimal intervention. His dog whistles are heard loud and clear by folk who were never going to change their mind anyway, yet we are force-fed this idea that fascists deserve to be heard so they can be put in their place (which is in the White House, apparently). We will undoubtedly see repercussions of his "bad politics" again when he appears at the Open Future festival run by *The Economist* with the blessing of the Editor-in-Chief.

The reaction to Bannon being disinvited has been utterly predictable and embarrassing. Instead of giving him the Milo treatment, we're meant to believe that he still has something worthwhile to say, therefore we must avoid driving him underground like the troll he is. All the minorities are suddenly invisible and we have white people being asked to discuss issues that don't even affect them. It's easy for them to claim that it's only fair that good ole Steve gets to say his bit when they aren't in the firing line.

I say this while knowing full well that I could be invited on and elegantly explain why his presence is unnecessary but it would need to be amplified by a white voice for anyone to actually take it seriously. It's a catch-22, but I'd still much rather prefer if white women like Ella Whelan didn't get to use their time on TV to discuss bigotry as if it's of the same urgency as not liking pineapple on pizza.

The Steve Bannons of the world have always existed in one form or another, as have his less successful counterparts Jared Taylor and Richard Spencer – both of whom enjoy peddling the absurd myth that compared to white people most ethnic minorities are savages with inferior intellect, which has given even the dumbest of racists delusions of grandeur. As if systematic racism wasn't enough fun, we're also forced to listen to the tedious rhetoric of the many power-hungry fascists desperate to become the new Hitler in skinny jeans.

None of this is far removed from the daily lives of people of colour. Everything filters down, from racist agitators through politicians and the media to harassers in the street, dirty looks in the pub and humiliating treatment by police and border officials, It's why we have to prove ourselves to be overly competent for a job a white people can just walk into. It's why you tend to only see one minority at a time on TV shows. Sure, Bannon and his cronies aren't directly responsible for the fact that it took Friends nine seasons to feature an ethnic minority. But they are responsible for othering minorities to such an extent that we are dehumanised *en masse*. We don't actually have to be exterminated or physically assaulted to be harmed by them; we just have to exist.

It's in the details. It's in the hostile environment he encourages which places ordinary muslims under intense scrutiny. It's in Brexit. It's in the attempt to suppress black voters in the US through gerrymandering, voter ID laws and purges of voter rolls. It's in the way that people compliment my mother on her excellent English despite the fact that she was born here. It's when people consume and espouse the *Daily Mail* while buying it from my immigrant father. It's when people ask me where I'm really, really from. It's when my ability to speak another language is used to question my Britishness. It's when the US can create a law and casually refer to it as the Muslim ban.

Every time I and my clearly Muslim name travel to the US, my boarding card has the dreaded SSSS on it. This ominous sequence of letters is why I'm stopped and searched at every port of security for clearance. It's why sniffer dogs nose through my colourful sun dresses and why I'm aggressively manhandled multiple times as the pat downs increase in their humiliation.

I factor this into my holiday plans the way most people factor in sunscreen. Amongst a long list reminding me to pack an adaptor, I also calculate and set my alarm so I'm at the airport obscenely early so these extensive security checks don't risk me missing my flight.

Like Steve Bannon, I, too, thrive on attention. While he cries out for a race war, I mostly ask people not to send me racist death threats for informing them that "naan bread" means "bread bread" so saying naan alone will suffice. It's controversial stuff. My existence and those like mine are constantly tainted by the influence of the alt right in a myriad of ways of which I am lucky to be at the milder end of.

Regardless of the topic, like most women of colour, I can't tweet, write an article or appear on TV without receiving racial abuse, whether that be someone taking umbrage with my skin tone, referring to me as a terrorist or accusing me of trying to implement Sharia law. In order to pursue my career, I have to accept racism fuelled by the likes of Bannon as a consequence of my ambitions. It's especially wild when you realise I'm just a young working class Muslim woman from a small town in Scotland who spends most of her time discussing pop culture and writing comedy.

That's the crux of the matter. Most minorities, including Muslims, are incredibly ordinary people busy binge watching Netflix. But Steve Bannon is set on turning the western world against us with the promise that we're all secretly nefarious beings who need to be ousted from society – one we helped build and defend, no less.

So yes, Steve Bannon is dangerous to me, and no, I don't think his racism has a legitimate place in some healthy marketplace of ideas.

The Rehabilitation of Gordon Brown

Jamie Maxwell

Gordon Brown is back. Again. Earlier this week, to mark the tenth anniversary of the financial crisis, the former prime minister treated us all to another nakedly self-serving political intervention.

In two separate puff piece interviews – one with *The Guardian* and one with the BBC – he issued a series of stark claims and denunciations. The world is "leaderless" and "sleepwalking" towards a second economic crash. New Labour "did not know what was going on" in Britain's financial sector in the run-up to 2008. Tory austerity was a mistake. Politicians must resist retreating into "nationalist silos [of] populism and protectionism."

There's nothing particularly controversial about Brown's main point – he is right to flag-up the risk of another crisis, although he's hardly the first person to do so.

It's everything else he says that I find problematic. Let's be clear: Gordon Brown bears a sizeable share of responsibility not just for the 2008 crisis itself, but for the catastrophic mishandling of its aftermath and for the current atmosphere of nativist toxicity in British politics.

Let's start with New Labour's relationship to the UK banking industry.

In 2001, the Blair-Brown government established a new Financial Services Authority (FSA) designed to streamline regulatory constraints on the City of London and consolidate the UK's global "competitive advantage." The FSA swallowed up nine separate bodies into a single agency in order to provide – as Brown boasted at the time – "not only light but limited regulation" of British banks.

The result was a spectacular failure of oversight. Britain's regulatory watchdog wasn't properly equipped to discipline the banks if it suspected they were doing something wrong. In fact – perversely – its chief function seemed to be to make life easier for them.

What's more, in 2009, FSA head Adair Turner told a parliamentary committee that the agency had come under political pressure to further loosen restrictions on financial institutions. "There was a philosophy rooted in political assumptions which suggested the key priority was to keep it light rather than to ask more questions," he said ('Gordon Brown helped fuel banking crisis – FSA head').

There is, of course, no doubt about who was applying that pressure or why. This is what Brown told the City in June 2007, three months before the collapse of Northern Rock:

"I want to continue to work with you in helping you do [your job], listening to what you say, recognising your international success is critical to that of Britain's overall, and considering together the things that we must do to maintain our competitiveness: enhancing a risk-based regulatory approach, maintaining our competitive tax regime, and [keeping] our main rate of corporation tax the lowest in the G8."

So the suggestion that New Labour was blindsided by City malfeasance doesn't stack up. On Brown's watch, the government did everything it could to encourage risk-taking behaviour within Britain's dangerously over-sized and unruly financial sector.

Brown is equally culpable for the austerity regime that came into force in 2010.

Granted, he was one of the leading global advocates – alongside Barack Obama and the US Federal Reserve – for stimulus spending as an immediate response to the crash. And, had he won the 2010 general election, he wouldn't have cut expenditure as recklessly as David Cameron and George Osborne did.

Nonetheless, Labour's 2010 manifesto was crystal clear: from 2011 onward, deficit reduction would be the government's overriding priority. Indeed, Brown went into the election pledging a series of "tough choices" on Britain's national finances. These included £15bn worth of "efficiency savings", £11bn worth of "operational efficiencies", a public sector pay cap, welfare reform, an increase in National Insurance contributions, and £20bn worth of "asset sales" – or privatisations – by 2020.

Moreover, Brown's tenure as chancellor was characterised by an overwhelming PR obsession with 'fiscal prudence' and 'budgetary discipline.' He may have significantly increased key aspects of social spending, but he did so by balancing the increases out with tax hikes in order to keep public debt low, run annual surpluses, and manage inflation.

Ultimately, Brown's sensitivity to the charge that he was financially irresponsible lent credibility to Osborne's later (manifestly false) claim that Britain had to eliminate its deficit before it could return to economic health. In other words, many of the major decisions Brown made at the Treasury framed and reinforced the political rationale that Cameron and Osborne used to justify austerity.

Which brings me to my final point. Brown did a lot of ideological grunt work for the right in terms of the economy and spending cuts. But he shamelessly bolstered its social and cultural narrative, too. In and out of power, Brown has repeatedly appealed to the worst atavistic tendencies of the UK electorate.

On a trip to Tanzania in 2005, he told reporters that the UK should "celebrate" its colonial past. In 2009, he argued that "British jobs" should be reserved for "British workers." And as recently as June of this year, he was calling for a crackdown on immigration as part of a broader package of policies to help "address people's anxieties" over Brexit.

All of this highlights the emptiness and cynicism with which the ex-chancellor is currently trying to salvage his political legacy. He wasn't duped, as he now claims, by the criminality of the UK banking sector – he enabled it. He wasn't opposed to austerity – he championed it. And he doesn't find populist language unsettling – he uses it himself when it suits him.

Brown might be right about the inevitability of another economic crash. But if we want to handle the fallout from the next crisis more effectively than we did the last one, he is the last person we should be listening to.

Cranstackie

Dougie Strang

The weather's glorious, the days shift towards mid-summer, and although the first stage of lifting lockdown has begun, most of those who love to walk and climb in the Scottish mountains are still unable to do so. There are, of course, more important concerns, but the ongoing lack of access to the hills is keenly felt. The following is an extract from a book-in-progress about a month-long walk in October in the North West Highlands. It's offered here in solidarity with all those who are looking out windows and poring over maps, tracing routes they'll be glad to one day walk.

Many of Scotland's bothies are maintained by the Mountain Bothy Association. They are free to use and open year-round, though the MBA is a registered charity and welcomes donations. All bothies are currently closed due to Coronavirus.

I was sitting on a chair by a table at a window, drinking tea from my tin cup. The table was stained and blistered with candle wax and the sun above the ridge was warm through the window. A grey wagtail fluttered at the glass, as though it was trying to find a way in. Three times it flew to the glass, before being cast aside by the wind. Its breast was pale yellow, like primroses. Earlier, I'd opened the front door and all the internal doors, to let the bothy breathe. They had to be wedged with old roof slates to stop the wind from banging them shut. When I opened the doors, the space inside the bothy seemed to expand like a lung, stirring ash in the hearth and swirling dust that sparkled in the let-in light.

The evening before, I'd crossed the Bealach Horn, the high pass between the mountains of Arkle, Foinaven, and Meall Horn. It was dark by the time I scrambled down into Strath Coille na Feàrna, 'the strath of the alder wood', using the line of a deer fence as guide and clutching the fence wire in places to lower myself. There was no moon and few stars and it took a long time to walk the last two miles to the bothy.

Strabeg Bothy was once a shepherd's cottage, with upstairs bedrooms and a bathroom with a toilet that flushes into a septic tank. There's no running water, but there are buckets to fill from the river. The cottage sits on a knoll at the bend where Strath Coille na Feàrna opens out into Strath Beag, 'the little strath'. From my chair at the window, I could see a silver birch growing out of a ruined stone byre. The sun was full on my face. It was a dazzling day, a high-energy day, but too windy to go anywhere exposed, despite the attraction of the stony ridge of Cranstackie to my west. Up there today I'd be beaten by the wind, cast aside by it; so I went out to wash my socks in the river instead and gathered dead branches for firewood. The wind pummelled the reeds on the slope that led down to the river, so that the slope was alive with their movement. It looked like an attack, as though the reeds were sweeping up against the solidity of the bothy.

The wind increased through the day, toppling my stack of drying firewood and flailing the alder trees by the river, snapping branches. I was impressed that the bothy kept its roof on. At sunset, I watched clouds moving fast across the summit of Cranstackie, while the wind bellowed in my ears like the stags I'd heard earlier in the strath. The mountain glinted like gun metal. Inside, the walls muffled the sound of the wind, but at times the force of it shook the ceiling and it felt again like an attack – one that the bothy was only just withstanding. I sat by the fire, the storm amplifying the pleasure of small treats: dry socks, two chocolate digestives, a candle on the mantle above the hearth, whisky in my cup; and I thought about the people who'd lived here before, without electricity or telephone, with no road in and their nearest neighbour two miles away. When I went outside to pee before bed, the sky was clear of clouds and bands of pale green light were rippling across it, fading then strong, then fading again: Aurora Borealis; Na Fir Chlis in Gaelic, 'the Nimble Men'.

Next morning, I walked up the strath in the wind and rain, following the tree-line below Creag Shomhairle, 'Sorley's crag'. The woodedness of Strath Coille na Feàrna is a delight. A note in the bothy explains that the deer fence is in place to protect the trees that are there and to encourage regeneration, with the eventual aim of extending the woodland further. The path dodged its way amongst the trees and between boulders that had split and fallen from the crag above. Across the river, Cranstackie rose in armoured plates of stone. I disturbed a heron ahead of me on the bank of the river and it flew upstream, landed, then flew again. I found myself involved in the strath, as though I wasn't just passing through, as though the chores of gathering firewood and scooping buckets of water from the river were a form of participation. In the morning, when I woke and rekindled the fire in the hearth, it was in communion with all those who'd done so before.

My plan was to wander up the wooded side of the river and gather enough firewood so there'd be a dry stack for whoever next visited the bothy. Towards the head of the strath, there's a bealach that leads over and down into Strath Dionard, below Foinaven. It's called Bealach a' Chonnaidh, 'the pass of the firewood'. Early maps show that Strath Dionard has long been treeless, so the people who lived there, at Carrachandubh, would've crossed the bealach to Strath Coille na Feàrna to collect firewood. The name evokes the act, and I thought of gathering a bundle of fallen branches, packing them in my emptied rucksack, and carrying them over the bealach. It would be a way of honouring the name, but it would be a wasted journey: there are no longer people who'd welcome the wood at Carrachandubh.

The wind had dropped a little in the night; it was still too strong for the heights, but I'd taken waterproofs and oatcakes just in case. The further up the strath I went, the more I was drawn to Cranstackie. Despite the weather, I wanted to walk on the glinting stone of its ridge, and I could trace with my eye the route I'd take to climb it. When I crossed the river, I gave up the pretense of looking for wood, and before long I was following the course of a stream up onto the mountain. On the lower slopes, in the gully of the stream, there was a single holly tree with tattered leaves and berries that were desiccated by the wind.

I was walking on a large patch of unbroken rock: dark grey gneiss, almost black, like the flank of a giant whale that had breached through the crust of the earth. Veins of white quartz rippled through the gneiss. The rock was so smooth, each step had to be measured, like walking on ice, even with the traction of the Vibram soles of my boots. Nothing had changed here since glaciers scoured the rock. Such scales of time were beyond my grip.

I'd set out to gather firewood and found myself on the ridge of Cranstackie. The wind made the skin of my face ripple against the bone of my skull, and to move forwards I had to lean into it, walking at an angle to myself. There were no detached stances up here: it was too real, too risky, too hypothermic. With my hood pulled low and chin tucked into my fleece, I looked directly across at the northern peaks of Foinaven. I've never been so intimidated by a mountain. This wasn't a rounded, grassy-sloped sleeping giant. It was furious, spiked, a prehistoric-monster mountain, with twisted seams of gneiss and quartzite. Around its summits, clouds fumed.

Confronted by so much stone, life seems more obviously precarious. I thought of the poet Hugh MacDairmid, and the time he spent in another stony landscape. For nearly a decade, through the 1930s, MacDairmid lived with his second wife Valda and their young son on the island of Whalsay in the Shetland Isles. They lived in poverty in a cottage with a peat fire and wooden crates for furniture, surviving their first winter there on a diet of fish and potatoes gifted to them by neighbours. It was a difficult time, physically and psychologically. MacDiarmid writes in a letter that he was a man "brooding in uninhabited islands." From that brooding he wrote 'On a Raised Beach', a long poem that contemplates the stones of West Linga, a small island off Whalsay. MacDiarmid faced the hard stuff of material reality, the 'lithogenesis' of creation, and sought to articulate his faith in an eternal creative force at the essence of things. I find the poem's language alienating: it reads at the start like a glossary of geological terms; but there are also lines of great beauty and insight. MacDiarmid writes of the stones: "Their sole concern is that what can be shaken/Shall be shaken and disappear/And only the unshakable be left."

The ridge was pathless. I picked my way along it, amongst a jumble of broken quartzite slabs, jarred by the wind but aware of how present I was: what can be shaken/Shall be shaken and disappear. Unexpectedly, I found life on the ridge: there was no soil or turf, but there were trees, extraordinary trees. They were an Alpine form of juniper, a prostrate variety, with tight, flat growth, spreading horizontally, rooted in cracks and crevices in the rock. The largest trees were only the length of an arm, but their branches were vibrant with evergreen needles, each clutching a handful of small blue-black berries. Once I had an eye for it, I began to see a sparse forest on the ridge. Some of the trees had trunks that were as thick as my wrist, representing decades of growth, maybe hundreds of years; stunted but surviving, thriving even, on their terms.

The weather closed in as I approached the top of Cranstackie, with thick cloud and whipping rain. I turned back before reaching the summit cairn, spooked, aware that all around me, invisible in the mist, there were steep crags dropping away. I was grateful to climb down below the cloud and feel the wind lessen in the lee of the ridge. Sitting in the quiet of a gully, I tried to figure out some kind of coherence between the mountain and its shattered stones and the green world of the strath below. I'd picked a sprig of juniper from the ridge, with three berries on it. I took it out of my pocket and put one of the berries in my mouth. The taste was bitter, resinous, intense.

Cranstackie is nowadays translated as 'the rugged hill', but older references clearly state the name as Crann Stacach, where crann is 'tree', and stacach can mean 'rugged, peaked, or rocky'. It seems the name might actually refer to the presence of the juniper trees. Either way, having climbed up into the stone world of the mountain, I was glad to find them there. Hugh MacDairmid, brooding on Whalsay, self-absorbed and intellectually isolated, admired the indifference and "barren but beautiful reality" of the stones. I preferred the juniper trees, their vulnerability and tenacity, their intense, compact aliveness; and I wondered about Valda, MacDairmid's wife, how she'd managed, bringing up their child in poverty, coping with her husband's solipsism.

Back down in the strath, I took off my boots and socks to ford the river, and kept them off to keep them dry, crossing the bog and moor barefoot, with my trousers rolled to my knees. A snipe rose two yards in front of me and twisted away. It was well dressed for the moor, its feathers striped pale and darker brown like patterned tweed.

I stopped and filled my water bottle from a stream fringed with bright green water-cress. The cress tasted mild, earthy. With my knife, I carefully harvested a bunch – it would go well with oatcakes and cheese – and thought of the words attributed to Suibhne Geilt, the medieval bush-mystic of Celtic folklore. Remembering his time wandering in the wilderness, he says: "Though you like the fat and meat which are eaten in the drinking-halls, I like better to eat a head of clean water-cress in a place without sorrow." The wind was at my back as I crossed the strath, bending the grass and reeds in great waves so that it seemed as though I was surfing back to the bothy.

The Art of Living Together

Mairi McFayden

This month I was at The Ceilidh Place in Ullapool for the annual adult Fèis Rois gathering, a three-day festival of tuition in traditional music, song, dance, Gaelic language and culture alongside fringe events, gigs and late-night cèilidh sessions in pubs all over the north west's cultural capital. There is such a spirit of community here. For many, this is a chance not only to meet friends old and new, but to learn from the great tradition bearers – such as fiddler Aonghas Grant or Gaelic singers Rona Lightfoot and Cathy Ann MacPhee.

This year the Fèis also welcomed a group of singers and musicians from Brittany, who threw a fest noz into the mix; two blind music students from the National Academy of Music in Bucharest and a young musician who is working hard to raise awareness of autism. Music has such an incredible power to connect, to bring people together.

The whole weekend was a life-affirming and hopeful reminder of what is important to hold on to in the face of it all. With the relentless daily news cycle headlining the triple crisis of climate change, mass extinction and inequality alongside escalating trends of populism, isolation, alienation, uncertainty and disconnection,

211

creating spaces for connection and conviviality is more vital now than ever.

A particularly special moment was the performance of the 'Kin and the Community' project Sgeulachd Phàdruig Mhoireasdain – one in a series of short films bringing to life audio archive recordings alongside newly composed music as a soundtrack to a life story. In this instance, we learned of the life of musician Pàdruig Morrison's own grandfather, Peter (Pàdruig) Morrison, a man who survived the First World War and lived as a crofter in Grimsay, North Uist. The audience witnessed past and present fuse together as Pàdruig and friends accompanied his forebears in real time, unlocking layers of memory and meaning and inviting us to reflect on who we are and where we come from. Inspired by and created under the guidance of fiddler and composer Duncan Chisholm, this work of creative ethnology is a moving reminder of what it is to be human.

We live in a society that has forgotten to value what it is to be human, in a world where far too many people get left behind. Our economy cares not for localities, cultures, ways of life or the cohesion of kin and community. The pervasive growth-at-all-costs model – upheld by all of the main political parties and mainstream media – is so narrowly focused on the pursuit of profit, productivity and measuring GDP that it fails to count the damage it wreaks on the environment or the health, well-being and dignity of its citizens.

What can we do to resist and reclaim our lives, our communities, our planet?

Reclaiming the Commons

Across the globe, the commons movement is growing and reclaiming hopeful alternatives to the dispiriting status quo of market economics, challenging the deep pathologies of contemporary capitalism and suggesting cooperative, egalitarian and participatory alternatives.

Deeply rooted in human history, it is difficult to settle on a single definition of the commons that covers its broad potential for social, economic, cultural and political change. The commons includes natural resources – land, water, air, forests, food, minerals, energy. It also encompasses our cultural inheritance – the traditions, practices and shared knowledge that make society possible and life meaningful. Commoning is the lived expression of conviviality, understood as the 'art of living together' (con-vivere). Put most simply, perhaps, the commons is that which we all share that should be nurtured in the present and passed on, undiminished, to future generations.

The movement to name and reclaim the commons has roots in the struggle of English commoners against the 'enclosures' of the 15th, 16th & 17th centuries by the rising class of gentry who expropriated common land for their private use; and later, in both Lowland and Highland Scotland, the dispossession of the Clearances. These enclosures severed a deep connection to the land and destroyed local cultures, paving the way for the industrialisation, colonisation and globalisation of the modern world.

In the 21st century, it is not just land and resources that have been enclosed by capitalism, but almost all aspects of life itself. The modern tendency towards turning relationships into services, commons into commodities, human into machine has been described by commons scholar David Bollier as 'the great invisible tragedy of our time.' The 'new enclosure' can be seen in the patenting of genes, lifeforms, medicines and seed crops, the use of copyright to lock up creativity and culture, academic knowledge behind paywalls and attempts to transform the open internet into a closed, proprietary marketplace, shrinking the public domain of ideas, among many other examples.

The endgame of this process is the enclosure of the mind and the co-option of dissent. The absolute triumph of this system is demonstrated by the fact that so many of us have lost the ability to imagine our way out. As Naomi Klein has written, we are 'locked in, politically, physically and culturally' to the world that capital has made. We are up against the formidable capacity of global capitalist and colonial systems of power to enclose our sense of the possible.

Connection and Conviviality

Despite the rapid encroachment by capitalism on the commons, much of what we value in terms of quality of life is still created outside the spaces of economic exchange, through the voluntary association of friends, neighbours and citizens. Convivial co-operation is very much alive in scattered enclaves and in communities – in the home, the library, local clubs, community gardens, community land trusts, or simply in an open-mic night, cèilidh or pub session. These are the places and spaces where the impulse and catalyst to strike and kindle sparks of change, creativity and transformation are to be found.

The carrying stream of traditional music is a cultural commons. Every song, pipe march, slow air, jig or reel has its own story to tell, connected to the language, histories and memories of people, places and lives lived. At its heart, traditional music is a shared activity, a community practice, drawing on wells of deep communal and collective memory, passing from previous generations to the curiosity, ingenuity and dexterity of the next. The tradition has been created by many hands; first in the minds of individuals, but often reshaped – altered simply through the human process of forgetfulness or given new life by those with a desire to innovate. There is the spirit of the commons too among those who are generous with their passion and talents, willing to share and pass on their knowledge through playing and teaching.

This music does not represent some parochial caricature of a bygone age, but rather a living, breathing culture that is as contemporary today as it ever was. Rooted in place, it has a life force and an energy that demands to be reshaped, to continue, to be passed on.

Traditional music has always resisted mainstream commodification, despite the success of the 'creative industries' in packaging this music as an export brand for global consumption. While the brand-driven individualism of neoliberal economics demands of all artists to be professional entrepreneurs – and while some may enjoy or benefit from this situation in financial terms –

214

many more sit precariously and uncomfortably within such a dehumanising ideology.

It is important to name it too: the neoliberal ideology and discourse of the creative industries belongs to the same story of economic growth, and is therefore enmeshed and implicated in the wider process of climate breakdown. It's all connected.

This is not an argument to get rid of money or markets; neither is this an argument for an economics of scarcity or against regeneration. This is an argument for transforming and releasing ourselves from the grip and structures of contemporary neoliberal capitalism-as-we-know-it. Our very survival as a species depends on it.

Capitalism moves fast. We need time to slow down, reflect, remember, resist and make space for what really matters. When we slow down, our experience of being human swells. Our sense of possibility augments and swells with it. Paulo Freire wrote that it is our vocation to become more fully human. What he means by this is that we must move from existing as human objects to be acted upon towards becoming subjects who think and act with critical consciousness, liberating our imaginations and transforming the world.

We might think of reclaiming the commons as reclaiming our past and our future, reclaiming what it means to be human, to be alive. If, somehow, we are able to come together to confront and overcome the desperate challenges that lie ahead, we might just find a world far richer in possibilities than the one we leave behind.

Patchy and Negligible

Claire Squires

Claire Squires, Professor of Publishing Studies, University of Stirling on the Scottish Review of Books controversy suggests it reflects a closed clubbable world divorced from contemporary Scotland.

In the age of diminishing print book review space, the decision to defund a well-established literary magazine might seem questionable. Indeed, initial public reactions to Creative Scotland's rejection of the Scottish Review of Books' funding application concurred. The SRB, established in 2004, and – until last month – in regular receipt of Creative Scotland funding, published a quarterly print version via the Herald, with a partially paywalled online version. Creative Scotland's decision, announced the SRB, would mean it would no longer produce the print version.

Following these initial reactions, a further article appeared in the Herald by its literary editor Rosemary Goring, who is also an SRB co-editor and board member (as well as married to its editor Alan Taylor). The article was republished last week on the SRB's website, under the provocative headline, 'Is Creative Scotland more dictator than facilitator?'

I read the statement with fascination – and a sense of growing disturbance. A disturbance which, as I started to tweet about it, struck a chord with many in Scotland's literary community.

In the statement, SRB made public the grounds on which it had been rejected. Creative Scotland withdrew funding but with the encouragement to reapply for a 'considerably enlarged' amount which, apparently, would move the SRB away from an '(unpaid) cottage industry' to paid staffing. Creative Scotland also asked for ('imposed') a 'higher degree of editorial and board member diversity, thereby meeting Creative Scotland policy'.

Where was the controversy, I wondered? Who would not want a professionalisation of editorial staff that might enable individuals who otherwise could not afford a volunteer role; and a diverse staffing base?

Conversations around diversity and inclusion in publishing and literature are loud at the moment, and rightly so, given the industry's preponderance of white, middle-class workers and writers, as well as its gender pay gaps, glass ceilings and centralisation in the south-east of England. Industry initiatives and publications are working to make long overdue positive change, enabling people of all demographics to be involved in the reading, writing and publishing of books. Academic research including Anamik Saha's AHRC-funded research in collaboration with *The Bookseller*, Melanie Ramdarshan Bold's work on the (lack of) inclusive UK YA writing, and my own on publishing's 'diversity deficit', adds to the evidence base. And while there might be justifiable criticism of the efficacy of some activity – such as novelist Pat Barker's recent comments that industry initiatives are 'fashionable' rather than concerted – it should come as no surprise that a Scottish Government-funded entity such as Creative Scotland has an Equalities, Diversity and Inclusion policy to which it expects funded organisations to adhere.

But the SRB found Creative Scotland's urge to diversification unacceptable:

'While as wide as possible a range of talents, voices, background and experience is important, the pre-eminent consideration for anyone pulling the strings [...] is quality and originality. These are the foremost consideration, after which all other matters must join the queue.'

Was this statement effectively telling people under-represented in its pages and its management to 'join the queue'? To add salt to the wound, Goring added that:

'Imposing BAME diversity targets [...] in a country whose ethnic profile is at best patchy and in some cases negligible, is to put the implementation of an inarguably important principle higher than any other consideration.'

The phrase 'at best patchy and in some cases negligible' spread across social media, with Scottish writers, publishers and literary sector workers of colour temporarily changing their profile handles, and suggesting Edinburgh publisher 404 INK assemble an anthology with that title. But the banter sat alongside a real unease at the phraseology, its whitewashing of Scotland's general population, and of its literary sector, aspirant writers, and readers.

Even the briefest of surveys of writing and publishing in and from Scotland demonstrates that quality, originality and artistic excellence is being produced by people of colour: from publishers and magazines such as *BHP Comics* and *The Selkie*, writers including current Makar Jackie Kay, Leila Aboulela and Chitra Ramaswamy, plural and diverse festival and event programming, and groups including the Scottish BAME Writers' Network.

The SRB statement also contained an assumption which habitually meets any act of positive discrimination: that equality measures cannot also be enablers of (artistic) excellence. It assumes that people of colour are inhibited by a lack of 'quality and originality', rather than by prejudicial structures and gatekeepers. While the inter-relationship of aesthetics, critical judgement and demographics is complex, evidence has repeatedly shown that across the literature/publishing sector, and the creative industries more widely, there are systemic and institutionalised barriers to equal access, fair representation, social and creative justice.

To call Creative Scotland, then, as the SRB did, a 'dictator', or even 'a manifesto-waving, policy-driven arm of an increasingly authoritarian state' is histrionic – and perhaps betrays anti-Scottish Government roots (Nicola Sturgeon is notably a regular contributor to the literary scene, including a key note speech at 2019's Scottish Book Trade Conference and through chairing book festival events).

Creative Scotland is an easy target, and nobody would claim its recent decisions and processes are beyond reproach. But media reports continually underplay its role in literary successes – for example, a lengthy and informative *Scotsman* article on the 'rebirth' of Scottish publishing (following the Man Booker International award to Jokha Alharthi's Celestial Bodies) failed to mention it funds Sandstone Press, Alharthi's publisher – or indeed any other publisher.

At the end of my Twitter thread, I expressed the hope that what can emerge from the defunding of the SRB is some form of a Scottish review of books (lower case intentional) that takes on board key principles both of literary and artistic endeavour, but also, crucially and centrally, of equalities.

My call to action – 'So who's in?' – received enthusiastic response. It wouldn't surprise me if something emerges soon...

55 Years Ago in Madrid

Stuart Christie

55 years ago this week 18-year-old Stuart Christie from Partick was arrested while carrying explosives to assassinate General Franco. He was later alleged to be a member of the Angry Brigade, but was acquitted of related charges. He went on to found the Cienfuegos Press publishing house and in 2008 the online Anarchist Film Channel which hosts films and documentaries with anarchist and libertarian themes. Here he remembers his arrest:

I've just been reminded it was 55 years ago this week that I was arrested in Madrid by the Gestapo-trained Brigada Político-Social (BPS). Around this time of night, 11-12 p.m., I was still being interrogated on the second floor of the Dirección General de Seguridad in the Puerta del Sol (El Ministerio de la Gobernación).

I remained in their direct custody for three days before being transferred downstairs to the infamous subterranean cells, los sótanos, under the jurisdiction of the Jefatura Superior de Policia de Madrid, the policia armada (the grises). Subsequently we were brought back up to the BPS offices for further interrogation, as and when required.

Being a UK citizen, just turned 18, and with the regime sensitive to the negative media and diplomatic impact my trial

221

would have in the wake of the international outcry that followed the previous year's judicial murders of Julian Grimau, Joaquin Delgado and Francisco Granado, my treatment was relatively benign.

I was pushed around a bit and had my face slapped and hair pulled, but it was nothing compared with that dished out to my Spanish-born comrade, Fernando Carballo Blanco, whose torture I was forced to witness through a two-way mirror.

They pistol-whipped his wrists while he was tied to a chair and subjected him to relentless kidney punches. His wrists and midriff were still massively bruised when we met up after our release from solitary confinement two weeks later in the patio of Carabanchel prison.

Also, for the record, although it's a good canard, I wasn't wearing my kilt when arrested — or indeed at any time during my travels; it was folded, neatly, under the flap of my Bergen. Also, although arrested on the 11th of August the DGS sat on the news for five days until August 16.

Paul Winzer, the head of the Gestapo in Spain, was based there throughout the Civil War. Seconded by Heinrich Himmler to the Madrid Embassy in the mid-1930s to monitor German leftist activists during the Popular Olympics of 1936 he was in Barcelona on 18 July when the rising took place. Appointed adviser to Franco's general staff, Winzer later organised and supervised the notorious concentration camp at Miranda del Ebro (Burgos) through which over 65,000 Republican prisoners passed. The BPS was established by decree on 24 June 1938 and overseen by Winzer who was appointed to the Nazi Embassy in Madrid in 1939. Although he was known to be in Madrid in the early part of 1945, by April he had disappeared from view and never faced justice for his crimes against humanity. Surprise, surprise!

The Jobby, Brazil and Nuveen

George Kerevan

Where there's smoke there's fire: How Edinburgh got into bed with a US investor linked to wholesale deforrestation in Brazil.

WHAT connects the burning of the Amazon rain forest with Edinburgh?

The answer lies at the top of Leith Walk, where they are building a veritable Babylonian ziggurat. Actually, it's a new hotel – as if the capital needed another one. But the inappropriate and megalomaniac bronze-coloured design of this monstrosity is fitting given the developer is one the world's nastiest private equity funds. In truth, the new St James Centre is a monument to a city transformed by runaway development – aided and abetted by the local council – into a poster for neoliberalism.

The company behind the £850m ziggurat (plus the inevitable retail space and luxury flats) is called Nuveen Investments. You've probably not heard of Nuveen. It is the working arm of TIAA, an American financial services conglomerate that just reached an out of court settlement with clients who sued because of alleged mis-selling – so what's new in the world?

Chicago-based Nuveen/TIAA is one of the world's top three asset managers, along with BlackRock and Vanguard. These are companies that invest in property and shares on behalf of rich clients. Nuveen has nearly a trillion dollars under management, roughly the GDP of the Netherlands. What does Nuveen do with this cash and why is it in Edinburgh?

Sadly for capitalists, the global economy is not what it used to be. Profit rates are down thanks to excess competition, especially from China. Plus central banks have spent the last decade printing money to keep interest rates rock bottom, which means that investing in government bonds yields next to nothing. So what do you invest your billions in?

Nuveen thinks the answer lies in land and commercial property, both of which yield rent. Rent is safe, sustainable and can be ratcheted up year-on-year. Besides, there are another three billion extra folk expected on the planet by 2050 and God isn't making any more land – a point Nuveen makes forcefully in its presentations to clients.

Hence Nuveen is putting its cash pile into high-end commercial property developments (such as St James Centre) and particularly... agricultural land. Nuveen is now the world's biggest private owner of farmland, which it rents out. For instance, it is the second biggest owner of vineyards in the United States by acreage. And in Brazil, Nuveen is now the biggest foreign holder of land, which it snaffling-up hand over fist. It owns 300,000 hectares in Brazil, equivalent to four per cent of Scotland.

SOMETHING'S BURNING IN BRAZIL

Since 1970, over 700,000 square kilometres of the Amazon rainforest have been logged or burned – often illegally and often stolen from indigenous peoples. The cleared space has been turned into farmland, especially for soybean cultivation and cattle ranching, both for the global export market. As well as murder and loss of biodiversity, the loss of forest adds to global warming by depleting the world's biggest natural carbon sink.

Nuveen has been attacked by local activists for purchasing farms whose ownership was subject to legal proceedings concerning the validity of land titles – farms which have seen high rates of deforestation. Alert to criticism and the threat of legal action, in 2018 Nuveen announced it would not burn rainforest habitat in Brazil or buy land that had already been burned.

However, in 2019 a coalition of environmental organisations – including Friends of the Earth, GRAIN, National Family Farm Coalition, and Rede Social de Justica e Direitos Humanos – accused Nuveen of duplicity. Using satellite photographs, they claimed that Nuveen was culpable in the extension of illicit land burning to Brazil's tropical savanna lands in the Cerrado region, south of the Amazon basin.

Savanna is mixed grassland and woods, rather than dense rainforest. The Cerrado is the largest and most biodiverse tropical savanna on the planet, and a major sink CO_2. In recent years it has become the main frontier for the expansion of large-scale, industrial plantations in Brazil. Over the past decade, the Cerrado has seen 50% more deforestation than in the Amazon, with the loss of over 40,000 square miles of habitat.

Within the Cerrado, Nuveen has already purchased 25 farms covering 288,000 acres. Satellite images show this Nuveen land overlaps with areas where there has been a heavy concentration of forest fires. In the past year, according to this satellite data, the number of illicit fires in the has actually doubled.

Nuveen's alleged prohibition on deforestation is carefully framed as referring to the Amazon, not the Cerrado. It is also in this region where major land ownership disputes with local peasants are ongoing.

GETTING EDINBURGH'S FINGERS BURNED

Nuveen's business model is to drive up financial returns by raising rents everywhere. That counts for its tenant farmers in Brazil and for anyone renting property in the St James Centre. Yes, there will be (low paid) retail jobs and making beds in the luxury hotel at the new

St James Centre. But the mega-profits sucked out of the development will head to the US, and thence to Nuveen's Asian investors. Edinburgh is being sold for the proverbial mess of potage. Just like Brazil's poor peasants.

Here's the really sad thing.

Nuveen is the world's biggest owner and investor in commercial property. Yet the Scottish Government (through its Futures Trust) and Edinburgh City Council were persuaded to put £60m of public cash into the St James project, supposedly to "unlock" Nuveen's money by proving free surrounding public infrastructure. Even with a conservative annual yield, Noveen and its Dutch partner will make £60m every year in rentals.

Notes from Underground #7: I Only Have One Prediction for You

Dougald Hine

Notes From Underground is an ongoing series from Bella's commissioning editor, Dougald Hine, reflecting on the deeper context of the new climate movements. The first six essays looked at what makes the current wave of climate activism different, how conversations about degrowth are reaching inside political institutions, and where we might look for hope – as well as the implications of 'climate emergency' declarations and the Green New Deal, and the common roots of Extinction Rebellion and the gilets jaunes. This week we move into Part II of this series: Knowing What We Know. These essays are also available as a podcast and on YouTube.

The walk from the station cuts through the modern shopping streets, then across the channelled river, its banks lined with the painted fronts of older buildings. The afternoon sky is a flawless blue, but there's an edge to the air that wouldn't have been there a few weeks earlier. On the steep path that runs up past the castle, you have to stay alert for the cyclists who come flying the other way. It's the first of September, the first day of a new academic year in this old university town.

The lecture theatre is a cave, down a wide flight of steps, in the basement of one of the newest buildings. There are no seasons underground, here in the bright fluorescent light and the conditioned air. The rows of seats fill up with students, notebooks at the ready, phones set to silent, poised on the threshold.

I have been asked to give the opening lecture of the year at the centre for environment and development studies. During their courses these students will hear from researchers who work at the front line of climate change: earth scientists, ecologists, ethicists, engineers, political economists and economic anthropologists; people with PhDs and academic publications behind them. I am none of these things, and through the weeks of late summer, I've been wondering what I could say that might be some help as they grapple with the knowledge that is coming their way.

'I want to talk about the future,' I say, 'but I'm afraid I don't have any charts or projections. There won't be one of those quadrant diagrams with four scenarios for how the world might look in 2050. This isn't going to be the kind of talk which ends with a list of eight things we can do that will make it all turn out OK. In fact, I only have one prediction for you, and I don't think there's anything we can do about it, and it's this ...'

Click the remote control, the first slide hits the supersized screens behind me, big letters spelling it out: 'WE ARE ALL GOING TO DIE.'

A gentle pulse of laughter passes through the cave, and something eases. Any audience faced with an unfamiliar speaker starts with the fear that it may die of boredom: the sooner you can allay this fear and establish shared signs of life, the more chance there is of going somewhere together. There's more, though, as we ease into each other's company: a sense that parts of us are welcome on this journey – parts that might not ordinarily show up in a room like the one in which we meet.

We are all going to die. You, me, everyone who either of us ever loved, our closest families, everyone who might remember our faces or our names: all of us, we are all going to die.

This is not an apocalyptic prophecy, it is only to state the quiet fact of our mortality, the undramatic reality of personal extinction that waits for each of us, sooner or later, somewhere down the road. Yet many of those who study or work with death have come to the conclusion that there is something strange about modern Western society and the way it handles this reality. The Canadian author Stephen Jenkinson, who worked for decades with patients approaching death, suggests that North America has become a 'death-phobic' culture. Across the developed countries, there seems to be a difficulty in facing death that sets our current ways of living apart from the ways in which people have lived in other times and places.

I want to suggest that this difficulty is tangled up with the difficulty we have when it comes to knowing, coming to terms with, and acting on our knowledge of a thing like climate change. Way down in the roots of the mess in which we find ourselves, there is a subterranean connection, a shared thread that I want to follow.

For that matter, those among us who have done the most to sound the alarm are not free of this root tangle. Western environmentalism is surely haunted by the same ghosts as the death-phobic culture out of which it came. When we look at that famous image of the Earth from space, I can't help thinking that our sense of its fragility is overlaid with projections of an unreconciled fear of our own deaths. When we talk about extinction, we call up the shadow of another ending – smaller, yet seemingly total, voiced aptly enough in the words attributed to Ayn Rand: 'When I die, the world ends.'

I don't mean to charge my friends in the environmental movement with Randian solipsism, only to own that we too come out of a culture whose attitude to death is skewed enough to make such a statement thinkable. To know a thing like climate change, with all that it implies, to see and speak clearly about it, I need to start with death: to come to terms with my own mortality, not as an inconvenient fact, a thing to try and avoid thinking about, nor as a world-ending event, but as an intimate knowledge, a mystery that makes me who and what I am. Knowing that the body in which these thoughts are cradled will someday be burned or buried, that the world will close quietly around my absence, that this is the ordinary course of events, releases me to be vulnerable and dependent as I always was, a part of processes whose time is vastly other than my own.

Almost a decade ago now, in a brightly lit office space one block from Trafalgar Square, I was introduced to a man who proudly produced a card which he carries in his wallet at all times. The card declared his Lifetime Membership in the Cryonics Institute. For around the cost of the flashy car another man might have bought to mark his midlife crisis, he had become one of the two thousand people worldwide signed up to have their bodies frozen cryogenically at the point of death so as to benefit from as-yet-uninvented medical innovations which will allow them to be restored to life.

On one side of the card was a set of phone numbers to be called immediately in the event of death, to summon the team that would collect his body; on the other side, instructions as to how the body should be handled in the meantime. This mostly involved ensuring that the head was surrounded with ice. I thought of the new layers of anxiety which this investment must introduce: what if no one finds the card? What if there is no ice on hand? What if the institute goes bankrupt and has the plug pulled on its freezers before the necessary technological progress can be made? I'd swear his hand was cold as I shook it, as though the process were creeping backwards and slowly freezing him alive.

Most of us have a gut-level reaction to this kind of scheme for cheating death. We feel that something is astray. There is some shared sense of the distinction, offered by John Michael Greer, between a problem and a predicament. A problem has a solution: you can fix it and it goes away, leaving the situation much as it was beforehand. A predicament has no solution; it is something you have to live with, and you can do a better or worse job of living with it, but you cannot make it go away. When we encounter someone who treats death as a problem rather than a predicament, we have a sense that he is making a category error.

Let Greer's distinction sit with you for a while and you may come to suspect that we don't have as many problems as we think we have, given that many things labelled as problems are more likely to be predicaments. In *The Long Descent*, Greer illustrates the difference with a thought experiment: suppose that you could go back in time to a prosperous agricultural village in the English Midlands, somewhere in the early years of the 18th century, equipped with the knowledge of the Industrial Revolution which lay around the corner; suppose you could convince the villagers of the scale and the speed of the changes ahead, the destruction that is coming:

"Within a century, every building in the village will be torn down, its fields turned into pasture for sheep, and the farmers and cottagers driven off their land by enclosure acts passed by a distant Parliament to provide wool for England's cloth industry and profits for a new class of industrial magnates. For the young men of the village, England's transformation into a worldwide empire constantly warring with European rivals and indigenous peoples overseas prophesies a future of press gangs, military service, and death on battlefields around the globe. For a majority of the other residents, the future offers a forced choice between a life of factory labour at starvation wages in bleak urban slums and emigration to an uncertain fate in the American colonies. A lucky few will prosper spectacularly by betting on ways of making a living that nobody present on that autumn day has even imagined yet."

Suppose your listeners took all this on board and asked you what they ought to do. What would you tell them?

It is a question without an answer, Greer suggests, because what they are facing is a predicament. It's not that there is no course of action worth taking, it's that none of them resembles a solution. Many responses are possible, some wiser than others, none of them assured in its consequences, except for the assurance that they will not lead to the continuation of the way of living which these villagers have known.

The industrial society whose coming marked the end of that village world would prove more confident in its capacity for solving problems than any way of living that had gone before it. It would come to see the world as a puzzle, a set of problems to be solved; yet over time, more and more of the problems it encountered would be the consequences of its earlier solutions. Meanwhile, it seemed to lose the knack of recognising a predicament, or knowing what kinds of actions still make sense when faced with one. Even now, when its world faces forces of disruption quite as overwhelming as those which broke across that English village, the only responses it can imagine are solutions: innovations that would allow us to resume a pre-existing trajectory of progress, growth or development, only with solar cells and vat-grown meat.

Seen through the industrial lens, even death cannot be recognised as a predicament. We react to the category error of cryogenics, but a more diffuse version of the same logic has shadowed modern medicine, which starts by seeing death as failure and ends in drawing out the lives of its beneficiaries at all costs, hooked up to every kind of machine, in the earthly limbo of the dying. Meanwhile, the rest of us – the living – defer the encounter with the predicament of mortality as long as we can, keeping ourselves distracted, until it catches us unprepared, well along the journey of a life, in a phone call bringing terrible news, or among the magazines and posters of a hospital waiting room. It is this deferral of the encounter with death that marks us out, that makes our ways of living seem so strange.

The novelist Alan Garner was born in rural Cheshire in 1934. His memoir of a wartime childhood, *Where Shall We Run To?*, is a testimony to the lived experience of a world too easily romanticised. What struck me reading it was the unremarkable presence of death. A group of American GIs march past the front porch of the family cottage where Alan is playing with his toy gun, and their officer commands them to salute the delighted little boy. In a sentence, at the end of the chapter, we learn that their homebound ship was sunk and all those young men lost at sea. Yet it is not just the war that brings death to the village. Another chapter tells the story of one of the evacuees, urban children billeted with local families for the duration, a bright girl who becomes a favourite playmate. Again, almost in passing, we learn that she dies of a common childhood illness. In a world where penicillin had not yet reached mass production, this was the ordinary course of events, that at some point in childhood one of your friends would be off sick from school and not come back.

Any reckoning with the deferral of death, the distance we keep from the knowledge of mortality, must start with the remarkable achievements made in the prevention and treatment of common diseases as old as human civilisation. The greatest part of the changes in life expectancy over the 20th century came from public health rather than high-tech medicine. Any sane response to the predicament our societies face in this century surely includes the attempt to bring this knowledge and practice with us into whatever futures lie ahead.

Modernity has two faces, suggests the decolonial thinker Walter Mignolo, as inseparable as the faces of a coin. He calls them 'the shine' and 'the shadow'. If the changes in the prospects for surviving childhood are among the brightest aspects of the way that death has changed in the era of industrial modernity, their shine is not the whole of the story. Seen from elsewhere, what defines this era may not be the triumph over death so much as its systematic outsourcing. The world system which made industrial society possible was founded on the destruction of worlds, not only in rural England, but more brutally across the globe. The conquest of the

Americas involved the extinction of 80 to 90 per cent of the indigenous population, a multi-generational genocide in which the impact of introduced diseases was compounded by military, economic and biological warfare. The raw materials that fed the new industrial economy were grown and mined by victims of the new industrial slave trade, black bodies bought and sold and disposed of at will. This systematic savagery was not a side story to the main drama of industrialisation, still so often presented as a history of ingenious white men and the unforeseeable consequences of their inventions: it was a necessary condition for the viability of the industrial economy, and it is a process that persists, in varying forms, to this day.

Small wonder, then, if the discovery of the Anthropocene – the new geological epoch which names the dawning recognition of our predicament – appears from elsewhere as the return of the outsourced. As Mario Blaser and Marisol de la Cadena write in *A World of Many Worlds*:

"The world of the powerful is now sensitive to the plausibility of its own destruction in a way that may compare, at least in some ways, with the threat imposed on worlds sentenced to disappearance in the name of the common goods of progress, civilization, development, and liberal inclusion."

As the Nishnaabeg writer Leanne Simpson told Naomi Klein, 'It's been the end of the world for somebody all along.'

There is a further sense in which industrial modernity stands outside the frame of all other ways of being human together, as a uniquely death-fuelled society. All life feeds on death. All enduring human cultures have been shaped by the need to be worthy of what we take. Much of the ritual and story by which humans have found their bearings in the world has at its heart the cultivation of awareness and gratitude for the deaths of the animals and plants that give us life. The need to be worthy is not just a moral aspiration, a desire for a sense of dignity or self-justification, but a practical necessity. Either we make our lives a part of a cycle of gift, or we become an engine of depletion, bringing about a desolation from which we will not escape. The tapestry of myth carries memories of the ways we have ruptured this cycle and the work that has gone into mending it, time after time.

The fossil economy breaks the possibility of such a cycle. How many million years of dying in the forests and seas of the ancient world goes into one generation of living the way we have been doing around here lately? How could our lives ever be worthy of so much death? What could we possibly give back? Committed to dependence on these vast underground reserves of death, the only response that remains to such questions is to silence them, to extinguish the ways of living which embody them, to make them unthinkable.

This is where the geological story of a death-fuelled economy converges with the outsourcing of death, the elimination of indigenous cultures and the reduction of black bodies into factors of production. The argument is powerfully made by Kathryn Yusoff in her book *A Billion Black Anthropocenes or None*:

> "The movement of energy between enslaved bodies in plantations, plants, long-dead fossilized plants, and industrialized labor is a geochemical equation of extraction in the conversion of surplus."

The story of our predicament cannot be told without recognising these violent connections and the economic drive that links them.

One evening in the first days of the year, between the news of Australia burning and an assassination in the Middle East, my partner sees a story about a meteor shower that's due. Outside, the sky is clear and I catch sight of one straight away, a bright flash travelling across the sky, like a silent firework. So we pull out the sun-lounger from my in-laws' conservatory and lie under blankets, staring up. While we wait, my son wants to be told the names of the constellations. He's not yet five, but he knows there are two names for everything, Swedish and English, even when these are only two ways of pronouncing names older than the languages we speak: Orion, Taurus, the Pleiades. The last time I saw Alan Garner, he told me there's new research on the resemblance between the Greek constellations and the figures seen in the sky by Aboriginal people in Australia, the similarities strong enough to hint at common threads of myth leading deep into prehistory, stories carried out of Africa.

'How does it work when you wish on a falling star?' my son wants to know. 'Does the thing you wish for just pop up, out of the ground?'

His eyes are wide with recent memories of Father Christmas and the cartoons he's been getting to watch on his grandparents' TV. Suddenly I understand why he was so keen on this impromptu astronomic outing.

'I'm going to wish for a Paw Patrol fire engine,' he announces.

I don't know how to disentangle myself or my family from this way of being, this web of extraction that surrounds us with objects that seem to pop up, magically, out of the ground. I don't even know how to frame the question, how to name the work that's called for. (It's not a problem, I remind myself, it's a predicament.)

One thing I know that helps – one piece of the work – is to gather and share the embers of other ways of being, blowing them gently into flame together, knowing how much unfinished history we carry with us. Listening to those who have more experience than I do of the ways life has been made to work in other times and places, one theme I hear is how much work goes into making a grown-up. It's not just something you become by virtue of surviving childhood, or sitting out enough years in schoolrooms and lecture theatres. When the time comes, it takes a work of initiation on which much of the life of your community is focused. You have to be cooked in the flames, I've heard it said, and the frame of initiation which your culture builds is the vessel that gives you a chance of coming through the fire.

Among the stories and skills acquired in such a process, among the experiences described by those who have gone through it, a common element is some form of ritual death. On the threshold of becoming a grown-up, you are taken through a staged encounter with your own mortality, an encounter which is taken with the utmost seriousness. I'm thinking about this, and about the clumsy, risk-filled encounters that bridged this gap as I stumbled into adulthood, and a thought comes: so that you do not meet your death for the first time, when it comes for real.

To be a grown-up, it seems to me, is to live alert to consequences; to know the cost of your living. It is hard to be a grown-up in the world that we have made. The cost is almost unbearable. No wonder our culture seems built to keep us distracted, to postpone the encounter with consequences until the last possible moment.

If I set a lot of store by the ways in which people have made life work in other times and places, this is not to romanticise the lives of others. There is no way back, nor would we want one. The lives of our ancestors were hard in ways we do not like to think about – and for this reason, they could not afford the kind of carelessness to which we have been accustomed. Cushioned on millions of years of fossil energy, veiled by the impersonal logic of commodity exchange and the Emerald City magic of the shop window display, the level of detachment from consequences which has been normal, even necessary, for participation in our death-fuelled societies of consumption was until quite recently the preserve of mad emperors. Our ancestors could not afford this carelessness – and nor, it turns out, can we.

The Capital of Amnesia

Christopher Silver

"*Nostalgia doesn't create good policy. Nostalgia dragging you back to a year that is gone and a place and time that is gone doesn't give you a good way of looking to the future. The only thing that gives you a good way of looking to the future is looking at what you want to achieve and taking meaningful action on how to get there.*"

– Adam McVey, Leader, City of Edinburgh Council

"*And many times throughout her life Sandy knew with a shock, when speaking to people whose childhood had been in Edinburgh, that there were other people's Edinburghs quite different from hers, and with which she held only the names of districts and streets and monuments in common.*"

– Muriel Spark, *The Prime of Miss Jean Brodie*

One reason that people choose to live in cities is because they are able to be surrounded by thousands of others with radically different experiences of it. Few cities demonstrate this better than Edinburgh – a capital city that voted not to be a capital city. The AIDS capital of

239

Europe so quickly transformed into the hyper-financialised "inspiring" capital (like most cities struggling with the impact of gentrification today – a concentrated AIDS crisis is a telling common factor). "One of the world's must-see destinations," or a city with the same clout as Sheffield or Nottingham – but with a castle, a Parliament and a festival? The Enlightenment's "Athens of the North," or Tom Stoppard's "Reykjavik of the South"?

A mess of diverse contradictions – any city's past is its greatest resource, and the bedrock of all its imagined futures. But in the city that first gave the historic a leading place in modern life, the public writing-off of collective memory is particularly bizarre. The political leader of Edinburgh claiming that 'nostalgia doesn't create good policy' is a bit like his counterpart in Venice claiming that canals don't make good policy. Nostalgia, Liz Lochhead's 'national pastime' is fundamental to Edinburgh. To banish it from the debate on what the city is for and might become, represents an act of rhetorical clearance.

The significance of nostalgia to Edinburgh's culture probably stems from the fact that it was among the first cities in the world to seek to comprehensively remake itself. It is not hard to imagine a kind of longing amongst the first residents of the immaculate and spacious New Town, for the rich social mix of the filthy and cramped Old. It is easier still to think of the first residents of Muirhouse or Niddrie, finding in the promise of urban improvement only a void where community and street culture used to be. With the near-complete gentrification of tenements in the city centre, such nostalgia for the shared space of the close and the back court, seems strangely ahead of its time.

But in their way, Councillor McVey's remarks are familiar enough. They're essentially a reheated and localised version of Blair's 2005 claim that debating globalisation is like debating "whether autumn should follow summer." There is no alternative, and the loss that many people of Edinburgh feel in relation to their city, is simply inconvenient baggage.

Edinburgh is now undeniably the beating heart of the Scottish economy. Tourism, financial services, food and drink, energy — the holy quartet of contemporary Scottish capitalism are all, in their different ways, fundamentally extractive. They all, despite the Blairite dismissal, remind us of the fact that the awesome irresistible force of globalisation is destructive and unsustainable. Globalisation might be all-pervasive, but it understands the price of everything and the value of nothing. Within this world view, to think that the residents of a small northern European city should get special treatment is palpably unfair. Still, the implicit admission of decline in the city leader's acceptance that Edinburgh was a better place to live ten years ago – "no shit!" – was unusually candid.

McVey was addressing a tourism summit, and referring to a citizen who suggested they'd have preferred living in Edinburgh a decade ago — before the contemporary problems of affordability and overtourism reached their current pitch. Before the symbolic ruin of Princes Street Gardens, before one of the world's most rapacious hedge funds was given leave to destroy an iconic skyline, before AirBnB turned the Old Town's tenements into a vast and unregulated playground for rent-seeking.

It is too much, apparently, to imagine the democratic role of a councillor as something other than the guardian of a product: singular and sellable. McVey notes Edinburgh's place right at the top of 'liveability' rankings, as underpinning its draw for tourists. But if local government has no use for the city's past in policy making, it might at least consider more nuanced views of what a city is for – rather than citing an index created by an asset management firm, which placed the Scottish capital ahead of London and Paris in 2018 (unsurprisingly, given the competition, affordable rents are not factored in here).

In 1961 Jane Jacobs, visionary critic of mid-20th century urban planning, wrote that the great concentrations of people which define urban spaces: "Are the source of immense vitality…because they do represent, in small geographic compass, a great and exuberant richness of differences and possibilities, many of these differences unique and unpredictable and all the more valuable because they are."

But for Jacobs this vitality is dependent on relatively stable neighbourhood economies and street life — providing an organic array of local services and public goods that planning seldom achieves, and that dramatic shifts in change of use often destroy. When a city neighbourhood starts to garner a certain level of commercial investment, she notes:

> '... the locality will gradually be deserted by people using it for purposes other than those that emerged triumphant from the competition — because the other purposes are no longer there. Both visually and functionally, the place becomes more monotonous...The locality's suitability even for its predominant use will gradually decline... In time, a place that was once so successful and once the object of such ardent competition, wanes and becomes marginal.'

Such a process is now writ-large across Edinburgh, and decline can already be seen on the horizon — if you can see past the Deliveroo cyclist running a red light to pay the rent, or weave your way around multiple walking tours jostling for pavement.

Take me to Abaton

Mike Small

"*Abaton (from the Greek a, not; baino, I go), a town of changing location. Though not inaccessible, no one has ever reached it and visitors headed for Abaton have been known to wander for many years without even catching a glimpse of the town. Certain travelers, however, have seen it rising slightly above the horizon, especially at dusk. While to some the sight has caused great rejoicing, others have been moved to terrible sorrow without any certain cause. The interior of Abaton has never been described, but the walls and towers are said to be light blue or white or, according to other travellers, fiery red. Sir Thomas Bulfinch, who saw the outline of Abaton when traveling through Scotland from Glasgow to Troon, described the walls as yellowish and mentioned a distant music, somewhat like that of a harpsichord, coming from behind the gates; but this seems unlikely.*"

— *from My Heart's in the Highlands, Edinburgh 1892*

As we glide (dis)gracefully from one phase of this Memetic, hyper-normalised dystopia to another, Scotland's odd status feels like Abaton: a place and a space blinking in and out of existence.

243

We are borderless, seamless according to Jackson Carlaw who wrote:

> "It is ridiculous to suggest Nicola Sturgeon could close the border. There is no border – we are one United Kingdom."

Without definition you don't exist.

The recurring thread of Unionist thinking from 2014 and well before is that Scotland doesn't exist in any meaningful way. The well worn and famous phrase of the campaign from Lord George Robertson is worth remembering:

> "There is no linguistic differentiation, no great cultural discrimination, that might argue for independence like it does in some other countries. In Flanders or Belgium, or Catalonia and Spain they say they want to become an independent state. But they've got language and culture … we don't have any of that here."

'You don't have a culture.' 'You don't really exist' are two of the strongest arguments in the armoury of an increasingly beleaguered Union, whose old baubles and icons of unity: the Monarchy and the Palace of Westminster, are not so much tarnished and discredited as broken.

The deep irony is that having sold-off and privatised many of the institutions that might act as a bond of 'Britishness', the Conservative and Unionists are now dependent on our support for the National Health Service, an institution they have derided and undermined for years.

The queue for writers to quash any perceived differentiation has been a long and consistent one, it may stretch even longer than that of those claiming, remarkably, that the coronavirus experience has destroyed the case for independence. Sure, the differences in culture and society can be over-emphasised, as a global culture unites people in different countries. But to deny any difference at all is a sign of desperation.

And the strident calls for unity and borderless nations strikes an odd note with the stench of English nationalism still in the air after the debacle of Brexit still lingers with its toxic xenophobia and exceptionalism.

This is a new level of Morbid Unionism, in which the task must be to cleave to the entity of 'Britain' muttering "UK:OK" even if it means, literally, a higher death rate. Any divergence from the Mothership cannot be tolerated or even considered. This is Britain as the Borg cube. Resistance is futile. As the British governments response to pandemic is revealed to be what can only be described as criminally negligent leading to thousands of avoidable deaths, the Unionists response is to revert to a default position of fealty and deference and to demand the same of others.

As we descend into further crisis, the Prime Ministers response is a sort of confident bonhomie mixed with some Churchillian rhetoric. It's Trump without the bleach.

In this crisis its essential not just to reiterate "we exist" but also that we have agency and we will act – in self-defence – as we need to. Sturgeon has been scrupulous in trying to NOT make party political advantage out of this. She has been – rightly in my opinion – careful to try and be as co-operative as possible with the British government. She, like the rest of us, is making it up as she goes along. She, like the rest of us, has never had to cope with this situation before. She has said: "My only interest right now is to fight this virus, and anyone who is trying to use the immediate challenges we are facing, or trying to twist what I am saying ... will not find me willing to play ball."

But as the mishandling of the crisis spools out through the cracks in a pliant jingoistic media, the pressure for her and Scotland to take a different path increases dramatically, whatever the political cost.

For the geographically curious, the border between England and Scotland runs for 96 miles between Marshall Meadows Bay on the east coast and the Solway Firth in the west.

It exists.

Liminal Land

All of this, stating the obvious, is a pity.

Scotland has for a long time been in a liminal state, halfway through a transformative ritual – neither what we were previously, nor what we are to become. The tensions a country can experience when it is at a threshold of choice are what we've all been going through for the last thirty years or more. But this national conversation, this constitutional moment has now been deepened with the rupture of the virus experience. As the philosopher Richard Rohr writes:

> "Liminal space is an inner state and sometimes an outer situation where we can begin to think and act in new ways. It is where we are betwixt and between, having left one room or stage of life but not yet entered the next. We usually enter liminal space when our former way of being is challenged or changed—perhaps when we lose a job or a loved one, during illness, at the birth of a child, or a major relocation. It is a graced time, but often does not feel "graced" in any way. In such space, we are not certain or in control. This global pandemic we now face is an example of an immense, collective liminal space....In liminal space we sometimes need to not-do and not-perform according to our usual successful patterns. We actually need to fail abruptly and deliberately falter to understand other dimensions of life. We need to be silent instead of speaking, experience emptiness instead of fullness, anonymity instead of persona, and pennilessness instead of plenty. In liminal space, we descend and intentionally do not come back out or up immediately. It takes time but this experience can help us re-enter the world with freedom and new, creative approaches to life."

Our ability to "begin to think and act in new ways" will be crucial, and this is not just a case of looking to our leaders, it is down to all of us, it is a community and a societal challenge.

The opportunities in this liminality are endless but must be cultivated. There is the chance to emerge from the lockdown freer and more appreciative of each other and the sort of society we can create. Coming out of the lockdown must mean coming out the Union, but it must mean much more than that.

All the signs are that the crisis is worse than we are being led to believe. The FT today suggests that the the data indicates that the Coronavirus deaths are more than twice the hospital toll.

Those advocating a public inquiry haven't grasped the scale of the predicament. The idea that we replace the British state with the Scottish state, British capital with Scottish capital and business as usual with business as usual with a saltire, isn't good enough. It never was. The idea that we replace rampant inequality with Lion Rampant inequality and that we fail to use this opportunity to remould our economy into an ecologically viable one, is now just unthinkable.

We need this to be an epiphany, somewhere between Gunn's Atom of Delight and Robertson's Republic of the Mind. As we settle in our new interior world and worry about the past, we must look to the exterior and plan our future.

We must not allow this future to remain like Abaton, an unreachable destination.

When I Needed a Neighbour

Alison Phipps

When I needed a neighbour.
Were you there, were you there?
When I needed a neighbour.
Were you there?
And the creed and the colour and the name won't matter
Were you there?

Sydney Carter, the English singer songwriter and poet —
conscientious objector in World War II and committed pacificist —
wrote this song, well known to many from school assemblies and
protest marches.

It's written in my tradition. A tradition of whole-souled non-
violence and whole-body listening which is fiercely contemplative,
critically liberatory and hopeful in song, and lamentation.

It is a song for a people made in a strand of the religion which
calls itself Christianity which sits with deep unease under such a
label today, and for good, good reasons.

But it is equally a strand passionate about the enduring truth in
the goodness of news of the life-giving force of forgiveness, mercy,

justice, repentance, liberation. It imagines a better way of being together. A commonwealth of love.

I sang this song through the anti-nuclear campaigns of the 1970s; the apartheid struggle of the 1980s; the environmental conscientising of 1990s and in solidarity with displaced peoples again and again and again. These days I hum it in the kitchen, and to my grandchildren too.

An anthem.

A lullaby.

Strengthening and soothing.

And we need songs and anthems if we are going to be whole body listening, lively people.

If we are to be neighbours, again.

The words have been playing as a sound track to the new found local neighbourliness of the time of confinement we are rather lazily calling 'lockdown'. 'Lockdown' is prison discourse; 'lockdown' is curfew language. 'Lockdown' doesn't come with 'care packets'. Ask any refugee who has experienced detention.

Neighbours are not always easy people. I know that when a neighbour destroyed the garden I'd made I was devastated and felt violated. Neighbours can be wanton in destruction. Too loud, too lonely, too indifferent. Neighbours can be hurt people who will hurt people, and you might just be the nearest to hand. And that's all.

'You weren't there' is the visceral scream from our black neighbours just now.

It's not like this scream has not been present amongst us as enduring testimony. It was there when the Egyptians took the Israelites into slavery, and it was the passing over of the plagues that brought their liberation and their singing.

It's not like this scream was not present in the genocide of slavery. You don't need to spend more than a moment in the song 'By the rivers of Babylon' to know how people, black people, have suffered and died.

'You weren't there' was the loud, angry internal voice that played through my whole being in September 2015. Closely followed by the self-righteous 'where the hell were you?' when the pitifully few of us who normally met to try and do the enormously burn-out inducing twin tasks of aid and advocacy with people seeking asylum in Glasgow, found our normal meeting spaces stowed out with people shouting 'I welcome refugees'. There was a competition to care and be seen to care in a somewhat unedifying scramble to hold the mic and claim new resources.

Neighbours, eh!

As one of the many standing-room-only meetings ended in that time I locked eyes with a refugee colleague and we spoke telepathically, knew what each other was thinking, bit our tongues, and got on with the work of capacitating the newcomers, now friends, allies, and enacting welcome and hellishly difficult, patient listening and explanation ("No, there is no recourse to public funds for these family members, no, they get £37 in vouchers to live on, yes, there is indefinite detention in the UK").

At a different point in my journey, people had done this work with me, too (you know who you are, and I am still profoundly grateful). Because there is no short cut, no other way. Because we need to learn and begin again and they don't make a pill for this. It's education.

I sat down to write this because Bella put out a call:

Bella Caledonia - @bellacaledonia - 2 June 2020

Call out to faith leaders to step up and in to talk about the moral vacuum in public office, state brutality and our unprocessed grief and anger ... anybody out there ... ?

I'm not a faith leader but I am led through discernment, prayer, study, wisdom and a ragged faith.

In the four books, in my tradition, which record wisdom of a man who died violently, unjustly and lived a life fused with love, there is a posthumously recorded set of parallel and contradictory stories and maxims he is said to have spoken to those living in anger and hope under Roman occupation, and with lying, thieving, cowardly, corrupt leaders (you can draw the parallels).

"Walk the extra mile"

"Turn the other cheek"

"If someone wants to sue you and take your tunic, give him your cloak also"

It's a sad testimony to the power of theology in the service of empire that it took the twentieth century theological genius of Walter Wink to unravel and draw out the defiant non-violence, and comedy of these statements when heard by people living under Roman Occupation. Context matters and where the church turned these statements into pious statements Wink shows, in 'The Powers' trilogy, how they would have landed with the listeners back in the day. Spiritual jujitsu – using the force of the enemy to unmask their power, and make room for a levelling, and equality, and a pause for a new possibility.

Just to take the first – because you can read more in Wink's trilogy– to walk an extra mile isn't to just do more giving unthinkingly. In Roman Occupied Palestine it was a rule that a Centurion could ask an occupied subject to carry his pack from one milestone to the next, but, crucially, no further. The Romans were clever, and subtle in their enslavements. As, of course, are we. But the imagine of the subject then grinning and putting the centurion in a position of precarity by carrying it two miles, and forcing them to have broken their own rule, is a very different thing to tholing it.

The Iona Community, of which I am a member, has lived out non-violence as a rule of life over its 82 years of existence, not always well, but as a fierce and urgent commitment. A community now largely of great elders and wisdom-holders, it has resources aplenty for these times. It's Rule of Life is one which has both kept and broken me daily for over twenty years. Think of institutions which stand for justice and solidarity in Scotland and you'll find a member of the Iona Community, or someone influenced and formed within its sphere of influence and parenting, quietly (or not so much) getting on with the work of dismantling the old and building the new. Shelter; Medical Aid for Palestine; The Cyrenians; Scottish CND; SCIAF, Christian Aid, Poverty Truth Commission, Water Aid; Extinction Rebellion to name just a few of the places where the liberatory and non-violent commitments in the Rule of the Iona Community to living a certain way, day in day out and with accountability to others, find their human and fresh, material expression.

The churches in Scotland have not had a great record of keeping to the second most important of the two commandments they are given to live by: to love their black neighbour as they love themselves. Aid, yes, aplenty, inspiringly so, sack loads, not just cups of sugar, but that's not the same as loving themselves. Most of the many, oh so beautiful nineteenth century churches in Glasgow are also, with a bit of digging in their histories, products of the slave trade and the imperial wealth stolen by the Second City of Empire. The established Churches in Scotland are still very white in their complexion and their welcomes are not often true integration but assimilation or toleration, like the offer of a room to a black congregation for worship. It's not nothing but it's not non-violent liberation and the work of justice.

This week, nonetheless, all the major churches have made necessary, good enough statements.

The former Archbishop of Canterbury Dr Rowan Williams, has gone further and condemned the president of the United States for idolatry. And he didn't do this by preaching to the converted, but in an article in the *Financial Times*, that newspaper which has long worshipped the idol that is money.

Whilst easy to critique the performative statements, and there is plenty of black scholarship doing just that, they are also part of the necessary work, but they are no more or less than the folk in the stowed-out room I described, coming late to awareness and action. Because we need it all – slogans; banners; protest marches, bodies bending to their knees unaccustomed to bowing down in any form of solidarity or humility, silence, elite institution making statements and reparations, but we also need the spiritual action that endures and is passed down via our elders, from generation to generation, in the stories and testimonies of turning the tables that we have largely banished from the churches, sanitised in the scriptures and neutered in the public square.

When I needed a neighbour.
Were you there?
Were you there?

It has to be asked twice for it to hope to be heard.

It's a time of finding a way to be there, collectively, not just as lip service or lived-service in churches, to be enduring neighbours, locally and globally – not the easy, fuzzy stuff of cups of sugar, or borrowed ladders – but the hard stuff, the day in day out, drives you crazy loving of neighbours as ourselves.

Sanctuary is an old Scots law of protection. If we aren't making sanctuaries everywhere, then our words and statements are empty, are ashes. Because refuge, the asking for it, the protesting for it, the taking of it, is a refusal to live in permanent violence. A protest is a refuge for those you stand alongside. Straining to go the extra mile for the planet, for black lives, the overturning of the tables of the sickening greed that is what our economic and military systems worship, these allow for a space where together, we can make things new, and heal, the hard way.

Protesting may not do anything or change anything and God knows but the Iraq war protests didn't exactly stop that war. But it does do something.

It's a way of being there.

When I needed a neighbour.
Were you there, were you there?
When I needed a neighbour.
Were you there?
And the creed and the colour and the name won't matter
Were you there?

Magical Thinking

Rory Scothorne

As part of a new series 'Routes to independence' #RouteMap we explore the competing ideas and options for gaining self-determination, looking at parliamentary, extra-parliamentary, conventional and unconventional ways forward. Rory Scothorne explores problems with the idea of 'Maxing the Yes'.

Slavoj Zizek once observed that "on today's market, we find a whole series of products deprived of their malignant property: coffee without caffeine, cream without fat, beer without alcohol," and so on. In Scotland we might add: hegemony without power. How else to describe Scotland's nationalist movement, which seems to expand its dominance of the political scene on a daily basis, yet cannot secure a legitimate vote on its most fundamental goal?

Zizek argues that this pervasive "virtual reality" reflects a new, self-limiting hedonism where "everything is permitted, you can enjoy everything, but deprived of its substance which makes it dangerous." This was always the neoliberal genius of devolution: a means for Scots to express – and even enjoy – their own distinctive political identity, which simultaneously withheld from nationalism the thing that makes it dangerous – state-making power.

Some nationalists don't even notice the difference. Everyone has stories of school friends offered a "joint" stuffed with shreds of innocent greenery who would hazily proclaim its effects, sometimes even after the big reveal. Scottish nationalists are still puffing away on a damp, tasteless wad called the "sovereignty of the Scottish people" several months after Boris Johnson waved away Nicola Sturgeon's request for a "Section 30" order like a passing cloud of smoke.

Another request for a limited expansion of Holyrood's borrowing powers from Scottish Finance Secretary Kate Forbes – more modest than even Scottish Labour's 2019 manifesto proposals – has been similarly rebuffed by Rishi Sunak. As polls for independence now suggest, these denials offer a sort of perverse placebic thrill in themselves, in a wider culture where disempowerment and exclusion are virtues. But those polls are still an effect of powerlessness, not a solution to it.

Post-democracy

The phenomenon of politics as virtual reality isn't uniquely Scottish. It is a feature of "post-democratic" politics worldwide, as the global loosening of regulations on capital has produced a drastic shrinkage in what even the most powerful states can and can't do with their last dregs of sovereignty. But "post-democratic" implies that there was at some previous point a "democratic" politics in Scotland. In fact, the two arrived at the same time. When democracy shuffled into Scottish public life in 1999, it did so with a manacled jangle, prevented from running away with itself by the iron link of globalisation and Westminster supremacy.

The result has been a politics increasingly defined – to a globally unmatched extent – by mere representation. It doesn't matter that Scotland cannot stretch its constitutional legs without permission, nor that almost all the key economic powers with which we might gather some momentum towards real self-determination have been held at British or European levels. So long as the Scottish

Government can ensure that our political desires are represented and spoken for, it doesn't matter if they are never met.

But what desires are being represented? Certainly not "popular sovereignty" in any meaningful sense. Most people gave up on collective power long ago, for understandable reasons. Reclaiming even a fragment of mass agency, after decades of right-wing revolution, endangers those very spaces 'beyond' politics – friendships, families, work, culture, identity – into which humanity has retreated from neoliberalism's onslaught.

The common unionist refrain that the last independence referendum "divided families and friends" is part of the right's effort to exploit this retreat: how dare the nationalists politicise people's refuge from the daily disempowerment of post-democratic politics? Right-wing culture war turns these last, desperate barricades of collective life into further ammunition to be used against those trying to defend it, and blames its defenders for the bombardment.

Manufacturing Consent

Scottish nationalism's continued advance in spite of these tactics reflects the particular power of nationhood to link these private reservoirs of meaning to their public defence: observe Sturgeon's repeated discussion in recent interviews of the immense burden of her political responsibility. Much of that burden is genuine, especially when it comes to running those administrative elements of the government that keep things like healthcare and education running; but that's not why she talks about it so much.

What Sturgeon offers to the Scottish people is a means of transferring, to someone more qualified and convincing than themselves, the grim, alienating work of publicly insisting on basic human decency in the face of its growing impossibility. As her Government's prioritisation of house-buyers over renters suggests, that doesn't mean she ever has to live up to her rhetoric. Again, Sturgeon's soaring approval ratings are a register of disempowerment, not a way out of it. The impossibility is factored in.

The excitement around recent independence polling has very little to do with the prospects for its political realisation, insofar as 'realisation' means the achievement of independence. The polling, to an astonishing extent, is the political realisation; for a sizeable contingent of the nationalist movement the mere demonstration of support is the goal. This is why polling figures are reported so enthusiastically on the front cover of *The National*, in full-page primary colours that transfigure data into spectacle. Spectacle, Guy Debord wrote, is "the sun which never sets over the empire of modern passivity." Its "means are simultaneously its ends." It "aims at nothing other than itself." The gigantic text-image of "YES MAJORITY: 52%" that dominates the newsstand is both the promise of self-determination and the full extent of it, in a post-democratic world where we have nothing to hope for but hope itself.

For decades, more fundamentalist nationalists have been enraged that the nation they believed in did not believe in itself, and insisted that there must be some conspiracy to divert Scotland from its natural, sovereign course. For many of these people, the new polling majorities for independence represent not years of careful persuasion and compromise – politics, in other words – but a divine revelation of the timeless national spirit. The National's readers derive far more meaning from the quantification of their cause in polling numbers and election results than they do from the messy, compromised politics hidden in the data. This 'grassroots' nationalism is characterised by a kind of passive idealism, measuring its success in terms of self-confident opinion, not power. Each further denial of power by Westminster only heightens the thrill of martyrdom, which then seeks anxiously to validate itself at the only possible terminus of national opinion: the ballot box. In devolution's sophisticated system of manufacturing consent, powerlessness breeds its own legitimation.

Political alchemy

This is perhaps the most generous way of understanding the new ruse to "game" Scotland's electoral system to secure a pro-independence supermajority in 2021. The proposal is that independence supporters split their constituency and list votes between the SNP and a largely identikit "independence party" to "Max The Yes". "Maxing" the Yes in this case means achieving a level of parliamentary representation for independence that substantially outstrips its actual popular support (something that has already been the case for years). What is baffling about this scheme is its overlap with a "Plan B" approach to independence strategy: the latter, which proposes extra-constitutional means of pressuring the UK Government, is rightly founded on the assumption that there is no level of Holyrood mandate for independence that Westminster has to obey. The relationship between "Max The Yes" and "Plan B" might be understood as an attempt to convert the artificial spectacle of an overwhelming electoral "mandate" into overwhelming extra-parliamentary force. If Holyrood defines the nation, and Holyrood has an overwhelming independence majority, then maybe through the alchemy of electoral faith the nation will stir itself into existence and take to the streets.

This is not serious political strategy but magical thinking, a collective derangement of the terminally online that has been whispered into reality by a handful of politicians, commentators and activists pursuing their own agendas, from anti-trans factionalism to Salmondista pot-stirring. As far as achieving independence is concerned, the problem with "Plan B" is that Scotland's cautiously parliamentary brand of nationalism does not translate naturally into militancy. In fact, by threatening to re-politicise the world 'outside' representation, it directly undermines the SNP's successful promise to speak on Scotland's behalf. "Max the Yes", meanwhile, is even more self-destructive. By calling the representative legitimacy of Holyrood into question, it undermines the whole edifice on which nationalism bases its popular appeal. The UK Government and unionist parties will broadcast Holyrood's faltering legitimacy to the world, and blame the nats for wrecking devolution.

Whether that is how Scottish voters will see it doesn't matter; the people who matter are the English voters who, until recently, had become increasingly comfortable with the idea that the Scottish people were genuinely moving towards independence through the legitimate, British institutions of devolution. With those institutions delegitimised as a nationalist stitch-up, it will be even easier for UK Governments to justify ignoring – and perhaps even repressing – Scottish demands in the eyes of English voters.

Decaf nation

Since the 1970s, the Scottish nationalist movement has gradually moved towards the realisation that Scotland's cultural identity is insufficient to mobilise people behind a break from Britain. Instead, independence must be a means to an end. Nicola Sturgeon has talked of two sides to her nationalism – "existential" and "instrumental". The SNP have adopted a "social democratic" identity. The "Yes" campaign gave room to the Scottish Greens, the SSP and non-party groups who made explicitly political arguments for independence, expanding the issue beyond its identitarian base.

The trajectory of the Yes movement since 2014 has abandoned most of this progress and returned nationalist ideology to the world of existential self-affirmation, its demonstrations decorated with only the most vacuous national iconography: saltires, lions rampant and unicorns. Some in that movement are now trying to replace the firmly pro-independence Scottish Greens – who want to actually do something with independence – with a fundamentalist party that boasts all the ideological nuance of an accounting scam. Nationalism's ongoing electoral success is – and will be – in spite of these people; its triumphs are powered by the stupidity, cynicism and nihilism of English politics, and the relative intelligence, principle and commitment of its existing representatives in the SNP and the Scottish Greens. The SNP's only major strategic failure has been not politically educating the mass movement they stirred into life just under a decade ago.

The reason independence still feels so far away to so many is not because the SNP are not being bold enough, but because the Scottish people have thus far demonstrated neither the means nor the will to overpower the British state for the sake of independence – or anything else. Indeed, beyond their electoral representation and the occasional public spectacle, it is hard to find evidence that the "Scottish people" even exist as a meaningful political force.

Scotland, in that sense, is just another facet of our virtual reality: coffee without caffeine, cream without fat, beer without alcohol, a nation without a people. It should come as no surprise that its nationalism has now produced a politics without a strategy.

Slavery Derived Wealth in Scotland Today

Iain MacKinnon

At the beginning of the 21st century at least 450,000 acres in the western and northern Highlands and Islands were owned by families with historical connections to transatlantic slavery. The revelations show the origins of landed power in Scotland's elite. Iain MacKinnon reports, with additional research by Andrew Mackillop.

Last month Andrew Mackillop and I published a report disclosing connections between landownership in the west Highlands and Islands of Scotland and the profits of plantation slavery. The full report, published as part of Community Land Scotland's discussion paper series on 'Land and the Common Good', is available here ("New research reveals extent of historical links between plantation slavery and landownership in the west Highlands and Islands".)

"Scores of estates in the West Highlands and Islands were acquired by people using the equivalent of well over £100m worth of riches connected to slavery in the Caribbean and North America. Many would go on to be leading figures in the Highland Clearances, evicting thousands of people whose families had lived on their newly procured land for generations. These are amongst the conclusions of a research paper titled 'Plantation slavery and landownership in the

263

west Highlands and Islands: legacies and lessons' published today, by two university academics – both from Hebridean backgrounds."

The report detailed research that discovered at least 63 estate purchases made by direct or indirect beneficiaries of slavery in the years between 1726 and 1939. These purchases covered more than 1.1 million acres of the west Highlands and Islands and the majority took place during the main period of the Highland clearances, with a peak occurring in the years immediately following the award of £20 million – £16 billion in today's terms – compensation for slave-owners for loss of their slaves as 'property' when slavery was abolished.

Including traditional families who already owned land in the area, slavery beneficiaries have owned a total of around 1.8 million acres in the west Highlands and Islands – amounting to more than 50 per cent of the area's land-mass, and approaching 10 per cent of the entire landmass of Scotland.

Our report was a historical account, although it referred to some of the consequences of these historical developments on the area today. During an interview that Andrew and I gave to the BBC Radio Scotland Out of Doors programme about our report we argued that our findings have the potential to be the beginning of an important, if at times uncomfortable, discussion involving landed proprietors about the importance of slavery derived wealth on the nature of landownership and use in the Highlands today, of which private estates are still a major part.

The Out of Doors team took us at our word and approached Scottish Land and Estates, a representative body for large landowners and country businesses, to get their views. Their chief executive told the programme that 'it is a bit of a stretch to leap from a review of social history and ancient connections to slavery as being a reason why communities should own land today.'

What follows is a response not only to the factual aspects of the statement from Scottish Land and Estate but a questioning of its underlying assumptions. Beginning with the latter: strictly speaking, the ancient period is that time in history before the medieval, and its end is generally dated at around 600AD. Our account of slavery beneficiaries buying land in Scotland is almost entirely late modern history. In the wider historical understanding, this is as close to contemporary history as it gets.

Over and above the statement's telling attempt to put chronological distance between current landholding structures in the west Highlands and Islands and British slavery, there is the one-dimensional understanding of history. Landlords consistently seek to benefit from the historical traditions and stories associated with their land and with their houses and castles. Past connections are readily, and understandably, utilised by Scottish Land and Estates to enable heritage tourism and generate a particular version of the Highlands and indeed Scotland in general. Dismissing one element of the past as irrelevant while promoting and deploying another version as key to the contemporary economic and revenue basis of many landed estates is not conducive to a fully informed and effective discussion of land, land use and community in the Highlands.

Then there are matters of accuracy. In the statement SLE's chief executive added: 'Indeed the authors of this paper admit themselves there are few if any families in the area who are major landowners today and who have any past connection to slavery.'

For the record, we didn't say this and it is not true.

Our report did not detail contemporary ownership by families with historical slavery links. However, in response to SLE's inaccurate representation of our work, and drawing on Andy Wightman's research published in 1996, we estimate that at the beginning of the 21st century at least 450,000 acres in the western and northern Highlands and Islands were owned by families with historical connections to slavery. For the avoidance of doubt, here is a list of landowners and acreages:

House of Sutherland 83,239
Cameron of Lochiel 76,000
Wills in Applecross 62,000
Duke of Argyll 60,800
Mackenzie of Gairloch 57,600

Burton of Dochfour 48,000

Macleod of Macleod (Dunvegan and Glenbrittle on Skye) 30,600

Schroder (Dunlossit on Islay) 16,500

Ellice (Invergarry & Aberchalder) 15,000

Martin of Husabost 5,200

Maclean of Duart 300

The only landholding in this list that is not taken from Andy Wightman's work is the Maclean of Duart estate on Mull which includes the clan seat of Duart Castle but which is too small a holding to feature in Wightman's analysis. The landowners given here don't map directly onto 'the west Highlands and Islands' as defined in the report, as we have added the Duke of Argyll whose main landholdings today are in mainland Argyll and the House of Sutherland whose holdings are today all in Sutherland. However, both families owned land in the nineteenth century in the west Highlands and Islands as we defined it in the report, and the Argyll family still hold some land there today. Further research may well confirm indicative evidence that the descendants of other families currently holding land in the Highlands were connected to the economy of enslavement.

We have not closely studied recent land transfers in the area, but understand that there has been relatively little movement of land among families connected with slavery since Andy Wightman's book was published. The late Lord Burton (who was actually a member of the Baillie of Dochfour family whose eighteenth and nineteenth century history is saturated by slavery) sold substantial west coast estates early in the twenty-first century, although the family are still major landowners elsewhere in the Highlands. It is understood that the although the representative of Martin of Husabost family died in recent years, the estate is still in family hands. However, the wider point remains. It's likely that somewhere between 400,000 and 500,000 acres of the western and northern Highlands today are in the hands of families which have benefitted from the profits of slavery.

That is not an insignificant amount. Indeed, it is that not much less than the acreage owned by the entire community land sector across Scotland at present. This comparison is one of many reasons why these important if uncomfortable discussions about the ways in which slavery derived wealth has shaped the current structure and patterns of landownership, and use, in Scotland need to take place. Contributions from landed proprietors are not only welcome but are an important element in such debates. But this input should be based on a holistic rather than selective understanding of the past and needs to be based on the facts.

Patriarchy, Theocracy and Tragedy: The Dark Shadow of Ireland's Mother and Baby Homes

Cait O'Neill McCullagh

Ireland's Mother and Baby Homes Commission Report: a mirror held up to the power of dominance, socialised diffidence and our own need to 'de-link' and connect.

On the 5 February 1984, people across Ireland – and throughout that worldly 'other' Ireland – the diaspora of millions living in London, Liverpool, Glasgow, Cardiff, New York, and right across the mapped circuit of the globe – read of the death of 15 year old Ann Lovett, and of her not-even-moments born, baby son, in Granard, County Longford, under the shade of a grotto shrine, like so many in Ireland, dedicated to Mary, both mother of God, and virgin; known to many Irish, in a kind of intimate-distancing, as 'Our Lady'. I recall my own 15-year-old self, reading the story in the pages of the *Leinster Express* and *The Kerryman*. These were our 'glocal' newspapers, bought every Sunday by my Irish migrant parents – living at that time in London – between attending mass; reciting their rosary prayers, and sitting down to a dinner of boiled ham, cabbage and spuds. This tricolor feast of green, white, and rose-gold scented the streets of our home-away-from-home neighbourhood of fellow Irish patriots. We were all, together,

269

suspended in the between-ness of being, in the sparsely descriptive language of the present day, economic migrants, settling for a time unspecified outwith the pale. Our culture – imbibed through novenas, nuns, and nights of porter and Powers whiskey, and singing from the back pages of the *Ireland's Own* magazine – was an intense and heady distillation through nostalgia of the Ireland of our parent's childhoods. It was an Ireland in large part created out of the union of church and state – the consummation of a particular relationship between morality and legislature in the precarity of the third decade of the twentieth century.

I remember the affective flow of furious, adolescent empathy as I pored over this story of a girl giving birth, in solitude, in the interminable Spring rain of an Irish Midlands town, with only a pair of scissors stashed into her pocket to cut the cord of nine months sustaining between her own body and that of her child. Like me, Ann was a convent schoolgirl, born in 1968, to parents who, themselves, had been born into the renovation of a becoming Republic, captained by Éamon de Valera, Taoiseach from 1937 – 1948. And like me, I imagined, in my own girl's heart-mind, that for Ann, that the one thing more terrible than enduring labour and giving birth for the first time, alone, and of losing her hold on that life, for herself and her newborn – poured out into a rain soaked road under the fixed, and distant, gaze of a statue – was to admit to being pregnant and unmarried.

In this last week, approaching the anniversary of Ann and her son's shared and lonely deaths – recounted in this recent article from the Irish Times – I have minded them both, while following news of the release of the Mother and Baby Homes Commission of Investigation's report, describing the containment of pregnant women and girls, and the births; confinements; dispersal into uncharted adoptions, and the too many deaths of their children in these religious and county run homes. The pitiful conditions of these homes-away-from-homes were also set up by 'Ireland's Own' – the polity that was generated in that union between a domiciled Roman Catholic Church and the governance of the Irish State – and continued to be upheld by them until 1998. These were conditions that Ann, herself, might reasonably have expected to experience, were her pregnancy to have become a public admission – both through her own volition, and, in that environment of the entangling of ethics; morality, and large government, through that of her family and community.

In considering how it can be that a family, and the wider kith and kin of a small town would not notice the pregnancy of one of their own, I looked to why my own engagement with these lives had been so urgent. It seems to us now – in these islands to the east of Ireland – in present-day Scotland, that we are separated by the undeniable physicality of the Irish sea. And yet, for millennia this water has been a road of 'community transmission' – to use phrase now commonplace in this time of pandemic.

The Irish communities making their worlding here were bound by the connective threads, and inter-generational flow, of a pervasive culture and historicity, that, along with the institution of the Mother and Baby Homes – founded also in Scotland and England – has accompanied their flitting, and becoming and belonging across these waters. Included in this transnational wave of belonging, are traits and behaviours that were cultivated through Ireland's postcolonial condition – a need to enact exceptionalism and differentiate from an instantiation of 'Britain', or more specifically, the imperial environment. This identity-building was vulnerable to reifying a pastiche coloniality. The new republic had not yet had the time or process to mature into the de-colonial thinking that activist academic, Walter Mignolo, describes as a 'pluri-versal' way of knowing; the kind of knowing that is needed for assembling more just, and therefore, more sustainable futures. For Mignolo, it is the sustenance of connectivity between all people – sharing and reflecting upon different, and also comparable, empathetic experiences, in a worldly, decolonial intent – that enables us to participate in 'an epistemology [de-linking] from the tyranny of abstract universals' [1]. To cultivate freedom with all folk, is to disentangle from the paradigm of dominant power that, from early modernity, has colonised the ways we produce and value knowledge, and whose knowledges; experiences, and voices are valued and heard. Among such abstractions, Mignolo includes those ideological traditions espoused in Christianity, Marxism and libertarianism that have been mobilised by the hegemony as totalising worldviews.

The particular vulnerability of twentieth century Ireland – likely generated by the perceived 'unusuability' of its colonial past – did not facilitate this 'de-linking' from the cultural and intellectual influences of this dominant paradigm. Pasts, undeliberated, because they are painful; complex; nuanced, and so consigned to the oubliette of public life, are not disappeared. They linger, ghosting our communities, and societies, and our future worlding. The non-reflexive suspension of key, formative aspects in the historicity of Irish people, trapped like relict wasp, preserved in amber, sustained the residue of imperium suspended in the expressions of a patriarchal society, still burdened, and burdening its members, with the weighty, unconscious power of internalised subjugation. Sociologist Avery Gordon has written about such haunting and its being a way in which abusive systems of power make themselves known; when the apparently 'over and done with' come alive.[2]

For Ann Lovett; for the mothers and children in Tuam; Bessborough; Stranorlar, and the 15 other institutions investigated for the Commission's report, and for the descendants of Irish people, scattered throughout the diaspora, this burden metastasised as the specific fear of 'bringing shame'. For the people that gave service to the idea that women and children could be institutionalised as they entered the life passage of birthing, this fear was valorised through an interpretation of a particular anthropology in Christian thinking, which Richard Holloway, former Primus of the Scottish Episcopal Church, has identified as 'the crushing idea that, simply by being born, human beings inherit a sinful, fallen nature, like a congenital virus that can only be remedied by extraordinary methods'[3]. In a state seeking to impose its 'Own' order across the uncertainty of change, it seems that the transmission of this viral fear inundated the still present embodying of the spaces of subordination created in the difficult past.

In the days following the joint funeral of Ann, and her posthumously named baby, Pat, the people of Granard, and of Ireland, more generally, constellated around one poignant question – 'how could this have happened, here?'. This same question has underpinned the reeling-keening reflex throughout contemporary Irish society, following the revelations of the living and dying, and cursory burying of 798 children at the home in Tuam. The names of each of these children have also been broadcast posthumously, through the vigilance and painstaking research of historian Catherine Corless, who grew up in Tuam, alongside the home, and whose ontology of commitment to the absent presence of these buried lives and stories has been a catalyst for the mandating of the Commission.

I am sharing these personal reflections, invoked by this recent, further opening-out of the experiences of thousands women and children across the expanses of Irish society in the mid to late twentieth century, not to deflect from the apparently casually incompassionate, and – in the words of the Dáil's elected representative for Galway West, Catherine Connelly – 'inhumane' aggressions inflicted upon those who found themselves the subjects of the state's solution to a constructed and then widely socialised problem. In truth, their stories are not mine to tell. Their voices still need to be encouraged, to be articulated apart from what Deputy Connelly has identified as a banalisation of the narrative in the report itself. Rather, I hope to share a connective perspective and an invitation to continue making connections; to propose that we understand these specific treatments of particular Irish women and children as examples of a global structural and systemic 'othering' – the isolation and marginalisation of specific groups of people to expedite constructivist, reductive and populist readings and applications of ideologies. These girls and women became pregnant in a variety of contexts including denial of access to knowledge, statutory rape, incest, and – we must acknowledge – through the generative gift of love itself. They were institutionalised within the paradigm of the mass socialisation of an idea that was germinated in a milieu where food, land, opportunity, and, it seems, the choice to be in the relationality of love, itself, were experienced as scarce resources. When we look now at a system that allowed for the poverty of compassion around these mothers and their children, I believe that we are also looking at a universally relatable phenomena – the social dispersal of pain.

In a post-colonial Ireland – itself experiencing still the birthing pangs of individuation as a nation, and calculating the economic costs and psycho-cultural labour of maintaining the long view of attaining independence from Britain – it was the unwed mothers and their babies who were applied like lint to the fissuring; absorbing a society-wide experience akin to what Australian Professor of Sustainability, Glenn Albrecht has characterised as 'Solastalgia'. This pain through lack of solace, is, Albrecht argues, unlike nostalgia the 'homesickness experienced by individuals when separated from a loved home ... is the distress that is produced by environmental change impacting on people while they are directly connected to their home environment'[4]. To see the in the granular detail of other's lives, the connections to our own reality; as it were, a perspective offered by the cosmological mirror of imagination and empathy that unites all living beings, is not a deflection – nor the glib reflex of false equivalence – but, rather a way of deepening our reflection upon the particularities of each one.

In this mirroring, as the names of the children and parents and the Mother and Baby institutions reported upon last week, are recovered and recalled, we might ask, along with the people of Ann Lovett's Granard, 'how could this have happened?'. We might, also, find ourselves in reflexive self-preservation, calling out 'it could never happen here'. But it has, in all our 'heres', including in the so-named asylums that, in regions throughout Scotland, operated as social oubliettes for the keeping out of sight and mind of 'them': people with intellectual disabilities, neuro diversity, and countless other conditions and ways of being that were characterised as aberrant. It continues to happen in the marginalisation of contemporary asylum seekers and the de-personalisation, including disenfranchisement, of all who are currently migrating and settling and, together, looking for becoming and belonging in the Scotland we are today – highlighted in aspects of the work of researchers in Scotland including Philomena de Lima, Katerina Strani-Jefferson and Lina Fadel. There is a call to us all in Catherine Connelly's plea, directed to her fellows in the Dáil Éireann. It is an invocation to desist from naturalising, and turning into social truths, popularist values formed without giving time to pluralised debate, the dialogue that enables meaningful engagement of thought and action.

Such collaboratively deliberated thinking and acting is based on developing the kind of critical attentiveness modelled by Tuam's Catherine Corless. Such a practice is an education in attention with and for all people, including with ourselves. As European and Scottish ethnologist Ulrich Kockel proposes, this learning comes from quickening our interest in people's actions, and their contexts of environment and historicity[5] – the way people understand themselves as having pasts, in this present, and in the futures these understandings are shaping. Edinburgh-based and Whalsay-formed anthropologist, A. P. Cohen, calls this knowing how to know, 'appropriate knowledge'[6]. It is a concept far from the appropriative power of omniscience that dominates the worldview of societies that, as Mary Ratfery[7] wrote of twentieth century Ireland – and most of the world – are governed through a 'dangerous reality' that in positioning some of its members as inferior, a society inculcates diffidence to the way they are treated. This diffidence also inures us to awareness, attentiveness and vigilance concerning who is visible, and who is made invisible, in our societies.

To understand how forming values influences behaviours, decision-making and consequences, we need to seek out out the lived experiences of people who appear to be 'not us'. And we need also to make strange what has become all too familiar, naturalised, facing into our own individual, community, and national historicity, including the hauntings we might prefer to remain invisible, silenced, and indeed, buried. Understanding where we are, and we how got here does not mean giving ourselves up to versions of history that will appropriate us in a grasp of 'pastness'. What it can be is a process of recovery, a rigorous concern to identify; know appropriately, and practice the intention of de-linking from the harmful entanglements that persist in our present – those abstractions that distract us from connection and from realising futures that are just and sustaining, in a Scotland, and in a world, where all lives are can be welcomed, named, and 'let leave to live'[8].

[1] Mignolo, W. (2007) 'Introduction', *Cultural Studies*, 21(2-3), 155-167.

[2] Gordon, A. F. (2008) *Ghostly Matters: Haunting and the Sociological Imagination*, Minneapolis: University of Minnesota Press, p.165f.

[3] Holloway, R. (1999) *Godless Morality: Keeping Religion out of Ethics*. Edinburgh: Canongate, p.46f.

[4] Albrecht, G., Sartore, G.M., Connor, L., Higginbotham, N., Freeman, S., Kelly, B., Stain, H., Tonna, A. and Pollard, G. (2007) ' Solastalgia: the distress caused by environmental change', *Australasian Psychiatry*, 15(sup1), S95-S98.

[5] Kockel, U. (2007) 'Reflexive Traditions and Heritage Production', in Kockel, U. and Nic Craith, M. (eds.) *Cultural Heritages as Reflexive Traditions*, Basingstoke, Hampshire: Palgrave MacMillan, 19–33.

[6] Cohen, A. P. (1993) 'Segmentary knowledge: a Whalsay sketch', in Hobart, M. (ed.) *An Anthropological Critique of Development: The growth of Ignorance*, London: Routledge, 31-42.

[7] Raftery, M. and O'Sullivan, E. (1999) *Suffer the Little children: The Inside Story of Ireland's Industrial Schools*, Dublin: New Island Books.

[8] Shepherd, N. Shepherd (2008) *The Living Mountain: A Celebration of the Cairngorm Mountains of Scotland*, Edinburgh: Canongate Books.

Passing the Mundair Test

Raman Mundair

Raman Mundair presents an idea — akin to the Bechdel Test — on how we should assess the artistic and creative representation of people of colour (PoC) in theatre and other forms of broadcasting.

When I heard about Rebecca Hall's film *Passing*- based on Nella Larsen's 1920s novel that explores the practice of racial passing — I immediately wondered what skin did Hall have in the game. I wasn't aware that Hall is actually of mixed heritage — a complicated ancestry that includes African American roots, yet this was not something that immediately comes to mind when I consider the body of her work.

It's common in our culture to know titbits about our celebrities so why did we never hear about this aspect of her life? Perhaps it was thought irrelevant, or maybe of no value? Or did it seem like a fact that disturbed the Rebecca Hall brand? Hall is frequently cast as the smart, understated femme fatale, or a rare English rose. Does it matter? It does. I have no doubt my 7, 9 and 11 year old self would have felt differently had I known Freddie Mercury was Indian in heritage. My school life would have been different had I known that the rock stars my white peers were revering like Slash and Eddie van Halen were not in fact white.

I am a fan of old black and white movies, and have enjoyed them from childhood. I would have had a different experience had I known that Merle Oberon was in fact of Indian heritage. Oberon was born in India to an Indian mother. She ascended to stardom through suppressing her origins and Oberon, rather than disown her mother, passed her off as a servant. Carol Channing, John Gavin and Raquel Welch are amongst the stars I watched and later learned were all passing.

And then there is the music industry – where we find Norah Jones whose father was no less than the maestro Ravi Shanker and more recently Charli XCX – who is of Gujarati and Scottish heritage. XCX is the mastermind behind the fabricated indie pop group Nasty Cherry – an experiment in popular culture engineered by XCX as an attempt to create the group she says she would have liked to see growing up. Yet Nasty Cherry is far from diverse and on the surface presents as four, edgy, Gen X, white girls. On closer inspection I find that the lead singer does in fact have Latino heritage but this is not part of the identity she asserts. Her chosen community is a white hipster space. She is not presented as rooted in a diverse heritage or from a wider community with a rich, complex, thriving culture. Instead she is aspirationally white.

To see positive representation of myself as a person of colour (PoC) in the arts makes a huge difference to me and would have made my younger self feel a little cool, a little less hidden, quiet shame of feeling wrong and out of place. It would have encouraged the possibility and freedom to think that I could be rock and roll. That I could be Hollywood. That I could be the National Theatre. That I could be Top of the Pops. That I could be the National Opera. That I could be ballet. Representation matters. Passing is a warped privilege. It is a twisted head-space that robs our imagination. Yet, it is, of course, a survival strategy. It's about presenting yourself in a palatable, acceptable, non-threatening way in order to exist and function in the sea of default whiteness we all swim in. But it murders more than it allows to take root and live. It's worth clarifying that the term 'whiteness' does not describe white people, but instead the insidious and attritional impact of the underlying and systemic power structures of white majority communities and culture.

Passing in this context is a form of operating and surviving whiteness and white majority communities. It comes into play when you are unable to be the non-threatening exception, the only person of colour in the village, town, office etc. As a person of colour you may find yourself in a context where your cultural capital and stature is measured in relation to whether you are an exception – the only Black person, Black family in the village for example as opposed to being a member of a growing, functioning and blooming, wider Black community.

A tragic yet interesting feature of this is that it can impact the way PoC see ourselves and each other. An example of this is when a PoC has capital in a predominantly white community, space or culture and another PoC arrives, joins or is employed. Often there isn't immediate solidarity, if at all. Because the oppressive structures and systems of whiteness create an environment where a PoC's sense of personal safety is attached to being the exception, the only one, the novelty, which in essence all asserts one thing to whiteness: I am not a threat.

Another PoC arriving disturbs this survival strategy. The first PoC feels threatened because their security exists in being the only one. Safety is being scarce and on the down-low, being of use and interest. Having a role, serving a need, but not presenting as being part of something wider, bigger, stronger. Not asserting that you are from a rich, powerful cultural heritage and ongoing community that in fact has a history that precedes whiteness.

Recently I heard the brilliantly eloquent Marcus Ryder, an academic, executive producer and co-author of 'Access All Areas: The Diversity Manifesto for TV and Beyond,' talk about representation and ideas of community. He asserts that currently, what we are used to seeing is single or 'exceptional' Black and brown characters. They are often the only Black character inhabiting a functioning white community or a majority white community.

Black communities on screen on the other hand, are portrayed almost exclusively as dysfunctional. While many of the Black people portrayed in a drama set in a non white community may be likeable, the community they are set in is normally seen as anything but.

The message that comes across loud and clear is that while there might be good Black and brown individuals, Black and brown communities are a problem. Black and brown communities are 'others' to be feared, to be reviled, to be treated with suspicion. It suggests that if you are a good, positive Black person you should want to leave the dysfunctional Black communities as quickly as possible. That representation of Black and brown characters intrinsically include aspiration towards a proximity to whiteness.

These are of course unspoken, coded messages. They are set up and we are primed to read them. We are constantly imbibing these implicit negative views about Black communities and we'll often see similar messages about South Asians on screen – where there might be positive, individuals from the Indian subcontinent, the community is invariably problematic – the trope that is perpetuated is a community that promotes forced marriages and creates potential terrorists. The same with Arab communities and East Asian communities (tired tropes where communities can't speak English, run a restaurant or shop, are obsessed with money, gambling and gang culture etc.) Yet in reality the fact is while dysfunctional Black and brown communities certainly do exist [as there are dysfunctional white communities], there are also good, positive functional and flourishing Black and brown communities.

What we need to see in terms of representation and what resonates with and changes people, is the portrayal of community and this is what has been missing in so much of the diversity debate. An example of this is the award winning television drama, Killing Eve. We do not see any reference to Sandra Oh's character's Korean heritage, until she has left her white husband, lost her job – a job where she is predominantly working with white people, and she has hit a complete emotional and psychological rock bottom. At that point, she takes a job in the most stereotypical of East Asian occupations – she works in a Korean restaurant. It occurs to me that the writer and producers probably thought that this was a stroke of diversity enhancing genius, but the way it actually lands is this: although they cast Sandra Oh in a role originally written as a white character, they failed to represent her as rooted in a community that is held in high regard, status or value.

The subtle messaging is that no-one would ever want to be part of this particular community if they could avoid it. The character Sandra plays only returns to this community when all is lost and she has nowhere else to turn. What is this telling us? That specifically in this character's case, her power and autonomy lies in the context of whiteness and not in her community and heritage. The message is you may share some of your community and heritage if you must but only in small, palatable, preferably food related contexts. This sounds very familiar to me. It's the same wider societal messaging around diversity and culture: we allow your food, music etc. to cross borders, to exist within whiteness on a commodified basis but we don't want the communities this abundance is rooted in.

When there is representation that exists outside the context of whiteness, such as the 2020 Sainsbury Christmas advert depicting a happy, warm, Black family enjoying Christmas dinner, it resonates and was welcomed by Black people. Why? Because it shows a happy functioning Black family in the context of their community. It represented the powerful, implicit possibility that Black people can be happy without white people. It's not stating that white people make the Black family unhappy, it's not about racial trauma, it's the revolutionary idea that as a Black person you can be happy and whole with your own and that you don't need white people to achieve happiness. This clearly was a radical, new imagining and representation and it clearly touched a nerve and the reception the advert received is not at all surprising. If Killing Eve had been set up in this way we would have seen Sandra Oh's character maintaining her power and happiness and being part of a functional Korean community.

BLM and the murder of George Floyd has seen a lot of people within the creative industries reflect on issues of race and representation and this has taken on more urgency and there is a buzz around the concept of Authentic Representation. What is not clear or fully realised is what this would actually consist of and what does it look like? Ryder suggests that it must fundamentally include representation rooted in community. I would agree and go a little further.

Recently British East and Southeast Asian media advocacy group, BEATS, rolled out a ground-breaking new representation measure for the U.K. broadcasting industry. The initiative is fashioned after the Bechdel Test, which evaluates portrayals of women in media, and the Riz Test, a measurement of Muslim representation inspired by Riz Ahmed's rallying 2017 speech about diversity.

I propose the Mundair Test. A simple checklist which should be considered at the start of projects rather than tacked on as an afterthought or token gesture.

I call for the following when it comes to artistic and creative representation of people of colour (PoC) in theatre and all forms of broadcasting:

Representation that shows PoC:

-rooted in communities, not just their own but how they code switch between other spaces and belong in multiple spaces.

— in functioning friendships, relationships & communities that mirror their heritage.

— in the intersections of different worlds and experiences in a nuanced way and reflects actual PoC lived experience.

— happiness is not dependant on white people.— do not exist to compliment a white character but are a fundamental part of the narrative and have a functioning world outside of whiteness.

– without a focus on race based tragedy and trauma – that is to say that it should not be the sole intent of why the PoC exists in the narrative and that is all that they can bring in terms of their character's story.

– communities across class in a nuanced way. We are not all in gangs, living on estates or running corner shops or high caste medical professionals.

– with functioning visible or hidden disability that doesn't focus on tragedy or trauma.

– queerness that doesn't focus on tragedy, trauma or hyper sexualisation.

– women that doesn't exoticise, fetishize or involve any hyper sexualisation of them.

In short, I call for representation that affords PoC the same humanity and complexity that whiteness offers itself. Seeing and showing ourselves and representing PoC as part of a community and not in isolation is a revolutionary act. It shows we survived. We thrived. We stood our ground. We connected and forged a community. Being part of a community is not only subversive, it is seen as an outright threat and we rarely see it represented well or with any integrity or authenticity.

White systems, structures and establishment intuitively know this, perhaps on a deep, buried level. They know that presenting a mirror that reflects, uplifts and truly represents PoC simultaneously destabilises the sense of white self and that's precisely why they choose not to do it, encourage or reward it.

Mainstream awards like the Oscars and Golden Globes are perhaps a questionable barometer of success but what gets left out is significant and casts a glaring light on what is seen as more palatable and mainstream. The fact that Michaela Coel's I May Destroy You was left out of all the categories for the Golden Globes announced recently is very telling. Coel decolonised British drama and successfully created a world that showed PoC rooted in community and friendship and not reliant on whiteness for happiness. Her Black characters were authentic, true and engaging and had genuine autonomy and that is something we rarely see. We should be beyond passing and making ourselves palatable, we deserve authentic representation that offers a chance to re-calibrate tired narratives and offer quality art and entertainment that actually makes a difference.

Prince Philip was the Godfather of Anglo-British Nationalism

Adam Ramsay

In the year before Prince Philip was born, 1920, the British empire was the largest it would ever be. The year after he was born, 1922, Charles Francis Jenkins demonstrated the first principles of the television.

The changes driven by decolonisation and the invention of the modern media, between them, could easily have ended the reign of the House of Windsor. The fact that they didn't, the success of the British monarchy in transitioning from the divine rulers at the apex of history's biggest empire to the celebrities at the centre of a modern nationalist project built on TV and the tabloids, was, in large part, because of the duke of Edinburgh, who died today at 99.

As chair of the Queen's coronation committee in 1953, Philip proposed a radical idea: why not televise it? The result was the most-watched TV show in history at the time, doing more than anything else to make television a mainstream medium.

The next day, a *Daily Express* journalist wrote that the show "set up brilliant new standards in linking the crown with the people"; viewers, he said, "virtually rode with the Queen through London and stood near to her in the ancient Abbey itself".

By grabbing such a vast audience and directly — or so it seemed — involving them in the once-distant rituals of the state, Philip fathered a whole new phenomenon. And the tension between the institutions he pulled together — TV, the tabloids, and the monarchy — became the tripod on which Anglo-British nationalism hung, as the empire fell apart.

Philip also became an icon of this world view: his racist 'jokes' were carefully delivered in a cheeky tone as if he was a naughty boy mocking some kind of power, when in reality, he was the one with the power. It's a tone he perfected: I remember him using it when we joked together on the three occasions I met him. But what they hid was something more insidious.

Philip's uncle and mentor, Louis Mountbatten, was the man who did more than anyone else to partition India. Indeed it was extraordinary that William Windsor named his son Louis after one of the greatest criminals of late empire and yet has since gone on to say the monarchy is "very much not a racist family".

The atrocities of the late British empire — from concentration camps in Malaysia to castrations in Kenya — were quietly ignored. The decorative function of the monarchy was always intended to mask the violence of the state, and Philip played a vital role in bringing that screen to life in the 20th century.

If modern nations are imagined communities convened by the media and feudal states were family affairs, then the new relationship he arranged fused the one with the other, giving birth to a gaudy heritage of Churchillism, imperial revisionism, Thatcherism and, most recently, Brexit.

Of course this relationship was always tense. But it was Diana who briefly mastered it, before it killed her. As Anthony Barnett has argued in his book *The Lure of Greatness*, she transformed herself into the first celebrity populist, who Trump obsessed over.

Now, the godfather of Anglo-British nationalism has died just as it enters a crisis, with riots in Northern Ireland as Loyalists realise the risk of Ireland uniting, elections in Scotland likely to advance the movement for independence, the Harry-and-Meghan rift and a deep loss of faith in the British ruling class.

And so we can expect the institutions of the Anglo-British nation to desperately peddle their usual message. The BBC's Nicholas Witchell, a wibbling belligerent of monarchical propaganda, is already prostrating himself on television. Tomorrow, the tabloids will smear themselves in red, white and blue. Conservative politicians and the Labour figures who like to hide behind them will bellow mournful tears of sorrow.

But the truth is that 99-year-olds die, and their eras dissipate.

TV and tabloids are no longer the vivid and exciting formats they once were. They've been replaced with social media and streaming websites, which have formed different kinds of audience: audiences who aren't amazed simply to be allowed to watch the affairs of state, but insist on participating in them; audiences who it's much harder to bind into national borders and tell which 'we' they belong to. Audiences who, through their connections with each other, find their understandings of the world start to shift. Audiences who, in the case of Netflix's 'The Crown' are now able to access a less propagandised version of their history than the British press presents.

Harry and Meghan's split from the royal family was driven by this divide: they wouldn't tolerate being bound into the toxic racism of tabloid Britain, and instead launched themselves as a transatlantic king and queen of Instagram. And they represent a generation. Anglo-British nationalism has largely failed to make the leap into modern media. For younger generations on the UK's periphery, Scottish, Welsh, and Irish or Northern Irish identities are more common. And for England, who knows?

Anglo-British nationalism was already waning. Today, its godfather passed away. And once its mother has gone, who knows how long it will survive?

The rise, fall and rise of party and movement and the Changing Idea of Scotland

Gerry Hassan

The National Movement in Scotland, Jack Brand, Routledge

The SNP have been in existence for a long time and a serious electoral force since the 1960s. But at the same time there have been few studies of the party that have contextualised it within the wider nationalist movement and the changing nature of Scotland, and that have attempted to analyse and understand the dynamics of this relationship.

The National Movement in Scotland by the late Jack Brand, a political scientist at Strathclyde University, is a landmark study of the party and wider currents, first published in 1978 and now given a timely republication by Routledge in its 'Routledge Library Editions: Scotland' series alongside an impressive number of titles earmarked for bringing back into print.

Brand's study came at a critical time in not just the evolution of the SNP but of the constitutional debate – and in Scotland's understanding of itself. It caught the SNP on a rising tide of support and momentum, which had become evident from the mid-1960s, that saw them breakthrough electorally in 1974 when devolution become one of the central issues of Scottish and British politics.

Brand's book goes up to the year before the ill-fated 1979 devolution referendum and ascendancy of Thatcherism – all of which put Scottish politics in cold storage for a period including the SNP.

Brand explores a variety of factors to assess if they potentially contributed to the rise of the SNP and the nationalist movement. He addresses the changing nature of the Scottish economy and in particular growth and unemployment in relation to the rest of the UK; class politics and voting; Scottish identity; literary nationalism and the role of intellectuals; younger people and generational change; and the role of Scottish institutions such as the media, churches and football.

Even with the passing of time this is a riveting study, offering insights into thinking on the Scotland of the 1970s that shed light on the present and on current debates. Brand contends that the old traditional Scotland before the rise of the SNP was 'a leaderless nation' – a place with distinctive authorities and institutions but where a large part of elite society defined themselves in relation to England and London where political and economic power sat.

Brand's opines that numerous actors contributed to the rise of the SNP. There was the post-war relative economic divergence between Scotland and the rest of the UK around the period 1958-59 when Scottish unemployment hit 100,000 for the first time post-1945, against the backdrop of Macmillan's Toryism boasting that 'you've never had it so good' – a comment which didn't translate well into a Scottish environment. The subsequent UK 1959 election produced a Tory majority of 100 seats but saw Scotland deviate from the UK pattern and swing to Labour: a pattern which continued in 1964 when Labour were returned across the UK.

This was in the context of class politics changing, dissatisfaction with the Conservative and Labour parties; and the older institutional anchors such as religion and deference beginning to wither. All of this contributed to a new political landscape emerging – one conducive to the SNP which the party aided from the early 1960s onward by becoming an organised, disciplined force that could run campaigns and make an impact at by-elections even before Hamilton.

Remaking the idea of Scotland

The sum of this was that Scotland was remade as a political space and nation, as Brand observed of the 1960s: 'For the first time since the late 1920s Scotland was the centre of her own stage undistracted by foreign wars or worries.' Discussions about Scotland's relative economic performance brought forth a debate about the role of the UK Government and economic policy, while intervention by Scottish agencies such as the Toothill Report of 1961 contributed to a growing awareness of Scotland as a nation and economic territory: Brand writing that this 'made Scottish people more and more conscious of Scotland as an economic unit.'

One observation of Brand's argument with the passing of time is that beyond the political and economic he is more general and less specific about this evolution of the idea of Scotland. For example, he cites the changing behaviour of football crowds at the Scottish men's national team, moving from in the mid-1960s singing 'God Save the Queen' to by the 1970s booing it and subsequently replacing it with 'Flower of Scotland'.

Also touched upon is the revival of folk music in the 1950s and 1960s and the role of the likes of Hamish Henderson and Maurice Blythman, and the connection to the emerging anti-nuclear weapons movement in Scotland and the rest of the UK over the same period – which produced a counter-culture where new songs of folk resistance were needed such as 'Ding Dong Dollar'.

What Brand doesn't fully address is the substance of the UK Government decision to place nuclear weapons in Scotland – with the US asking the UK for basing rights in November 1959, the first deployment at Holy Loch occurring in March 1961, and the decision on British Polaris confirmed in March 1963. The timing and salience of this issue overlapped with the economic debate about Scotland and contributed further to a growing awareness of a distinctive Scottish political culture, it being no accident that the rise of CND contributed to a new generation of radical young voices identifying with the SNP.

Another dimension that Brand doesn't explore at length is the geo-political and international framework of Scotland. Instead, he draws from an approach focusing on the internal dynamics of Scotland, leaving unexplored a detailed exploration of external factors. This discussion was alive at the time Brand was writing in numerous debates – including between historian T.C. Smout and Immanuel Wallerstein where the latter positioned Scotland's experience in changes in the global system of political economy, capitalism and imperialism. In this, the return of the idea of Scotland as a political force is linked to the crisis of Empire and the world system theory of capitalism.

Brand's account is commendable – and even more so in hindsight – as we can locate it in a contested transitional place about the decline of the old Scotland, its place in the UK and within the global economy. In the period preceding this a host of prominent Scottish writers were prone to apologise for the state of the country or underplay its potential.

James Kellas who was a trailblazer in academia and making study of Scottish politics respectable wrote in his 1968 *Modern Scotland* that: 'Only a leisured, wealthy society can support organised culture, and Scotland has never had such a society' – so much for 'the swinging sixties' in Scotland. Similarly, the nationalist writer Moray McLaren wrote in 1965 that 'a national movement ... [has] no place in the brief history of the Scottish nation' – this being despite his wish to will one into existence. This world was turned upside down by the breakthrough of the SNP in the 1960s, that scholars like Brand were trying to find a counter-explanation to the above sentiments.

Scotland from the 1970s to the present

More than forty years after it was written *The National Movement in Scotland* is still relevant, reaching down through the years to the present, providing historic insights centred on a critical period of flux and crisis that speak to current considerations.

Brand's main areas of concerns – the nature of the SNP's appeal, the relationship of the SNP's fortunes to the appeal of independence, the characteristics of the nationalist movement, how party and wider movement relate to each other, and placing all of this in the wider terrain of how Scotland has been seen and contested – are as alive and relevant today as when Brand examined them in the 1970s.

All these subjects need to be debated and examined in the present, and remain the subject of serious discussion and rigorous research and writing. It is true that in the years since Brand's study, and particularly since the advent of the Scottish Parliament and the ascent of the SNP as the dominant party of Scotland, that a veritable academic industry has arisen offering in-depth studies of the SNP and the effectiveness of devolution.

But even allowing for this there remain huge gaps and inadequacies in relation to the SNP and independence and the dynamics of party-movement relations; the different currents in the latter over time; the shifting balance between political and cultural nationalism; and recognising the need to understand the limits of nationalism and any debate dominated by its different expressions – particularly alongside the decline of the older Labour, Tory and Lib Dem traditions.

Then there are the practical questions which need serious work: the atrophying of democracy too evident in everyday life; the concentration of power in the Scottish Government; the incorporation of numerous public institutions and the groupthink which affects too many walks of life; and the thinness and lack of depth of many policy debates and research.

The answers to these are challenging and complex, but go beyond partisan party politics or positions on independence. It is salutary to remember that the old Labour order in its latter years was upheld by a mindset of judging whether people were for 'the party' or against it – and such an outlook never ends well anywhere.

Brand's account is in many respects from a different Scotland: a world where the old Scotland was dying but was still present and visible, where the SNP as an electoral force were still a relatively recent phenomenon, and where the emergence of the Scottish question could be framed without referring to Margaret Thatcher and Thatcherism.

The book provides an illuminating portrayal of the leadership culture of the party, characterised by Brand as collective, writing that the SNP would never present themselves to voters as 'the party of William Wolfe' who was leader then. This underlines how far the SNP have travelled and changed culturally, in power, within the party – and how they do leadership and present themselves in the age of Nicola Sturgeon (and before that Alex Salmond).

This brings forth the observation that is a necessity to reclaim and excavate substantive Scottish political and social texts that have contributed to charting and understanding the journey we are still on. This should be a more ecumenical exercise than just continually dragging out the same well-worn texts such as Tom Nairn's *The Break-Up of Britain*, *The Red Paper on Scotland*, George Davie's *The Democratic Intellect* and shrinking our understanding of past debates.

A recent comment from *The Times*' columnist Kenny Farquharson inadvertently underlined the threadbare intellectual nature of much public life when he observed: Andrew Marr's *The Battle for Scotland* was 'the best book on 20th century Scottish politics and the rise of the home rule movement.' In response to this, many – myself included – observed that it is a book with little substantive research and a superficial understanding of post-war Scottish debates. Understanding and remembering books of the quality of Brand's could be part of a process of a richer, deeper discussion that goes past the usual reference points.

Underlying the arguments of *The National Movement in Scotland* is the notion of the remaking of Scotland as a collective idea, and in Brand's analysis 'a gradual restructuring of the political consciousness of the Scottish electorate' – a fundamental shift that led to the rise of the SNP the impact of which still affects us.

There are many contested ideas of different Scotlands and many Scotlands in play all the time as old interpretations die and new ones are born. The re-emergence of Scotland as a political, democratic, social and communicative space is but one expression of that, and a Scottish political debate and culture of self-determination which recognised and nurtured this would be the richer for this – as would all of us.

ACKNOWLEDGEMENTS

This collection, and this entire publication is by definition a collective collaborative project. So there are too many people who have supported Bella from its birth and have contributed so much to its continued existence: of course all of the contributors to the book you are holding in your hands, but also the hundreds of others who haven't been included but have been published on the site.

Huge thanks are due to the many people who subscribe and donate and have supported us for years and bailed us out when things have gone badly, as inevitably they have done. The precarious nature of being a micro publisher makes managing Bella a labour of love.

The following require special thanks for their critical support and insights: Dougie Strang, Mike Gunn, Laura Cameron-Lewis, Luke Devlin, Chris Erskine, Douglas Robertson, Dial M, Mairi McFadyen, Neil Cooper, Justin Kenrick, Erin Devlin, Bob, Chris Silver, Gemma Smith, Iris Pase, Jim Monaghan, Murdo MacDonald, Iona Lee, Luke Campbell, Pat Kane, Peter Arnott, Raman Mundair, Vishwam Heckert, AL Kennedy; Iain Mackinnon; Jamie Maxwell; Cáit O'Neill McCullagh; Alastair McIntosh; Adam Ramsay; Paul Tritschler and many more.

I'd also like to thank my editor Roxanne Sorooshian at the *Sunday National*, my publishers Peter Burnett, Ambrose Kelly and Joshua Andrew at Leamington Books and my web developer Jonathan Stevens at Starbit. Special mention to long-time collaborators and friends on design and much more: Stewart Bremner and Harvey Dingwall.

I'd like to remember my friend Robert Hamilton who has passed away but who was always about listening and encouraging people, challenging lazy thinking and bringing ideas to the table. Bella continues in your spirit of resistance and solidarity.

This book is dedicated to Stacey.

ABOUT BELLA

Bella Caledonia is an online magazine publishing social, political and cultural commentary. It was launched in 2007 and came to prominence during the campaign period of the Scottish independence referendum that was held in 2014. The site is not affiliated to any political party.

Follow:

T: @bellacaledonia

F: @bellacaledonia1

IG: @bellacaledonia

VIMEO: @bellacaledonia

bellacaledonia.org.uk